# Twin Cities Sports

**SPORT, CULTURE & SOCIETY**

DAVID K. WIGGINS, SERIES EDITOR

## Other Titles in This Series

# Twin Cities Sports

## Games for All Seasons

**Edited by Sheldon Anderson**

THE UNIVERSITY OF ARKANSAS PRESS

FAYETTEVILLE

2020

ISBN: 978-1-68226-109-5
eISBN: 978-1-61075-678-5

DOI: https://doi.org/10.34053/scs2019.tcs

24  23  22  21  20    5  4  3  2  1

♾ The paper used in this publication meets the minimum requirements of the American National Standard for Permanence of Paper for Printed Library Materials Z39.48–1984.

Library of Congress Cataloging-in-Publication Data

Names: Anderson, Sheldon R., 1951– editor.
Title: Twin Cities sports : games for all seasons / edited by SheldonAnderson.
Description: Fayetteville : The University of Arkansas Press, 2020. |
    Includes bibliographical references and index. |
Identifiers: LCCN 2019017233 (print) | LCCN 2019021775 (ebook) | ISBN
    9781610756785 (electronic) | ISBN 9781682261095 (pbk. : alk. paper)
Subjects: LCSH: Sports—Minnesota—Minneapolis Metropolitan Area—History. |
    Sports—Minnesota—Saint Paul Metropolitan Area—History. | Sports—Social
    aspects—Minnesota—Minneapolis Metropolitan Area. | Sports—Social
    aspects—Minnesota—Saint Paul Metropolitan Area.
Classification: LCC GV584.5.M56 (ebook) | LCC GV584.5.M56 T85 2020 (print) |
    DDC 796.09776/579—dc23
LC record available at https://lccn.loc.gov/2019017233

*In memory of Keith Hardeman and Bill McKee*

# Contents

# Series Editor's Preface

Sport is an extraordinarily important phenomenon that pervades the lives of many people and has enormous impact on society in an assortment of different ways. At its most fundamental level, sport has the power to bring people great joy and satisfy their competitive urges while at once allowing them to form bonds and a sense of community with others from diverse backgrounds and interests and various walks of life. Sport also makes clear, especially at the highest levels of competition, the lengths that people will go to achieve victory as well as how closely connected it is to business, education, politics, economics, religion, law, family, and other societal institutions. Sport is, moreover, partly about identity development and how individuals and groups, irrespective of race, gender, ethnicity or socioeconomic class, have sought to elevate their status and realize material success and social mobility.

*Sport, Culture, and Society* seeks to promote a greater understanding of the aforementioned issues and many others. Recognizing sport's powerful influence and ability to change people's lives in significant and important ways, the series focuses on topics ranging from urbanization and community development to biographies and intercollegiate athletics. It includes both monographs and anthologies that are characterized by excellent scholarship, accessible to a wide audience, and interesting and thoughtful in design and interpretations. Singular features of the series are authors and editors representing a variety of disciplinary areas and who adopt different methodological approaches. The series also includes works by individuals at various stages of their careers, both sport studies scholars of outstanding talent just beginning to make their mark on the field and more experienced scholars of sport with established reputations.

*Twin Cities Sports* is the latest book in the series devoted to sport in a particular urban setting, following on the heels of *DC Sports: The Nation's Capital at Play*; *Philly Sports: Teams, Games, and Athletes from Rocky's Town*; *Baltimore Sports: Stories from Charm City*; *San Francisco Bay Area Sports: Golden Gate Athletics, Recreation, and Community*; *LA Sports: Play, Games, and Community in the City of Angels*; and *New York Sports: Glamour and Grit in the Empire City*.

The book provides wonderful stories of the varied and complex nature of sport in Minneapolis and St. Paul, referred to by editor Sheldon Anderson as "fraternal rather than identical twins." Like many fraternal twins, the relationship between Minneapolis and St. Paul is marked by an extraordinarily close connection as well as intense rivalry that was reflected in their sports at all levels of competition, over an extended period of time, and during all seasons. This fact is made clear in the pages of this collection as is the enormous pride that the inhabitants of the Twin Cities have always taken in their high school and college sports programs and professional sports franchises. Importantly, the inhabitants of an area known for its extreme weather, thousands of lakes, miles of walking and skiing trails, and assortment of indoor and outdoor recreation and sports facilities, rightfully have also always taken enormous pride in their unparalleled park system. In essence, perhaps no other city in the world has so effectively combined high level competitive sports programs and a park system designed to offer "healthy, urban spaces" for the recreational benefits of all citizens.

*David K. Wiggins*

# Acknowledgments

The strength of this anthology rests on the authors' thorough research and analysis of a wide range of sporting contests in the Twin Cities. The contributors represent a diverse group of university professors, professional writers, and journalists. Their hard work made my job easy. I would especially like to thank David C. Smith, who contributed to several chapters and read many of the others. Chris Elzey of George Mason University also made helpful suggestions to improve the book.

I am indebted to the Minnesota History Society for providing most of the photographs. The *Hutchinson Leader* generously contributed a photo of Lindsay Whalen. I would like to express special thanks to Gracia Lindberg, who created the maps of Minnesota and the Twin Cities.

The staff at the University of Arkansas Press, especially Jennifer Vos and David Scott Cunningham, were also indispensable in shepherding the book through production.

# Twin Cities Sports

# Introduction

At the end of Twin City filmmakers' Ethan and Joel Coen's *Fargo* (1996),[1] Brainerd, Minnesota, police officer Marge Gunderson, in an oversized fur-lined parka and big winter clodhoppers, tracks two murderous kidnappers to a remote lake cabin. Traipsing through the snow, she spots one of the culprits forcing a shoeless leg into a grinder. As she is arresting the hulking criminal, little Marge, in her droll, singsongy, cheery Scando-Minnesotan accent, surmises, "I guess that was your accomplice in the wood chipper."

All of what many people think about Minnesota is in the wood chipper scene: winter, water, wilderness, whiteness, and Marge's simple, honest *weltanschauung*. For almost thirty years, humorist Garrison Keillor, in his public radio stories about the small, mythical Minnesota town of Lake Wobegon, evoked this image of devout, sober, hardworking, unassuming Minnesotans who love walleye, hot dishes, and weak black coffee, while grimly suffering through long winters, giant mosquitoes, and lonely life on the prairie. Kids in Minnesota are content to be—in Keillor's signature sign-off—"above average." Even the state bird—the common loon—has no pretention.

Keillor conjured Minnesota as a place of bland, cold, colorless Nordic sameness, although the ethnic makeup of the state no longer conforms to this caricature. The state has the reputation of a forbidden land of relentless cold. For a third of the year, snow covers the landscape, and the lakes ice over. Green appears fleetingly in the short spring and summer, while browns and reds show up in the abbreviated fall season. International Falls, on the Canadian border, has the coldest average temperature of any town in the United States. The town is proudly called the "Icebox of the Nation."

The pale-faced Scandinavians and Germans who settled in the Twin Cities ate and drank white too—fish, pork, potatoes, corn, beer, and aquavit. The Finns and Yugoslavs on the Iron Range near Duluth skated on the frozen glacial lakes and ponds, forging an ice hockey tradition second only to Canada's.

The authors in this collection tell sports stories that are firmly rooted in Minnesota. Many chapters, such as David C. Smith's chapter on speed skating, could not be told about any other place. The Twin Cities' abundant lakes and streams, the Mississippi and Minnesota Rivers, and the extremes in weather are conducive to doing sport year-round. Twin Citians can find a fresh water swim, an urban fishing hole, a cross-country ski trail, an outdoor skating rink, a public park baseball or softball field, or a tennis or basketball court within a mile of any place in the metropolitan area.

All of the major Twin City sports teams pay homage to the state's geography, history, and fauna. There are no Red Sox, Reds, Jets, or Tigers, nicknames that have no direct connection to their city. Even before achieving statehood in 1858, Minnesota was known as the Gopher State, and although the little rodent was a menace to farmers, the University of Minnesota teams adopted the nickname. The cute critter is among the least ferocious college mascots. After years and years of Gopher football futility, in the mid-1980s the athletic department unleashed a new angry-looking Gopher in attack mode. People laughed at Goldy Gopher's rabid makeover, which did not fit into Minnesota's reputation as a nice, accommodating place. The friendly, smiling Gopher soon returned.

Minnesota and Minneapolis come from *mini*, the Dakota word for water. Minnesota's license plate boasts of "10,000 lakes"; the actual number is closer to twelve thousand, but who's counting? Minnesota has the largest percentage of surface water of any state. Minneapolis was known as the Mill City because of the lumber and then grain mills powered by St. Anthony Falls on the Mississippi River. In his chapter on pro football, Dick Dahl traces the legacy of the game back to the Cedar-Riverside Marines, beginning a tradition of aqua-fied nicknames. The Minneapolis Lakers began playing basketball in 1947 and won five National Basketball Association (NBA) championships in the 1940s and 1950s. As Stew Thornley notes, ironically the Lakers, playing in the winter, had to compete for dates at the Minneapolis Auditorium with the annual Sportsman's Show, where anglers and boaters shopped for their summer gear. The franchise and the moniker moved to lake-less Los Angeles in 1960.[2] Many Minnesota high schools are called the Lakers. In 1967 Minnesota got one of the original American Basketball Association (ABA) franchises— the Muskies—named after the lunker of all lunkers looming in the depths of Minnesota's fresh waters.

A National Football League (NFL) team arrived in 1961. Unlike the lowly Gopher, the football Viking is an imposing figure. The original Vikings gained infamy by plying the high seas to ransack and plunder in far off places. The new football team, playing on the oft snow-covered tundra at Metropolitan Stadium, invoked fear and trepidation in the likes of the fair-weather Rams from Los Angeles, whose Roman Gabriels and Bernie Caseys were no match for the Bill "Boom Boom" Browns and Carl "Moose" Ellers.

In 1967 the National Hockey League (NHL) added six new expansion teams. Minnesota got the North Stars. When that team left for Dallas in 1993, once again the nickname went too. (Dallas dropped the *North*.) The hockey happy state received an expansion team in 2000, aptly named the Wild. The timber wolf (or gray wolf) that prowls the woods of northern Minnesota got its due with a new NBA franchise in 1989. The Canadian lynx is a rare sight along northern Minnesota's Gun Flint Trail (the bobcat is more common), but Minnesota's Women's National Basketball Association (WNBA) team took the name in 1998, and the Lynx won four titles in the 2010s. In 2017 St. Paul's new Major League Soccer (MLS) team was dubbed the Loons, carrying on this indigenous naming tradition.

Minnesota has a deserved reputation for progressive politics. Minneapolis's parks, as Shannon Murray documents in her chapter, were conceived for the public good. The state has shared its assets from inception. Before becoming a state, the territorial legislature divvied up the public institutions; Minneapolis got the University of Minnesota, St. Paul the capital, St. Peter the mental hospital, and Stillwater the state penitentiary. Minnesota's Progressive movement was strong after World War I, pushed to the left by the socialists on the Iron Range. A third party—the Farmer-Labor Party—elected three governors, four US senators, and eight US representatives in the interwar period. In 1944 the party merged with the Democratic Party to form the Democratic-Farmer-Labor Party, which was a muscular force in Minnesota politics. The decline of the iron industry and the depletion of the ores in northeastern Minnesota has contributed to economic challenges in the region that have eroded some support for the DFL, which Sheldon Anderson argues was one of the reasons a former pro wrestler wound up in the governor's office in 1998.

For many years Minneapolis has been named the city with the best park system in the country. Shannon Murray's chapter highlights the express aim of public park founders to create healthy, urban spaces to serve the masses and to provide recreational programs.[3] The city's park leaders were way ahead of their time in preaching the health benefits of fresh air and sports to relieve stress. Tom Jones points out that, although golf was at first the purview of the rich, public courses were built to serve the middle and working classes. Tom Taylor notes that the Twin Cities' vast park system has facilitated soccer games for new non-European immigrants.

The stories in this anthology tell a tale of two cities, fraternal rather than identical twins. Minneapolis and St. Paul dominate the urban sports scene, but the professional teams in the Twin Cities are embraced in the hinterland as their own. The big state high school sports tournaments are held in the Twin Cities, creating a competitive urban-suburban-rural dynamic.

The rivalry between St. Paul and Minneapolis, as Dick Dahl and other authors note, has always simmered. The friendly competition emerged when there was almost nothing in the ten miles that separated the young towns and continued long after they grew into one metropolitan area. The railroad, stock yards, and river wharf made up St. Paul, while Minneapolis ran the grain mills powered by St. Anthony Falls.

The Catholic Irish and Italians in St. Paul thought of their city as a livable, unpretentious, slow-paced, neighborhood place. That ethos persists: in 2017 sales spiked for a T-shirt emblazoned with, "Keep St. Paul Boring."[4] Tom Jones relates that St. Paul began its annual Winter Carnival in February to assure people that it was possible to live through a Minnesota winter. Minneapolis wanted none of that lowbrow winter carnival nonsense. The city tried to fashion itself as a cosmopolitan "Mini-Apple" to New York City's "Big Apple." David C. Smith and Sheldon Anderson suspect that St. Paul is happy to have the hockey team Wild, leaving the rest of pro sports to Minneapolis.

This sibling rivalry has been good natured. The Vikings and the Washington Senators turned Minnesota Twins were the first teams in the NFL and Major League Baseball (MLB) to bear the name of a state rather than a city (the Twins often wear a cap emblazoned with "TC"). All of the major league professional franchises in Minnesota have followed suit. Civic leaders viewed the franchises as a state as well as metropolitan asset, and the teams consciously tried to appeal to outstate fans.

While Minneapolis was the driving force behind the acquisition of the pro teams, the city did not want to overshadow its smaller neighbor to the east. Metropolitan Stadium and Met Sports Center, the first homes of the Twins, Vikings, and North Stars, were purposely located in Bloomington, a suburb, partly to avoid the appearance of choosing sides in the civic rivalry.[5] Minneapolis had the minor league Millers, and St. Paul had the Saints, in both baseball and hockey. And so it went—and goes!

Although there is some truth to this imagined Twin City community of progressive, honest, humble sameness, the whiteness of the place has masked historical class and ethnic divisions. None of the chapters in this book deal solely with gender and racial issues, but the authors have consciously addressed those issues. For example, Tom Jones and Shannon Murray observe that public spaces were designed for the masses to play, but that women and minorities struggled to gain access to golf courses and other recreational venues. Jones explores discrimination against African American and women golfers, although he points out that the Twin Cities were out front in integrating Professional Golfers Association (PGA) tournaments. Gopher football teams were mostly white before 1960, but then the 1950 US census showed that a mere 1.6 percent of Minneapolis residents had nonwhite parents, and 2 percent in St. Paul.[6] The great Minnesota teams of the early 1960s, as Sheldon Anderson chronicles, were in part the result of recruiting black players from the segregated South, and a star black quarterback from Pennsylvania who could not get a shot at that position at other schools. The Gophers became integrated at the same time that Minneapolis was becoming more diverse.

Scott Wright focuses on the ethnic character of Twin Cities boxing history, which was concentrated in St. Paul's Catholic Irish and Italian communities. Brad Lundell and Anderson highlight the importance of professional wrestling to the Polish Catholic community in Northeast, Minneapolis; located on the same side of the Mississippi River as St. Paul, Northeast has more in common with that city. Pro wrestling was also a favorite of the Twin Cities' large Native American population, the home of the American Indian Movement (AIM).

Tom Taylor observes that soccer in the Twin Cities is an international game now, mirroring the increasingly diverse ethnic makeup of the metro area. On any given day, one might see East Africans, Vietnamese, and Latinos playing the game in city parks. Unfortunately, the inspiring story of 1999 World Cup champion goalie Brianna Scurry has not caused a significant uptick in the number of African Americans playing soccer.

Jon Kerr reminds us that the Twins' Calvin Griffith was one of the last baseball owners who made his money solely from his sports franchise. With baseballs costing a few dollars apiece, Griffith's players were not to throw them into the stands for souvenirs. Griffith's extended family depended on profits from the ball club. Blair Williams argues that Griffith brought in Tony Oliva and other Latin American players in part because he could pay them the bare minimum.

As Jon Kerr and Blair Williams argue, the Griffiths' seemingly overt racism in moving to lily-white Minneapolis was not what it seemed. The Griffiths had to make money, and paying players less and moving to a more lucrative market was a business decision. (The precedent had already been set with the Boston Braves' move to Milwaukee, the New York Giants' move to San Francisco, and the Brooklyn Dodgers' move to Los Angeles.) Today all of the owners of professional franchises—the Pohlads of the Twins, the Wilfs of the Vikings, Glen Taylor of the Timberwolves and Lynx, and Craig Leopold of the Wild—made their fortunes outside of sports before buying the teams.

The Twin Cities are in the vanguard of popularizing the country's most rapidly growing team sports, soccer and ice hockey. Few Minnesotans cared about the world's game when the Kicks came to town in the mid-1970s, and that short-lived love affair with soccer was as much fueled by tailgating and alcohol as it was with the sport. Nonetheless, as Tom Taylor contends, the legacy of the multiethnic Kicks lives on. Today youth soccer has more participants than football or baseball, and the Twin Cities is host to one of the biggest youth soccer tournaments in the world. The Minnesota Loons will give those kids inspiration to play at a higher level.

Ice hockey has always had deep roots on Minnesota's Iron Range, but as David C. Smith and Sheldon Anderson reveal, the game was strange to most of the rest of the state, and few high schools had teams. It was not until the last quarter of the twentieth century that the proliferation of indoor ice arenas, the professional NHL team the North Stars, and Division I hockey programs catapulted Minnesota to its standing today as the State of Hockey. The sad reality is that hockey and baseball, and to a certain extent youth soccer outside of Minneapolis and St. Paul, have become sports dominated by Minnesota's white population.

Readers here will not find a paean to a glorious history of great Twin City sports teams. The Gophers men's football and basketball teams, and Minnesota's professional franchises (with the exception of the Lynx) have not won a major championship in over a quarter century. The football Gophers were a national powerhouse in the decade before World War II, but the last Gopher Big Ten football championship came over a half century ago. The Vikings lost four Super Bowls in the 1960s and 1970s but have not been back since. Even the men's Gopher hockey team, drawing recruits from the State of Hockey, has won only two national championships in almost forty years (2002 and 2003).[7] The Twins won two World Series, in 1987 and 1991, the team's only major championship in nearly sixty years.

What happened? Was Mother Nature punishing the teams for trying to flee from the harsh elements by moving indoors at the Metrodome? Tailgating in the huge Metropolitan Stadium parking lot was a big draw for Vikings, Twins, and Kicks fans, but that outdoor fun was circumscribed at the downtown Metrodome. Minnesota was not the first to build an indoor stadium for football and baseball, but as Sheldon Anderson contends, in escaping the cold and snow, the Gophers and the Vikings not only lost home field advantage but their connection to the soul of Minnesota—to the nature, climate, and geography that Horace Cleveland, Theodore Wirth, and other developers wisely incorporated into their park designs. The Gophers and Twins have since moved outside, perhaps portending a return to the true character of Minnesota sports.

# Map of Minnesota

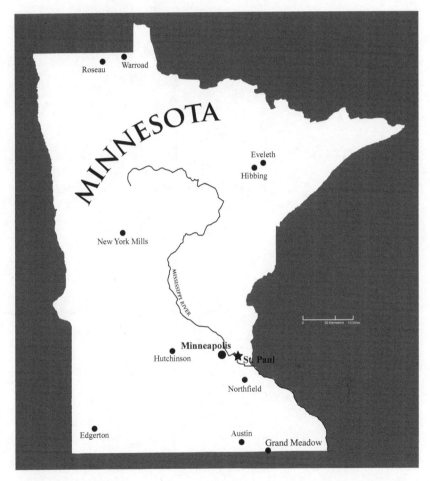

Maps by Gracia Lindberg.

# Map of the Twin Cities

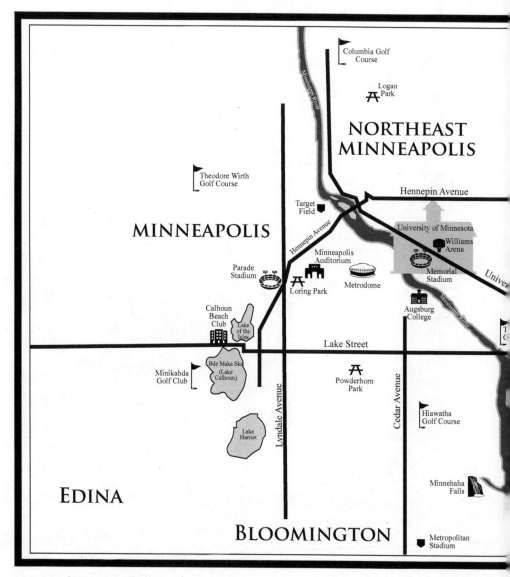

Maps by Gracia Lindberg.

# TWIN CITIES

Snelling Avenue

ST. PAUL

Lake Como

Keller
Golf Course

Lake Phalen

Johnson
High School

Hamline
University

DOWNTOWN
ST. PAUL

ty Avenue

n and Country
f Course

Marshall Avenue

Xcel
Center

St. Paul
Auditorium

## CHAPTER ONE

# From Parks to Recreation

## The Minneapolis Parks System, 1880s–1920s

### SHANNON MURRAY

In its infant years, the city of Minneapolis struggled to find its own identity. Civic leaders wanted to show that their city was not like others—especially St. Paul, its older sibling just a few miles away. Capitalizing on the only waterfall on the Mississippi River, Minneapolis was planned to be a great milling center for the Northwest and quickly became known as the Mill City.[1] Though economic success was important, civic leaders were keen to avoid a boom-and-bust company town model. In an effort to set their settlement apart from others and demonstrate that it was a city with culture and class, they turned to early landscape architect Horace W. S. Cleveland and charted out the city's future. He thought that parks were civic treasures because they were sites of healthful urban beautification and they served as key community-building places.

This chapter will focus on the development of parks and recreation in Minneapolis between the 1880s and the 1920s, a period during which parks became established as critical community spaces and indeed a major part of the city's identity. Through park board support and interventions by local social reformers, parks were developed as dynamic sites that went from passive green spaces to active playgrounds with organized sports and other recreations while always serving the community.

One factor in the success of parks in Minneapolis was that the park board was willing to alter them in response to the needs of the people. During the period under consideration, Minneapolis's parks underwent three main iterations: pleasure grounds, recreation parks, and active reform parks with

DOI: https://doi.org/10.34053/scs2019.tcs.1

playgrounds. Each type was influenced by early national trends in city planning work, social reformers, and the growth of commercial entertainments as well as the local perspectives of park board members. Each built accommodation, from pavilions and rectories to merry-go-rounds and grandstands, reflects the changing interpretations of the purpose of city parks.

The city's early parks were pleasure grounds, intended to provide passive respite from the hectic urban environment.[2] In the late 1890s, the Minneapolis park system was altered to accommodate popular recreation, part of an effort to make parks compete with emerging consumer entertainments. Light commercial elements such as lunch counters, dining rooms, pavilions with music and theater, and bicycle paths were all added to entice users. This set of formal accommodations helped to align the Minneapolis park board with social reformers' efforts to develop redemptive places that would provide a respite from cramped urban conditions and uplift the city's population.[3] The final iteration of Minneapolis parks that will be discussed here was the transition from recreation parks into active reform parks with playgrounds. The playground movement tied physical fitness with development of good character. It immediately gained local support, but it required changes to existing parks—specifically the addition of play apparatuses and structures like gymnasiums—in order to put it into action.[4] During a period of rapid urbanization, parks would hold a privileged place in the city's ideological and physical development. Parks played many roles as sites of respite and rest, play and spectatorship, but their consistent function was that of community spaces.

The early success of the Minneapolis parks system helped launch the city's reputation as more than an industrial outpost. The Mill City moniker saw competition from other titles like the "City of Lakes and Gardens" or the more awkward (but clearly emphasizing both industrial and aesthetic might) "City of Flour and Flowers."[5] While neither of those monikers really stuck, the importance of parks to Minneapolis's identity certainly did. Parks are defined as community spaces, integral to civic identity, and Minneapolis continues to rank first on national lists for having the best urban park system.[6] The role of parks in the city's development and unique character began in the early 1880s when a pioneering landscape architect was brought in to make a plan of growth for Minneapolis.

Horace W. S. Cleveland helped to define the field of landscape architecture. His complete visions for young cities set him apart from other practitioners in the late nineteenth century. Unlike the more frequently remembered Frederick

Law Olmsted, Cleveland prized the practical over the picturesque. In his 1873 book *Landscape Architecture, as Applied to the Wants of the West*, he argued that if cities grew with forethought and a dedication to spatial equality—the dedication to making space accessible throughout the entire city, many of the ills plaguing overcrowded American cities would be ameliorated.[7] He urged cities to acquire land while it was still affordable and to make sure that, in the long run, any development of park spaces was in accordance with the needs of the people (though at times these "needs" were defined more by civic leaders and social reformers than by the people themselves). Cleveland's book was based on a speech he delivered in the Twin Cities in 1872, and the published form was well received. Through his work in Chicago, Cleveland became connected with William Watts Folwell, president of the University of Minnesota. In February 1872, Folwell asked Cleveland to deliver a lecture at the university.[8] It became the basis for *Landscape Architecture* and began Cleveland's work in both of the Twin Cities.

In 1882 Cleveland was once again invited for a speaking engagement; he was subsequently engaged to make a plan for Minneapolis. Returning in July 1883, he presented his plan to the newly created Minneapolis park board.[9] The supporting document, titled *Suggestions for a System of Parks and Parkways, for the City of Minneapolis*, explained how his naturalistic approach would be expressed in Minneapolis. The accompanying map had simple red markings to denote future parks. There was a loop around the city—later to become the Grand Rounds—and four parks, one situated in each political ward for the city at the time.[10] His vision expressed the influences of the City Natural movement, whose practitioners "advocated that access to the beauty of nature should become a public right and not be limited to the fortunate few."[11] Cleveland's plan emphasized "natural" spaces through design interventions, which reflected his dedication to the city's natural principles. He especially highlighted the Mississippi River and advocated for interventions to improve yet preserve natural landscapes that would be otherwise unusable.[12] The park board approved of the plan, a decision that would forever change the form and spatial ethos of Minneapolis and its parks.

In 1886 Cleveland moved to Minneapolis and continued to work in his landscape architecture firm, designing parks, cemeteries, and private landscapes both in his new home and in other cities, including neighboring St. Paul.[13] He continued to urge the ongoing purchasing of potentially valuable lands to ensure that parks would be present in the inner city, not just the periphery

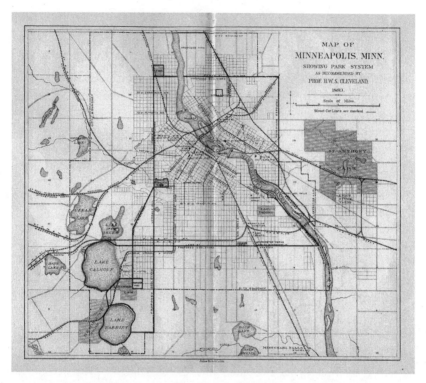

Horace Cleveland's 1883 'Suggestions for the Minneapolis Park System.' The red lines indicate proposed parks and parkways. *Source:* Horace William Shaler Cleveland, *Suggestions for a System of Parks and Parkways* (Minneapolis: Johnson, Smith, & Harrison, 1883).

where people would need carriages for access.[14] Over time he was supportive of changes in form to his original park designs to accommodate new types of recreation. Early park board leaders like Charles Loring and William Watts Folwell took the torch from Cleveland and worked to acquire land and cultivate appreciation among Minneapolitans for beautiful and functional parks throughout the city. By the turn of the twentieth century, the city had acquired most of the land Cleveland originally designated for boulevards or parks and added dozens of small neighborhood parcels to the system. The city's passion for parks grew, but the ways in which they were used and their physical forms changed over time.

Minneapolis's early parks were simple pleasure grounds, but their designs, locations, and use set them apart from similar parks in other cities. Pleasure grounds were spaces of "unstructured pursuits" that "encouraged family excursions and recreation" and "relief from the evils of the city."[15] In many American cities, they were exclusive sites despite being paid for by public money. New York's Central Park is one of the more prominent nineteenth-century examples of this. Cleveland was adamant that his parks would be for the people and criticized Central Park for its focus on ornamentation and its limited accessibility: "It will be no population of laboring poor that will dwell in [its] vicinity . . . it will be only on an occasional holiday that the toiling denizen of the central business marts, can afford the time or the means to go with his family to those distant gardens."[16]

Cleveland's dedication to spatial equality would become a foundation of Minneapolis's park system. The early parks that he planned in Minneapolis were also pleasure grounds in that they were designed for relief from urbanity and to be places for families to enjoy unstructured play, but they were purposefully planned to be accessible and to respond to the wants of Minneapolitans (or at least in the early years, to what civic leaders thought the people wanted). For example, there were some early accommodations for popular leisure recreation, such as ice skating in winter at Loring, Powderhorn, and Columbia parks or bicycling along newly created tracks along the park boulevard belt.[17] Thanks to Cleveland's influence, the early park board was dedicated to making improvements that it felt was in the public's best interest. This included maintaining features like floating bathing houses where people could bathe somewhat privately in the lakes, because they would satisfy the "wants of a very large proportion of our population."[18] Such provisions were not officially within the board's mandate at the time, but that it was considered an essential investment shows the social intentions of the early parks movement in Minneapolis.

Around the turn of the twentieth century, people's interest in passive pleasure grounds was diminishing. As the recreation offerings in the city's parks were proving increasingly popular—and the draw of commercial entertainments was becoming stronger—the board began to reconfigure some sites to ensure that parks remained relevant and popular public spaces.[19] This became part of the process of pleasure grounds becoming recreation parks, a transition that was marked by the broader accommodation for popular recreation activities and light commercial pursuits, such as lunch counters, dining rooms, bicycle paths, boat rentals, music shows in pavilions, and even a zoo.[20] These proved to be very attractive for Minneapolitans who, by their very presence, would support such transformations of the parks' roles.[21] These light commercial additions still emphasized parks as places of respite with picturesque views and, though there were detractors, represented the board's calculated move away from passive pleasure grounds to more active spaces.

Park leaders were encouraging of many formal changes, but they were also wary of commercialism's creep into pristine park spaces. The zoo at Minnehaha Park had started with a few deer, bears, and wolves. But as its popularity grew, so did its holdings. Within a few years it was being operated by the park board and there were wolves, swans, angora goats, a sea lion, guinea pigs, and a pelican, among many others.[22] Despite the growth of the zoo and its incredible popularity, superintendent Theodore Wirth found it to be cruel to animals and unbecoming of the Minneapolis parks system, so he closed it in 1907.[23] In 1904 the parks board agreed to allow a peanut stand, run by a private citizen, to be set up at the entrance of Minnehaha Park. Loring argued it was a "desecration of the park," but he was unable to convince the board to evict it.[24] He was not alone in this opinion. Landscape historian Daniel Joseph Nadenicek noted that Cleveland and Loring collaborated to quash an initiative to sell photos, "trinkets[,] and other Indian memorabilia" at Minnehaha, arguing that this invasive capitalism contradicted the purpose of public parks.[25] Still, these prominent park leaders—as well as the rest of the board—knew that if parks did not adapt and support the changes in recreation during this time, they ran the risk of losing visitors to emergent forms of entertainment like movies or dance halls that, they believed, had negative effects on the character development of Minneapolitans and, therefore, the city overall.

Loring considered Minnehaha a jewel in park board's crown, describing it as "one of the most beautiful and useful parks of this or any other city."[26] From the 1880s to the 1920s, the park saw a number of recreation-based changes beyond the zoo and peanut stand, and it stands as an excellent example of the changes implemented by the park board. Between 1893 and the 1910s, a number of additions to Minnehaha Park reflected the development of the city's recreation parks that encouraged activity and even light commercial pursuits. The park was a popular destination for Minneapolitans and was also touted as a tourist destination. In the 1893 Board of Park Commissioners annual report, Loring was delighted to inform readers that the land to finish Minnehaha Parkway, a route that connected busy Lyndale Avenue to Minnehaha Park, had been acquired.[27] Over the next decade, the board began making accommodations for bicycles along boulevards that connected parks, and to make Minnehaha Parkway an attractive and safe route for those enjoying the newly popular recreation of cycling.[28] In 1898 another bicycle pathway connected Minnehaha Park to a path that went to Fort Snelling.[29]

The park board's embrace of the bicycle craze was also reflected in the buildings they developed for Minnehaha Park. In 1899 plans for a new pavilion there were included in the board's annual report. Some of the amenities reflected the role of a recreation park as competition for commercial "destructive" entertainments such as dance halls and nickelodeons. The plans were developed based on provisions in similar parks in other cities, including New York's Central Park, Chicago's South Park, and Boston's Franklin Park. In the proposed designs, the pavilion's main floor was mostly an interior café hall with a covered porch and open pergola area. There were two private dining rooms and a small "ladies" room on the main floor, and a kitchen, large hall, and of course bicycle storage in the basement.[30] Locals truly enjoyed the park, but it also became an emblem of the city boosters' pride in parks as it was featured in multiple promotional pamphlets.[31] Such developed park spaces could be characterized as a departure from the early idea of parks as passive sites of relaxation in green spaces, but a crucial element of Minneapolis's parks is that the park board was not willing to maintain static sites in which the public had little interest. If parks were indeed for the people, they would need to be relevant spaces.

The success of parks as public spaces was not lost on Minneapolis's social reformers. Leaders of both the Young Men's Christian Association (YMCA) and Young Women's Christian Association (YWCA) in Minneapolis subscribed to the theory of environmental determinism—that environmental surroundings affected character development. Both organizations had national and local buildings with interiors that mimicked middle-class parlors to invoke a sense of respectability, but they could only fit so many clients inside at once.[32] In a city so well endowed with public park spaces, reformers began to target parks as ideal redemptive places that would act as "*sites of assimilation*."[33] By virtue of design and programming, these redemptive places would have formative effects on the characters of those who inhabited them. To make Minneapolis's recreation parks into active reform parks, though, changes to their forms and equipment updates were required. In most instances this was done by adding playground equipment; in others it was a more elaborate process with impressive overhauls of parks and the provision of supervisors to guide play of adults and children alike. In providing opportunities and spaces for organized play, Minneapolis was part of the national "sporting boom of the early 1900s," which "was supported by the rise of new theories of play that advocated organized youth sport, supervised by adults to control the behavior of youths ... [that] would build character, fitness, and morality."[34] Beautiful and functional parks would, social reformers believed, provide ideal environments for their programming efforts to mold the character of Minneapolitans.

Though Minneapolis had the park space needed, play equipment and recreation supervisors required new capital investment. In 1898 social reformers and civic leaders—including members of the park board—convened at a public meeting held at the West Hotel "to consider the playground movement" and discuss which parks were good candidates to be reconfigured into playgrounds.[35] The group lamented the lack of accessible parks for citizens living in the center of the city. Glenwood Park, in the far northwest of the city, was identified an ideal site for a playground, but "its only fault [was] inaccessibility by car lines."[36] This was a major shortcoming, as it would undercut Cleveland's principle of ensuring parks were accessible and usable for a broad audience.

Putting playgrounds into inner-city neighborhood parks was costlier than the park board budget could handle, though. Shortly after the meeting, the Minneapolis Improvement League sent a mailer requesting donations to facilitate new playgrounds. "What investment," it queried, "would insure better returns than providing a place where little children can have the benefit of pure air and sunshine and be free from the dangers and the pernicious influences of the street?"[37] In this mailer, it is clear that throughout each iteration of parks—from pleasure grounds to active reform parks—parks were consistently identified as clean, healthy spaces that were good influences on visitors. The mailer further stated that the new playgrounds would go in two congested areas—the first on a piece of land located on Thirteenth Avenue and Second Street South (just two blocks away from the red-light district), the second on Washington Avenue between Sixth and Seventh Avenues North.[38] Though uncomfortable with asking for donations, Loring defended the request by stating that playgrounds were crucial for civic health.[39] In what would be one of his last written works, "The Influence of Parks on the Character of Children," Cleveland, too, wrote in support of playgrounds. The text "addresse[d] the role of parks and nature in social reform, particularly for children in tenement neighborhoods."[40] The perspective would not have been shocking for those who knew Cleveland well; updating citywide parks to become playgrounds so that more children would have access to nicer, more modern facilities certainly fit with his perspective that parks were public spaces for the people. Although playgrounds had many supporters in Minneapolis, it would take a new park board superintendent to make them a reality.

In 1906 Swiss-born horticulturalist Theodore Wirth moved to Minneapolis to serve as the superintendent of the park board.[41] Like Cleveland, Loring, and Folwell before him, Wirth saw parks as fundamental public spaces. He also thought that parks should be structured in ways that accommodated changing public demands for the types of public spaces parks should be. Not entirely coincidentally, the first year Wirth was superintendent, the city got its first playgrounds. There were several sites located throughout the city selected to receive play equipment ranging from a "horizontal ladder" and "climbing poles" to "swinging rings" and "see-saws."[42]

Beyond these apparatus additions, Wirth was also responsible for accepting an offer from the local YMCA to lead recreation programming in the city's parks. In 1907 C. T. Booth became the first "Supervisor and Instructor of playgrounds," splitting his time between the YMCA and the city's parks.[43] The partnership marked a formal marriage between social reformers and the park board. Playgrounds provided ideal stewardship sites for character development. They did not replace polluted streets, barren courtyards, or movie houses as destinations for all children, but they were well attended. The partnership with reformers made parks more formal places with rigid rules. Booth advocated separating playground users by sex and by age, something that was a common practice in reform parks and playgrounds throughout the country, though less so in Minneapolis.[44] He also pushed for hiring recreation leaders, most of whom were connected with the YMCA, "to stimulate and organize sanctioned activities" as well as to ensure that those using the new equipment were properly educated on how to use them. However, supervisors also served to encourage certain behaviors. The Minneapolis park board defined its ideal leader as a man who "'should always appear neatly dressed, cleanly shaven, with well-groomed hair.'"[45] In other words: the recreation leaders had to be models of appropriate behavior, hygiene, and dress. By 1909—just three years after the first playgrounds were installed in Minneapolis—Booth reported that they had an annual attendance just shy of five hundred thousand.[46]

Reformers successfully exploited the park board's achievements. The board had acquired the land and worked to instill a civic ethos that prized parks as public places to be accessible by all Minneapolitans. But by insisting on having play supervisors in place and pushing for formal changes to the parks that would limit independent play in the neighborhood parks, reformers somewhat infringed on the early egalitarian park ethos that Cleveland, Loring, Folwell, and others had cultivated. Certainly, users continued to appropriate the park spaces for their own uses, but the early park designs of open grounds with a few recreation accommodations were becoming the minority.

Some Minneapolitans lamented the loss of parks as unstructured spaces. In a book of poetry inspired by Loring Park, Henrietta Jewett Keith wrote that "it is a thousand pities that modern life is so bereft of all those innocent festivities of the past. All our activities are on the lines of utilities and commercialism."[47] Still, recreation programs put on by the YWCA and YMCA kept parks as key sites of community development. In the first few decades after the first playgrounds and recreation accommodations had been installed, and parks truly became community gathering places. These shared spaces held everything from ski jumping and high diving to pageants and "community sings."[48] In later years, the YWCA specifically cited the playgrounds at several schools as being particularly useful for their programs.[49] Indeed, the playgrounds—as much as the parks in which they were situated—became a selling feature of Minneapolis. A 1912 booster pamphlet featured a watercolor of four girls running in front of a playground with swings and a slide with a backdrop of large, lush trees. The caption reads: "Nearly every neighborhood has a public play-ground for children."[50] The adoption of playgrounds and collaboration with reformers changed the parks and was a departure from the earliest forms of playgrounds, but their successes in keeping parks busy, relevant spaces to Minneapolitans was crucial to cementing their prized place in the city.

Making playgrounds out of existing parks required alterations to the form of the grounds. The proposed reconfiguration of Logan Park in the northeast section of the city is a helpful example of how such transitions were proposed and actually completed. In the park board's first annual report, that section of land was described as just over ten acres with "a level surface an is in the midst of the rapidly increasing population of that populous ward, and is reached well by the system of streets and avenues of the East Division as by the street car line."[51] Its original pleasure ground design had a bifurcated green space centered by a small fountain. Such ornamentation was typically out of step with Cleveland's design vision, but he added it as a concession because Logan did not otherwise have an interesting natural feature.[52] The south end featured large, open fields to facilitate unstructured play, and the north end had an extra set of pathways that divided up the lawns into smaller parcels that would better accommodate quiet and less-active recreation in the park. Logan's topography was flat and inconspicuous. It was this banality that made it a good candidate for a playground transformation.

Twenty-five years after Cleveland's original design, Wirth proposed a "transformation" of Logan Park that would incorporate structured play areas. The north side of the park was to be replaced with tennis courts, merry-go-rounds, sandboxes, outdoor gymnasiums, and a general recreation building. Booth's insistence that playground spaces be segregated by age and gender had clearly influenced Wirth's design for the park, as the outdoor gymnasiums were labeled specifically "Men's Out-Door Gymnasium" and "Women's Out-Door Gymnasium."[53] The southern half had scenic details, including curvilinear pathways and large green lawns. Flower beds interrupted the lawns, a design element that deliberately limited unstructured play opportunities that previously existed there. Moreover, the fountain—a purely ornamental addition to the park—was to be replaced by a wading pool, a more practical water feature that was more appropriate for Logan Park's transformation into an active reform park. In 1912 the board finally began construction at Logan Park. It would not, however, match Wirth's (very expensive) designs. The main surviving element was the field house and community hall. According to historian David Smith, "the Logan Park field house would be the immensely successful center of park board recreation programs and play host to numerous community activities, as well as a library branch."[54] Despite the addition's popularity, the initial costs were high, and without other partners stepping forward to build more, Logan Park was the only site of such accommodations until the 1950s.[55] The building was a physical marker of changes in the park board's vision. It accommodated year-round programming and brought in community partners such as the city library to park spaces. It was an active site and helped build and support community spirit in a densely populated section of the city.

Logan Park was not the only reconfigured site during Wirth's tenure as park superintendent. Within two years of the first playground being installed, as many as thirteen playgrounds existed throughout the city with equipment ranging from merry-go-rounds and swings to parallel bars and "basket ball [sic] goals."[56] Another site that accommodated facilities tied to the recreation and playground movement was the Parade, situated adjacent to Keith's beloved Loring Park west of downtown. In 1908, after more than three years of petitions by the YMCA, local high school teachers, and Wirth himself, the park board finally agreed to install an athletic park section there.[57] In some ways the Parade's development complemented that of Logan Park. Both were designated centers of recreation and their new designs would distinctly change the purposes of parks in Minneapolis. The Parade's athletic park provided programmed space for organized team sports and recreation. However, the Parade was unique because it also had a grandstand for people to watch others engaged in sports and recreation.[58] This accommodation appealed to yet another growing trend in recreation and play in the early twentieth century: spectatorship.

Spectacles were growing in popularity during this era, and sports performed in city parks quickly became part of the craze.[59] While the reconfiguration of smaller parks was intended to make it easier for more people to play and actively recreate, the addition of a grandstand contributed to a redirection of recreation in parks. This transition was part of the modernization of leisure, as "commercial entertainment, especially spectacles such as . . . professional sports, replaced self-generated and active leisure."[60] Organized sports were touted as practical and ideal means of keeping people fit and inculcating them with a teamwork mentality and respect for authority.[61] Professional baseball and league kitten ball, the precursor to softball, had taken off at the turn of the twentieth century in Minneapolis, and while sports that encouraged spectatorship initially got a chilly reception from social reformers, they became an acceptable form of entertainment once regulated.[62]

Kitten ball and baseball teams were formed by social and even work groups. Munsingwear, a major national knitwear company, offered both its male and female employees the opportunity to play on company-sponsored teams.[63] A Munsingwear-produced pamphlet described these teams, stating that "the games are enthusiastically watched by outsiders. We are proud of the Munsingites who represent us in the field of sports. They keep in mind, in play as well as in work, the ideal of teamwork, fair play and true sportsmanship."[64] The pamphlet shows the influence of national trends of recreation, organized sports, and spectatorship on local people, organizations, and park forms. The Parade grew to be a destination for all who were interested in watching or playing organized sports, regardless of age. The YWCA even identified it "with its numerous tennis courts and base ball [sic] and foot ball [sic] fields" as "the city's principal playground for adults."[65]

In a 1926 survey, the YWCA included a map of Minneapolis parks that indicated the types of recreation available at each park. The map showed the robust growth of the park system, which would not likely have been possible if it were not for the work of Cleveland and the early park board to acquire land and update park spaces to remain relevant to people's needs. When compared with

Cleveland's simple 1883 plan, the 1926 system demonstrated the dynamic roles of parks and the ways in which interventions and accommodations affected their form and purposes over time.

The map of available recreations in Minneapolis's parks demonstrated that the park board's ongoing efforts to provide varied recreation opportunities in these spaces throughout the city continued to develop after the period under consideration. There was no one, main, central park out of most of the population's reach. Nor was there one specific park that received investments at the expense of others (though this would become an issue in the parks system in the second half of the twentieth century). Accommodations for new types of recreation continued, as is evidenced by the three golf courses in place in 1926.

The transformation of park grounds reflected broader changes in the city's social development. Between the 1880s and the 1920s, Minneapolis's parks transformed from unguided, passive pleasure grounds to recreation parks intended to compete with commercial entertainments to active parks with playgrounds that gave children safe, guided spaces to play and adults the opportunity to play and watch organized sports. Cleveland successfully established an ethos of park appreciation in the city, and his successors worked to execute his vision after his death. The idea that parks were for the people helped guide the park board in keeping them dynamic, relevant spaces. Social reformers capitalized on the abundance of public park space in Minneapolis, but their programming helped to keep parks relevant and entrenched them as community spaces throughout the city. Minneapolis may never have become known as the City of Flour and Flowers, but the legacy of its parks and recreation continue to define and guide the City of Lakes well into the twenty-first century.

## CHAPTER TWO

# Fairways Open to All

## *A History of Golf in the Twin Cities*

### THOMAS B. JONES

Twin Cities' golf history offers a wide evidential fairway for the sports historian, seeded with several narrative possibilities (and as readers might wish, limited opportunities for badly shanked metaphors). The prominent role business elites and civic leaders played in the sport's early growth, the push for municipal golf courses, and the restrictions imposed on women and African American golfers are but a few of the topics worthy of attention. In effect, these past episodes fit a wider historical framework, allowing an exploration of golf as "more than just a game"—a sport that reveals much about the history of the Twin Cities and beyond.

The beginnings of golf in the Twin Cities can be traced to the 1890s and are linked primarily to an emerging class of business and civic leaders. In short order these bankers, lumber barons, grain merchants, real estate moguls, lawyers, judges, and dignitaries developed an enthusiasm for the sport and what it promised. What drew the Jaffrays, Pillsburys, Heffelfingers, Hills, Ordways, Raymonds, and others to golf, for the most part, mirrored what took place elsewhere in the nation at that time, particularly in regard to those of the same station and class. However, those in the Twin Cities who first established and promoted the game seemed to act in response to a unique blending of personal motives, class standing, and notions of civic responsibility.

Historians attentive to the enthusiasm golf stirred nationwide in the late nineteenth and early twentieth century have identified a variety of interrelated factors that serve as background for what happened in the Twin Cities.[1]

DOI: https://doi.org/10.34053/scs2019.tcs.2

Understanding the "why" behind this first golf craze demands attention to the interplay of industrialization, new economic roles and opportunities, technological innovation, advances in transportation (automobiles, commuter rail lines, and streetcars), urban and suburban growth, an expanding middle class, and the availability of inexpensive land for golf course construction. A changing attitude about work and leisure time; media ballyhoo touting the physical, psychological, and character-building benefits of golf for both men and women players; and a reactive drive to preserve status and traditions in face of a "new immigration" from eastern and southern Europe also help clarify why golf drew such growing, devoted attention.[2]

In another sense golf clicked with what early twentieth-century Americans imagined themselves and their history to be, not to mention what they thought it *ought* to be. Golf lovers endeavored to rid their game of its British aristocratic taint and transform it into a sport with a distinctly American ethos. In so doing, golf could fit into a cultural imagination much concerned with "identifying uniquely American things and . . . defining the unique character of that 'New Man,' the American."[3] To some, playing the game provided a contrived encore for the self-reliant, pioneering, lone individual in a determined quest to overcome nature's unpredictable domain and achieve success—a combination of Daniel Boone and Horatio Alger swinging a five iron and toting a self-improvement, golf-tip manual. Of course most people traversing the links did not directly envision a call-of-the-wild adventure or seek lofty cultural goals. A quick and efficient retreat from a rapidly modernizing world would do just fine.[4]

An early coterie of Twin Cities golf enthusiasts also welcomed such a retreat and likely found in the game a partial answer to "the adjustment that Americans (mostly affluent) made to the new city." This new city had greatly diminished a previous "sense of community," isolated urban residents from nature, and "plunged them into a rapidly declining cityscape." As historian Richard J. Moss summarizes, golf offered a chance "to reconstitute community," "revive a sense of belonging," and "reconnect with nature".[5]

Like their counterparts at St. Andrews (Yonkers, New York), the Country Club of Brookline (Massachusetts), and the Chicago Golf Club (Wheaton, Illinois), private golf club members in the Twin Cities also banded together to fill newfound leisure hours; clearly display their class status; experience the promised rewards of golf for a healthy mind and body; seek that aforementioned escape from a demanding, competitive world of work; and in playing the game, practice such treasured but supposedly threatened American values and characteristics as individualism, self-reliance, and hard work. These Twin Cities' private golfers no doubt also would have seized post-round, "19th hole" opportunities for new partnerships and dealmaking.

The honor of establishing the first golf course in the Twin Cities belongs to St. Paul. The Town & Country Club had its roots in a social organization, nicknamed the Nushkas, formed to promote and participate in the 1887 St. Paul Winter Carnival, an event hatched to dispel "mischievous rumors" that during the winter months Minnesota was unfit for "human habitation."[6] Within a short time, the club members acquired a stretch of land near the Mississippi River to build a stately (and comfy and warm) clubhouse. The site, overlooking the Mississippi River, included a picturesque surrounding stretch of land that was perfect for launching golf balls. In 1893 a handful of club members started play on a rudimentary, five-hole course.[7] The Town & Country golfing enthusiasts also would establish two short-lived courses nearby: the Roadside (1898–1902) and Miriam Park (1900–1902).

The Roadside course had a specific impetus for its founding. Embracing a national trend, the wives and daughters of the Town & Country members would have been attracted to golf for its "health and social attributes and especially because it was more appealing . . . than the alternative pastimes favored by Victorian females." As a midpoint between the sporting extremes of tennis and croquet, or bicycle riding and archery, golf seemed a "proper" game, allowing for time outside in a healthful natural setting, displays of fashionable and comfortable clothing, and a new (although limited) chance for male companionship.[8] Accordingly, the gentlemen of Town & Country gallantly launched the Roadside Golf Club, "primarily as a woman's golf club."[9]

In 1898 a Minneapolis-based contingent of Town & Country golf enthusiasts desired a more convenient golf venue. Impelled in part by a growing clash of differing business, cultural, and ethnic and religious "civic identities" with St. Paul, they set up a new nine-hole course to the west of downtown Minneapolis, reachable by streetcar.[10] Clive Talbot "C. T." Jaffray, future president of the First National Bank and Soo Line Railroad, played a key role in founding the Bryn Mawr Golf Club (Byrn Mawr means "great hill"), but he had a grander scheme in mind. On an idyllic bicycle outing with his wife and friends, Jaffray stopped to picnic on a hill above Lake Calhoun. He deemed the picturesque site and surrounding area as perfect for a golf course. And it was up for sale. The Minikahda Country Club opened to private membership in the summer of 1899.[11]

The Minikahda Club's founding and membership reflected the close relationship between private, country-club golfing and the larger concerns of the
city's business-social elites. Most of these Minikahda members already had
joined together at the exclusive Minneapolis Club founded in 1883. Historians
of the club have described it as a place where, "the influence of members,
expressed and exercised informally, has actually been the determining factor
in practically all of the important movements that have contributed to the
city's welfare and progress since it was organized."[12] Once the Minikahda Club
opened, these gentlemen had another venue for discussions and "were able to
merge their business and leisure lives and create a social oligarchy."[13] Without
doubt, hard-edged agreements on labor unions, commercial expansion, political power, and various business matters and opportunities would have found
a place in conversations on the golf course and over drinks in the clubhouse.
Leading members of the Minikahda Club also would find time to consider,
from different angles and perspectives, a growing need for municipal golf links.

By the early years of the twentieth century, Minneapolis and St. Paul housed
an expanding segment of white-collar workers and middle-class citizens with
discretionary money to spend, increased free time from the workplace, streetcar
access to different parts of both cities, a growing public park system, and cultural encouragement for sporting activities. Accordingly, this class of citizens
developed an interest in golfing and welcomed any efforts allowing them to
play within a reasonable distance and for a modest cost.

The citizenry of St. Paul and Minneapolis also had grown substantially
more complex in the late nineteenth century; accordingly, the Twin Cities
took on its share of the difficulties associated with life in other big cities, such
as New York, Boston, and Chicago. A raft of urban problems—overcrowding,
immigration, poverty, class conflict, public health problems, and a "declining
morality"—prompted serious concern among middle- and upper-class Twin
Cities residents. To meet these challenges, Twin Cities leaders and reformers
turned to some of the same solutions employed by their larger urban cousins.
Building public parks to help mitigate the social and moral ills of city life had
its first expression in New York City. Central Park opened in 1857 and set the
tone for an urban parks crusade that took off following the Civil War. The Twin
Cities joined that crusade and within a short period boasted an impressive
set of parks and parkways on both sides of the Mississippi. In large measure,
municipal golf would spring from a national public parks movement in which
the Twin Cities played a major role.[14]

The establishment of municipal courses before the Depression years owed a great deal to the efforts of private club members and civic leaders, who were often one and the same. Private golf clubs worried about what to do with a growing surplus of golfers on the waiting lists for club membership. Also, as their biographies reveal, many first-generation club members felt duty bound to open up golfing to the "man of moderate means, confined to offices and inside works and just the men who would become far more efficient machines, if they had a weekly chance to get a 'swipe at the pill' and get lungs full of fresh air."[15] As a breathless golf magazine article of the time urged, "Golf is and ought to be within the reach of all—poor or rich, as a mental and physical developer, and in the interest of a better and saner citizenship."[16]

Initially, landscape architects and planners envisioned Twin Cities parks "as areas to showcase naturalistic landscaping" thus affording for residents "a healthy refuge from the hustle and bustle" of life.[17] According to Horace W. S. Cleveland's vision of 1885, city parks would enable what the famous landscape architect termed "passive" recreations (walking, skating, picnicking, and other less active, non-sport activities). Keeping people off the grass seemed to be a major concern. Cleveland's passive recreation would soon yield to an updated, turn-of-the-century version, and the Minneapolis park board's Jesse Northrup, President of Northrup, King & Company, suggested a public golf course in his 1907 annual report. In less than a decade, Glenwood Park, a nine-hole course with sand greens located on Minneapolis's north side, attracted twelve thousand golfers in one year. By 1934, reflecting the supportive actions of the Minneapolis park board, five courses in the city hosted public play. The planning and decision-making that led to municipal golf at Theodore Wirth (1916, originally Glenwood), Colombia (1919), Francis A. Gross (1925, originally Armour), Meadowbrook (1926), and Hiawatha (1934) parks exemplified the connections between park board leadership and private club members.[18]

Across the river, St. Paul's superintendent of parks, Frederick Nussbaumer, favored active, organized recreation as an "important component" of his plans for Como Park's expansion. Town & Country golfing devotees had a project in mind to fit that ideal. A proposal for a "municipal golf links" to be located near and within Como Park, came before the St. Paul City Council in 1905. William F. Peet, insurance executive and member at Town & Country, described the outcome: "The plan was unanimously vetoed without discussion and with pitying smiles from our city fathers."[19] Adding insult to injury, the St. Paul newspaper carried an opinion piece that, in Peet's recollection, described golfers as "dudes, idlers, fools, degenerates," with the additional slam that "the game was the idiot's delight."[20] Despite such slights, idiocy apparently triumphed. By 1917 Phalen Park Golf Course hosted many a foursome of dandies, do-nothings, birdbrains, and louts. The construction of Highland Park (1928) and Como Park (1929) courses furthered opportunities for the golfing public. In addition, Herbert P. Keller, the former Mayor of St. Paul (1910–1914) and a prominent city leader, launched an initiative to construct a first-class, eighteen-hole public course. Named for its advocate, Keller Golf Course opened in 1929, and within a year hosted the first of several professional tournaments, including the longstanding St. Paul Open.

Overall, Minneapolis and St. Paul had accomplished a great deal before the Great Depression in building municipal golf courses and promoting public play. In 1925, according to a *Golfers Magazine* writer, the Twin Cities had "the best presentation of municipal golf . . . seen anywhere, as well as an excellent example of a city searching for the best means and methods for developing recreational facilities for all classes of people."[21] But as elsewhere across the country, the idealistic sentiments that played a part in the rise of Twin Cities municipal golf never stretched far from mainstream thinking about other matters. For when it came to it, golf had a decidedly reactive tilt with regard to matters of gender and race. Women might be allowed to play on certain days and within restricted times; African Americans faced rigid formal and informal discrimination.

In 1894 *Harper's Magazine* writer Caspar W. Whitney waxed rhapsodic about the country club golf scene, identifying its "one distinguishing feature" as "the recognition of the gentle sex." Whitney claimed no knowledge of country clubs where women were "not admitted either on individual membership or on that of *paterfamilias*."[22] Of course at that early date, the writer's purview did not include the soon-to-be typical country club, featuring golf as the quintessential recreation overseen by male members.

From the outset, women golfers would experience a not-so-subtle bias to go along with the era's societal disregard for women's rights and everyday being. A listing of the insults women golfers faced at private or public golf courses is familiar even today, despite some legal victories and hard-earned changes. No weekend, morning, or holiday play; no reserved starting times for tournaments; no representation on club governance committees; and banishment for divorcées were but some of the sexist rules a woman golfer encountered. From the pro shop, outright lying about available tee times was "par for the course." On one score, the Minikahda Club took exception from usual practice, granting women full resident voting memberships from the beginning. But tee times for women were limited, and none could cross the boundary markings protecting the sanctity of the men's bar and grill.[23]

Perhaps the wives and daughters of private club members did encounter situations where "social status protected them from ridicule or having their femininity questioned and made it easier to break social conventions."[24] But these instances would be the exception as reported by Anne O'Hagan in *Munsey's Magazine* (1901): "There is excellent and almost universal masculine testimony . . . that on crowded days nothing so discourages a man as women playing before him."[25] Many decades later the city leaders of Omaha, Nebraska, apparently had the same and usual thought in mind when they upheld a Saturday ban on women golfing. Why? "Women golfers are maddenly [sic] slow and would drive the men crazy."[26] Despite such male tizzies, women took up the game from the very start.

Despite her wry comment on male golfers' angst, O'Hagan saw many benefits about the sport for women's health, mental well-being, and social advancement. She insisted that "since the day when the Greek girdle became the Teutonic corset, no boon has been granted so great as the privilege of wearing shirt waists and short skirts." Women golfing had freed "half the race" (many of whom "could not distinguish between a cleek and broom handle"), to live a life better in "health, disposition, and dress."[27] With regard to this early-twentieth-century *zeitgeist*, Twin Cities women golfers, despite other indignities, likely agreed with O'Hagan. The Young-Quinlan Department Store, ever on the alert for fashion trends, advertised "some of the newest, striking originations in Golf Togs" ready for the "Golf Tournament-Town and Country Club sward."[28]

Playing golf or not, wives and daughters did not spurn the social aspects of country club life as it afforded a variety of occasions to mingle with the opposite sex. A mixed foursome or a club party could provide the perfect setting for a "courting ritual among sexes."[29] The Minikahda Club and Town & Country stayed open throughout the winter as places "of rendezvous for society folk," who braved cold and snow for formal dinners, luncheons, and teas.[30] The *Minneapolis Morning Tribune's* "Society Page" informed readers that "Devotees of the little gutta percha ball who are accustomed to playing in golf tournaments at the Minikahda Club" predicted a good coming season for golfing which had "proved to be one of the most popular pastimes with Minneapolis matrons."[31]

Winter Golfing at Columbia Golf Course in the mid-1920s. Minnesota Historical Society

Off the society pages and on the golf course, the women of Twin Cities country clubs did not waste much time organizing occasions for playing the game. In the early fall of 1915, over sixty golfers competed in a match play tournament at the Town & Country Club. That same gathering produced the Women's Minnesota Golf Association founded by women members of Minikahda, Interlachen, Town & Country, Northland, Lafayette and White Bear Yacht Club.[32] In time such competitions would produce an exceptional woman golfer, Minneapolis's Patty Berg, whose abilities and contributions to the game would extend far beyond her start at the Interlachen Country Club. Berg's career in golf encompassed some eighty amateur and professional tournament wins—including fifteen women's major championships. She also helped organize the Ladies Professional Golf Association (LPGA), serving as the organization's first president. In addition to all her golfing accomplishments, Berg's athletic exploits as a young girl in the Colfax Avenue South neighborhood of Minneapolis remain a biographical highlight. The future LPGA Hall of Fame golfer quarterbacked for the "50th Street Tigers" football team at age thirteen. The team included University of Minnesota legend Bud Wilkinson.

In 1901 the *Minneapolis Tribune* reported a growing interest in the sport among the city's African American population. Under the headline "Colored People Talk of Organizing a Golf Club," the newspaper noted an enthusiasm among the "colored folks" to play golf and to find a "suitable links for a new club." Scott Blake, one of the aspiring African American golfers, thought that somewhere towards the western edge of the city (between the Minikahda Club and the Interlachen Country Club) would make for a "very good nine-hole course." He promised others that at such a golf course "you will see some fun." Despite an optimistic start, the proposed golf course failed to materialize, but as the *Tribune* felt necessary to report: "Ever since there has been a rush for golfing outfits by the colored folks of the locality."[33]

Despite their passion for the sport, African Americans found *de facto* segregation and racial discrimination alive and well in the Twin Cities years beyond World War II. Denied entry to many restaurants, clubs, and even churches; redlined in housing; hired only as a last resort; restricted in location and access for a swim in public pools; prohibited from rooming in University of Minnesota dormitories; closed off in the balcony section of many movie theaters; and subjected to additional racial abuses and possible legal codes, African Americans of St. Paul and Minneapolis might well have thought twice about the local golf scene.[34] These new golfers had to scout out places and times to play with cautious appraisals. Indeed, until 1952, the Minneapolis park board did not allow black golfers to join any golf clubs (men's or women's) formed for play and recognized at its public courses.[35] It would be years before anyone other than white golfers trod the fairways of private golf clubs.

Subtle and flagrant prohibitions to playing aside, the sport had gained a strong foothold among black golfers by the 1920s. Many arrived at the first tee indirectly, first glimpsing the sport as caddies, greenskeepers, pro shop attendants, cooks, bartenders, and servers. Leaders in the St. Paul and Minneapolis African American communities also spotlighted golf by forming clubs and sponsoring tournaments. In 1931 the Twin Cities Golf Association (TCGA) organized formally and settled on a mission (1935) "to sponsor the advancement of golf among the Negro citizens" of Minneapolis and St. Paul.[36] Soon the African American golfers of the Twin Cities promoted a national tournament for men and women with competitors arriving from Chicago, Detroit, St. Louis, and Kansas City. Heavyweight boxing champ and avid golfer Joe Louis rarely missed an opportunity to play, winning what became the "Upper Midwest Bronze Amateur" prize in 1957.[37] Despite these grassroots organizational and promotional pushes, a significant obstacle remained for any African American golfer who dreamed of competing as a professional.

From its beginnings in 1916, the Professional Golfers' Association (PGA) held to policy that excluded "non-Caucasians" from membership. In a 1943 update of the PGA constitution, Article III (the infamous "Caucasian only" clause) made clear that African-American golfers could not be members of the organization or compete in tour events (except for a precious few, like the Los Angeles Open, where sponsors did not feel it necessary to secure PGA approval to have a successful tournament). In the long history of the "Caucasian only" clause, Keller Golf Course would be the setting of two significant actions against the blatant discrimination practiced by the PGA.[38] The first such action dates to the summer of 1934 when Robert "Pat" Ball, a black golfer from Chicago, attempted to play in the St. Paul Open.

By the mid-1920s, Pat Ball had earned his place as one of the top African American golfers around Chicago and beyond.[39] A determined challenger of the *status quo*, known among Chicago's African American golfers as one of "the prime movers of the game in the city," Ball refused to allow any Jim Crowism to restrict his passion for golf. Ball's approach was "to challenge the system without fanfare, like a mouse in the last church pew," although he practiced "a country charisma coated with a big city guile."[40]

In 1927 Ball captured first place at the Cook County Open, a US Amateur Public Links Championship, competing as the lone African American in the field. In that same year, he won the United Golf Association's second championship tournament (a title he would defend in 1929, 1934, and 1941). In search of a larger stage for his golfing skills and most likely, resolved to continue testing the "whites only" issue, Ball decided to enter the 1928 Philadelphia Public Links Tournament. As it turned out, the event officials denied Ball and another black golfer entry to the competition, despite the fact that he qualified in the first two days of stroke play. Ball refused to back off, especially since he had been accused of "disobedience" to the rules. He took legal action and won an injunction in common pleas court. Unfortunately for Ball and his fellow black golfer Elmer Stout, the injunction came too late for the pair to tee off as part of the match play finishing rounds. Yet buoyed by his continuing success on the United Golf Association (UGA) tournament circuit for African American golfers, Ball made his way to Keller golf course in 1934 for the fourth annual St. Paul Open.[41]

The PGA sponsored the St. Paul Open, and at that point in time, the tournament should have abided by the "Caucasian-only" dictate. But the professional golfing world's plan for excluding black golfers failed to register in the plans of one Chicago golfer. A "Robert" Ball showed up for the tournament and played each day with a field of some eighty white professional golfers, including such names as Harry Cooper, Walter Hagen, Tommy Armour, and Horton Smith who did his best as PGA President in the early 1950s to keep black golfers locked out.[42] It appears that no one officially called in to question Ball's participation in the tournament, and he finished thirty-third, after a disappointing 80 in the first round. A few weeks following the St. Paul Open, a sports column in the African American newspaper the *Minneapolis Spokesman* noted Ball's victory at the Minneapolis Negro Midwest Golf Tournament, and added: "He holds the distinction of being the first Negro ever to be entered in a major white tournament at the St. Paul Open." Two years later a *Spokesman* reporter heard that Ball might play again in the St. Paul Open. Recalling Ball's first appearance at the tournament, a "Golf Divots" article informed readers that the Chicago golfer "would have been trouble for some of the leading 'Pros' had it not been for a disastrous first round." Ball knew his "ABC's on the golf course," and it would be "a treat to see one of our boys in this big match."[43] It would be almost two decades in the future before that happened.

The 1948 St. Paul Open marked an essential moment in the struggle against the PGA's "Caucasian only" clause. Solomon Hughes of Minneapolis, a past champion UGA golfer, decided to enter the tournament, but he and another UGA top golfer, Ted Rhodes, would be turned away without a chance to display their considerable talents. The PGA was on the alert this time, and the organization had no qualms about asserting the specifics of its "Caucasian only" bylaw.

After his arrival in Minneapolis near the end of World War II, Solomon Hughes soon realized his dream of working as a golf pro did not accord with the prevailing racial prejudice. Hughes's job inquiries produced nothing, despite his previous experience teaching golf and his record of success on the UGA tour. "He thought he would be able to be a pro coming north," one of his daughters remembered. "Little did he know that racial segregation would follow him here."[44] To make ends meet, Hughes first took a job with the Great Northern Railway as a Pullman porter but made time to play, practice, and offer informal lessons at Hiawatha Golf Course whenever possible. Entering the clubhouse at Hiawatha proved a different story: African Americans were not welcome and were denied use of the supposedly public building. The same ban existed at other municipal courses in both Minneapolis and St. Paul. Hughes refused to let things stand, and with the help of his brother and fellow members of the Twin Cities Golf Club, eventually helped force an end to the discriminatory practice.[45]

Before moving to Minneapolis from Gadsden, Alabama, Hughes had forged a strong connection with boxer Joe Louis during the war years, possibly serving as the heavyweight champ's first golf instructor. After the war the two men remained in close touch, and Louis wanted his friend to travel across the country with him as a "personal pro" and money-match partner. Hughes had to decline the offer, but another welcome visitor to the Hughes' household, Ted Rhodes, signed on. During golfing stopovers in the Twin Cities, often spending time with the Hughes family in south Minneapolis, Louis and Rhodes would have voiced their opinions on the PGA's discrimination against African American golfers. Early in 1948 Rhodes, Bill Spiller, and Madison Gunther had filed a $250,000 legal suit challenging the "Caucasians-only" policy. By virtue of their top-sixty finishes in the previous week's Los Angeles Open, the three UGA pros qualified for the following week's Richmond (Oakland, California) tournament. The PGA refused to budge from its race policy.[46] The upcoming lawsuit and attendant bad publicity for the PGA held out a promising opportunity to keep up the pressure at the St. Paul Open. Hughes and Rhodes, with the "Brown Bomber" Louis in their corner, decided to go up against the PGA officials and enter the tournament.

Hughes mailed in the entry fees for himself and Rhodes, expecting a refusal.[47] The St. Paul Jaycees, longtime cosponsor of the golf event, returned the entry fees without delay. At this point a prominent and forceful voice in the African American community joined the fight. Cecil E. Newman, owner-editor of the weekly *Minneapolis Spokesman* and *St. Paul Recorder*, skewered the PGA's exclusion of Hughes and Rhodes and its duplicity in claiming the tournament to be an "invitational" rather than an "open." Editorials by Newman's hand also lashed out at the Twin Cities' newspapers and St. Paul civic leaders for a lack of "intestinal fortitude," in addition to placing money above principle. In a particularly damning but apt observation, Newman reflected that "it's one thing to editorially deplore race discrimination . . . miles away in the South, but still another matter to stand up against similar practices when found right here on our doorstep."[48]

Whitney M. Young Jr., future leader of the National Urban League and civil rights pioneer, took an early and active role in exposing the PGA's discriminatory actions and chicanery. As a local Urban League officer and new recruit to the St. Paul Jaycees, most likely knowing that Hughes and Rhodes planned to submit entrees to the tournament, Young asked his fellow club members if the upcoming golf tourney would be open to all. Jaycee officials answered yes. The PGA refused to consider that possibility, despite a last-minute attempt by St. Paul mayor Edward Delaney to somehow right the situation.

A day before the qualifying rounds, Mayor Delaney held an urgent, lengthy meeting with local tournament officials and Whitney Young, hoping to "solve the problem." The meeting failed to find the needed quick fix for several reasons, the most prominent being a lack of time for further discussion or legal action. At best, Mayor Delaney decided that any contract for a future St. Paul Open held at Keller Golf Course must include an anti-Jim Crow clause. Whitney Young commented to a *Spokesman* reporter that "the local Junior Chamber are making themselves a party to discrimination" by not pushing further for Hughes's and Rhodes's entry into the tournament. The Jaycees eventually did issue a statement critical of the PGA's "Caucasian-only" clause including a call for reform. The PGA eluded further embarrassment and later sidestepped the California lawsuit by pledging not to continue discriminatory practices. But the PGA would soon employ another trick—tested at the 1951 St. Paul Open event—designed to sustain its lily-white preferences for membership and sponsored tournaments.[49]

In 1951 Hughes once again set out to integrate the St. Paul Open with solid backing from the Jaycees. The PGA ignored that support and informed the Jaycees' tournament director, Ken C. Webb, that the "St. Paul Invitational Open Tournament . . . is a 'limited' field event" and "participation is restricted under the contract." As the contract specified, Hughes had to be a PGA member or an "Approved PGA Tournament Player."[50] He was neither. The PGA had preserved "Caucasian's only" with a song and dance worthy of a double-dealing office seeker. As a golf historian described the policy, "besides being an oxymoronic contradiction," the PGA's terminology ("Open Invitational") allowed "a host club to refuse to 'invite' a black golfer to an event" and yet "wring its hands and declare it had no control over a private club's policies."[51] The PGA's linguistic gymnastics failed to deter the Jaycees in the following year. After continuing growing local pressure directed against the PGA's rulings, the Jaycees stepped forward and once more invited Hughes and Rhodes to compete in the St. Paul Open. Primarily in response to a successful and well-publicized challenge at the San Diego Open—carried out by Joe Louis and UGA golfer Bill Spiller—the PGA made no attempt to block any competitors allowed invited status.[52]

The results of the 1952 tournament did not favor the first-time African American golfers. In his mid-forties, Hughes's most competitive golfing years were behind him, and Rhodes had difficulty shaking off "the pressure and the tension" he experienced during the first round. Although the official PGA "Caucasian only" clause would not be deleted until 1961, Hughes and Rhodes had played a key role in opening the future for other golfers—both amateur and professional. As one small salute to Hughes's accomplishments, a Minnesota golf tournament now boasts his name and "promises to bring new awareness and honor to a man who only wanted to play golf without racial restrictions."[53]

What might emerge as useful conclusions in the foregoing pages are, of course, more complex and deserving of additional research than at first glance. Nevertheless, here are some preliminary ideas and questions possibly of significance for the historian of Twin Cities' golf and other sports.

It appears that a close-knit group of business and civic leaders led the way in introducing, establishing, and spreading the game of golf throughout the Twin Cities. But how to fully, properly ascribe and explain the motivations and approaches of these leading citizens? In such a consideration, it is easy to lean towards either end of a continuum—self-serving elites versus public-spirited, upright men of influence. In terms of Twin Cities' golf, however, these movers and shakers and their actions are not easily identified as one or the other. In addition, did not the emerging municipal golf movement encompass more impetus and contributions from middle and working class golfers in St. Paul and Minneapolis than the present narrative presents?

In terms of the early experiences of African Americans, women, and other groups of Twin Cities golfers, the wish might be to stress a liberal-progressive tradition in favorable contrast with other US cities. Until recent years, the self-image of most Twin Citians routinely bypassed any conflict between ideal and reality. But the evidence brings much into question. How substantive were the legal and social changes that helped extend opportunities to play golf to a larger group of citizens? Do fundamental prejudices and exclusions at the golf course, though disguised as courteous, reserved, and mild-mannered "Minnesota nice," remain as widespread and irksome today? Did the golfing achievements of women and African Americans, both amateur and professional, help reshape local attitudes in a positive direction as some sports historians might posit?

What will the future historian write about Twin Cities golf? It appears at this point that golf is in decline throughout Minneapolis and St. Paul. Recent reporting indicates both cities have lost money and considered course closings. Public and private courses host fewer rounds and need more members. A study commissioned by the Minneapolis Park and Recreation Board (2014) labeled golf a "failing enterprise" and "in the grip of a death spiral."[54] To meet the difficulties, courses now recommend and advertise playing but nine or fifteen holes as an alternative for busy men and women. Cash-strapped courses consider food promotions and "cigar smoking events in outdoor tents" as ways to draw in more customers, who are not necessarily enamored with golfing.[55] FootGolfers (those who kick a soccer ball merrily down the fairway and into a large cup) can now share courses like Hiawatha and Colombia with traditional golfers. Simulated golf experiences also are in the works. At the Minneapolis-St. Paul International Airport, a twelve-thousand-square-foot space, packed with stimulators, a putting green, a virtual driving range, and a pro shop, is now open for waiting passengers.

What is next?

Envision a lone golfer approaching a fairway shot, dressed in business-casual togs, jabbering at a Bluetooth-connected, multipurpose wristwatch phone, and riding astride a Hoverboard device (with footholds resembling mock wing tip golf shoes). When not texting friends or checking email, the golfer will activate a virtual reality headset for handy golf tips and replays. One can only hope this modern-era hacker will escape the FootGolfers' errant soccer ball blasts from the neighboring fairway.

## CHAPTER THREE

# Aces on Ice

*The Glory Days of Speed Skating in the Twin Cities*

## DAVID C. SMITH

At a gala ceremony in the Radisson Hotel in Minneapolis on April 27, 1959, the Minnesota Sports Hall of Fame, in only its second year, inducted five new members. Two were speed skaters. One, John S. Johnson, had dominated the sport in its earliest days of the 1890s and had died twenty-five years earlier. The other, Ken Bartholomew, was still competing and would win another national championship, his fourteenth, before he retired a year later.[1]

Johnson and Bartholomew, feted that night by a rousing crowd and guest speakers Branch Rickey, Lefty Gomez, Patty Berg, and Jack Kramer, were the bookends on a period of speed skating history in North America that was often dominated by Minnesota skaters, and many of the sport's greatest races were held at the Hippodrome or Lake Como in St. Paul or Powderhorn Lake in Minneapolis.

By climate, topography, and culture, Minnesotans were ideally suited to excel at sports below freezing and to celebrate heroes such as Johnson and Bartholomew.

The vast majority of settlers in Minnesota in the 1800s came from other cold climates. New England, especially Maine, supplied most of the early immigrants from within the United States. They brought skating west with them. Immigrants to Minnesota from outside the United States were predominantly from northern Europe, especially Scandinavia, where winter sports had deep roots. In 1890 Minneapolis overtook Chicago as the principal destination of Scandinavian immigrants to the United States. The population of foreign-born

DOI: https://doi.org/10.34053/scs2019.tcs.3

Norwegians in Minneapolis more than tripled in the 1880s, making Norwegians the third-largest foreign-born group in the city after Swedes and Brits.[2]

In early recollections of life in Minneapolis, ice skating was fondly remembered as one of the few winter amusements. Adding to the popularity of skating was the fact that it was one of few athletic endeavors acceptable for women. Ice skating and horseback riding were the only "exertive sports" considered appropriate for mid-Victorian women. Skating gave women "a chance to exercise, exhibit athletic skills, and socialize in a proper setting."[3]

The people of Minneapolis and St. Paul enjoyed an abundance of skating opportunities, both public and private. In addition to skating on the river, lakes, and ponds, both cities had private rinks at multiple locations through the 1860s and 1870s. Entrepreneurs would erect a fence or wall around a lot, flood it, keep it cleared of snow, and charge admission to skate. Musical entertainment and fireworks were provided, and skating contests were promoted to attract customers.

The huge variable every year was weather. The Twin Cities were cold on average but not consistently. Many rink entrepreneurs were doomed by stretches of temperatures too warm for good ice or too cold for bad skaters. The *Minneapolis Tribune* lamented open water on the river in mid-December in 1868, but it crowed about six inches of ice on Johnson's Pond by the first week in November a few years later.[4]

The Minneapolis Board of Park Commissioners (BPC) was established by the Minnesota legislature and approved by a referendum in 1883. The board's first acquisition was the land around and including Johnson's Pond, which is now Loring Park. The pond was dredged and enlarged in the first winter it was owned by the board. In the second winter, however, about three acres of the frozen pond were cleared of snow, and electric lights were installed for skating.[5]

More importantly, in 1885 the BPC maintained skating rinks not only at the pond in Loring Park but created rinks on dry land in Logan Park and Murphy Square, two of Minneapolis's first neighborhood parks. Ice skating was the first *activity* ever sponsored by the park board.[6]

Skating remained more a form of recreation than of competition for decades. Although skating contests over long distances on the English fens and Dutch canals had existed for centuries, accounts of racing on ice skates in the United States did not appear with any regularity until after the Civil War.

Some of the biggest races widely covered by the sporting press featured the Norwegian champion Axel Paulsen in 1884. Paulsen toured North America that winter and drew large crowds wherever he skated. The proprietors of a Minneapolis rink prematurely announced that he would come to Minneapolis for an exhibition. Although the announcement was quickly withdrawn owing to a "misunderstanding," the apparent drawing power of Paulsen suggested there was considerable public interest in speed skating.[7]

Locally, one of the most important events was the creation of the St. Paul Winter Sports Carnival in 1886, featuring a life-size Disneyesque palace made of ice blocks. The Ice Palace had a skating rink within its royal grounds. Carnival organizers offered a prize for a five-mile race, as well as one for figure skating, which was the incentive for the formation of the first skating club in St. Paul.

In 1887 the Minneapolis park board also approved its first speed skating track—as well as a horseracing track on ice—at Lake Calhoun after acquiring the eastern shore of the lake in 1885.[8]

Axel Paulsen returned to North America in the winter of 1887—visiting towns such as Crookston and Fargo as well as Minneapolis—and again in the winter of 1888–1889. Paulsen's race against Rudolph Goetz over twenty miles at the Minneapolis baseball park rink in January 1889, drew a crowd of over five thousand "by actual count." The *Minneapolis Tribune* called the race the "sporting event of the year."[9]

Paulsen was not only fast but he also put on crowd-pleasing performances of "fancy" skating, which included a famous jump he invented that still bears his name: the Axel. His jump included a single spin, but the world of figure skating has now progressed to triple and quadruple Axels.

In the spring of 1889 Paulsen decided to make Minneapolis his home. He remained in Minneapolis for the summer of 1889 and started a cigar-manufacturing business. When ice formed on Minneapolis rinks in late 1889, skaters came to Minneapolis from around North America to race the world's most famous skater.[10] Paulsen's most serious challenge came from Hugh McCormick of New Brunswick, but McCormick was not the only famous skater in town. The world's top amateurs took the train west, too. August Frohman, the Dutch champion, came from Holland, and Joe Donoghue, the reigning world amateur champion, came from his home in the Hudson River town of Newburgh, New York.

During contentious negotiations between McCormick and Paulsen over venues, distances, and purses, other skaters raced. The most interesting and noteworthy was a scheduled race between American amateur champ Donoghue and the Dutch champ Frohman. The report of the race was brief. Frohman became ill before the race, so a Minneapolis teenager, John Johnson, took his place. Donoghue won the three-mile race easily. The newspaper claimed that while Johnson skated well, he was "far out of his class" against Donoghue.[11] Words to remember.

McCormick ultimately defeated Paulsen in three of four races that were held from Eau Claire to Minneapolis to White Bear Lake, and a bitter Paulsen moved back to Norway.[12]

When another winter blew in, the *Tribune* reported that "southsiders" were agitating for the organization of a speed skating club. The "southsiders" were the Normanna Club, a social organization of the city's burgeoning Norwegian population, which announced that it would sponsor a ball at Normanna Hall to raise money for a Normanna Skating Club and rink for the 1891–92 winter season. In a show of Scandinavian solidarity, the Club announced that the ball would feature the Normanna infantry, Swedish Guard, and Scandinavian Knights of Pythias.[13]

The Club's interest in promoting skating was part of a larger trend in the city. In 1890 the BPC acquired land for Van Cleve Park and approved designs that included a man-made pond, which would serve as a skating rink. The same year the park board acquired the land around Powderhorn Lake, a small lake in south Minneapolis, which would eventually be the most famous speed skating track in the United States. The park board also reported that in the winter of 1890 it was not unusual to see five thousand skaters on Loring Pond.[14]

Despite continued support for skating by the park board and commercial skating rinks, the Normanna Club rink on the corner of Minnehaha Avenue and Twenty-Fifth Street became the center of speed skating in Minneapolis for several years.[15]

In the 1891–92 season, Hugh McCormick, Paulsen's Canadian nemesis, had traveled to Norway to race Harald Hagen and had been defeated. The two men met again in Minneapolis at the Normanna rink in December 1892 as the *Tribune* proclaimed, "The ice kings are flocking to Minneapolis, the recognized center of the exhilarating sport of skating." Hagen easily defeated the Canadian a second time.[16]

Despite the Norwegian inspiration and sponsorship of the Normanna Skating Rink, it would be a young Swede who would make the rink famous. In early 1893, for the second time in four months, John S. Johnson stunned the world, leaving the sporting press incredulous. They did not believe what he had done either time.

The first was on a bicycle in late September 1892 at Independence, Iowa, when Johnson, then a wiry twenty-one-year-old, rode a mile on a bicycle in less than one minute: fifty-seven seconds, nearly ten seconds faster than the existing world record for a mile. The cycling press, especially in New York and London, had barely stopped sniffing at that performance when Johnson laced on ice skates and took to the Normanna Skating Rink in Minneapolis on January 21, 1893, and broke the world record for a mile on speed skates. Once again, Johnson's performance was met with a sneer from New York about whether the hicks on the frontier knew how to work stopwatches—or measure race courses. The *New York Times* was blunt: "Few persons here believe that Johnson ever performed the feat credited him."[17]

The skepticism about Johnson's cycling time perhaps was understandable because the only vehicle on Earth that had gone faster than his bicycle was a locomotive. The skepticism about his skating feat, on the other hand, appears purely parochial. As both cyclist and skater, Johnson had to travel East and to Europe to meet the local favorites to prove himself.

When Johnson skated at the national amateur championships at Red Bank, New Jersey, two weeks after his record-setting skate in Minneapolis, he faced the man considered the fastest skater in the world, Joe Donoghue from New York, who had won the world championship in Europe the previous year and whose family dominated American speed skating on the Hudson River. This was the same Joe Donoghue who had beaten Johnson when he stood in for an ailing August Frohman in Minneapolis more than two years earlier. Johnson certainly would have remembered that race, but whether Donoghue did is anyone's guess. Donaghue had trounced many hot-shot kids like Johnson. The *New York Times* headline expressed the amazing result of the rematch: "Joe Donoghue Badly Beaten, A Surprise from John S. Johnson the Northwestern Skater." Donoghue wasn't even the runner-up in that race, an honor that went to Olaf Rudd of Minneapolis in a race that "vindicated Minneapolis time keeping and track measurement."[18]

Johnson was the most famous of a generation of Twin Cities speed skaters that emerged in the 1890s in the wake of the excitement over high-profile races like those featuring Axel Paulsen. World records were set by A. D. Smith, a long-distance skater from St. Paul, and John Nilsson and Olaf Rudd, both from Minneapolis. Years later Johnson said, "Funny about those times. We had the skaters in the Twin Cities, but we had to go East to get the races. [Norval] Baptie, [Harley] Davidson, Nilsson and I usually went and took the prizes, but Lord, we left a dozen men at home that could have beaten the Easterners!"[19]

Smith's world records for twenty and twenty-five miles, set on a rink on Cathedral Hill in St. Paul later in 1893 were probably recognized by the skating world only because Johnson's incredible times, backed by racing success, won credibility for all Minnesota skaters. The following year Smith smashed all amateur and pro records for every distance from six to twenty miles at his St. Paul rink. John Nilsson also set speed records, which like Johnson's, were not eclipsed in some cases until the 1920s. Smith and Nilsson both remained on the racing scene for many years, Smith as one of the organizers of races in St. Paul and Nilsson as a racer, but more prominently—and lucratively—as a fancy skater who performed around the country solo or with a crowd-pleasing partner, Minneapolitan Minnie Cummings. At the national amateur skating championships at New York in 1904, Nilsson was a featured performer *between* races with his dazzling spins and jumps.

John S. Johnson's victories were impressively fast but not fleeting. Some of his records were not surpassed for thirty years during an era when equipment and facilities were rapidly improving. Part of his success may have been the result of being pushed by other competitive skaters. Another factor may have been the lines then being drawn between amateur and professional. The records established by Donoghue, Johnson, Rudd, and Nilsson were later classified as professional—not amateur—records and fewer and fewer skaters were racing as professionals.

In the early days of speed skating—the 1880s and 1890s—the sport was similar to prize fighting, wrestling, and horse racing. A skater would post a challenge to another skater in a newspaper, usually accompanied by a wager that was often deposited with the editor. When a challenger matched a bet, the race was on, usually with considerable side betting. The loser's stake was often used to create a medal for the winner. It was a naked sham to maintain amateur status while realizing some reward. Early on, Johnson, who was ostensibly a bicycle mechanic, abandoned the charade and raced for money. Johnson made the bulk of his income racing bicycles or giving exhibitions at venues that charged admission.

Interest in skating was such that *Popular Science Monthly* ran an article in December 1895 by R. Tait McKenzie entitled "The Anatomy of Speed Skating." McKenzie was a Canadian doctor, physical therapist, and sculptor who would later become the first professor of physical education at the University of Pennsylvania. The study featured anatomical measurements and nude photographs—in tasteful skating poses—of Johnson, another Minneapolis skater Olaf Nortwedt, and Canadian Jack McCulloch. The photographs illustrated the long thighs and deep chests of the skaters as well as their relatively undeveloped upper bodies. McKenzie listed Johnson's weight at the time as 144 pounds and noted that, although he was "unquestionably" the best skater at distances up to five miles, he could not complete three pullups. McKenzie also recorded that Johnson had a very slow and strong heartbeat of fifty-four beats per minute and that his pulse was "not easily quickened by exercise."[20]

Only three years after breaking onto the world skating scene with record-setting times, Johnson declined to participate in the 1896 national championship, even though it was held in St. Paul, because "there's no money in skating." Instead of two unpredictable months of skating in the northern United States, Canada, and northern Europe, he could race bicycles nearly year-round somewhere in the country.[21]

Thirty years after Johnson burst onto the national speed skating scene, Chicago's Bobby McLean, a world champion himself, was celebrated in the *New York Times* for breaking three world records in one day in 1923 at Saranac Lake in the Adirondacks. The *Times* reported that McLean had skated the fastest times ever over 220 yards (one-eighth of a mile), quarter-mile, and half-mile on the half-mile oval track on the lake. In two of those three events, the quarter- and half-mile, the records he broke had still belonged to John S. Johnson.[22]

After the immense popularity of speed skating in the early 1890s, interest in the sport waned. Part of the problem was unseasonably warm weather for a few winters. The decline in skating in general was worsened by the financial crunch that hit the Minneapolis park board in the years following the Panic of 1893. The only rink maintained by the park board in 1900 was at Loring Park, in contrast to the six rinks maintained in 1894. Still the *Daily Globe* wrote in 1900 that there was still "good reason" to rank the Twin Cities as "the skating center and stronghold of America."[23]

Lack of interest in racing on skates did not indicate a lack of interest in skating in general. The Minneapolis park board enlarged the warming house for skaters at Powderhorn Lake in 1902 and placed a new rink and warming house on the northern arm of Lake of the Isles a year later. A pickup in interest was indicated further by the application of a new Twin City Skating Club to use a park rink for races in 1905.[24] The next year Charles Loring donated a permanent two-story building beside Loring Pond, which had been named for him, for use as a warming house in winter. The Minneapolis park board was again maintaining eight rinks in winter, three of which were flooded by the fire department in neighborhoods without natural bodies of water.[25]

When Camden (now Webber) Park was acquired in 1908 in north Minneapolis, Shingle Creek, which ran through the park, was immediately dammed to create a pond that would serve as a skating rink. By 1915 Minneapolis park superintendent Theodore Wirth reported that the park board maintained thirty-seven skating rinks, seven hockey rinks, one skating race track, one horse race track on ice, thirty-four warming houses, eight paths across lakes, and eighteen sled and toboggan slides.[26]

Despite the popularity of skating, however, speed skating attracted scant attention from the sporting world. With little institutional or organizational support other than the provision of facilities, speed skating greatness depended on the emergence of extraordinary individual athletes. The few of those who emerged in the 1920s and early 1930s came from St. Paul's Hippodrome Skating Club. In 1908 the Hippodrome on the State Fair grounds in St. Paul became the largest indoor skating rink in the United States. A year later the Hippodrome Skating Club was inaugurated, which would produce many of the fastest Minnesota skaters for the next twenty-five years.[27]

The first was Everett McGowan, who may be the greatest Minnesota athlete no one has heard of. Minnesota sports fans talk about Bud Grant playing pro football and basketball, or Hamline's Howie Schultz playing for the Dodgers and the Lakers, or Dave Winfield being drafted in three sports out of the University of Minnesota, but Everett McGowan was paid to play five sports, six if you count fancy skating, which is how he made his living for much of his life. He was the only elite speed skater to have any success as a professional hockey player.

McGowan played professional baseball, football, and hockey, and had one unfortunate adventure in the boxing ring in addition to being a national champion as both an amateur and professional speed skater. As a fancy skater, he was one of the first performers for the Ice Follies as a pairs skater with his wife Ruth Mack and helped create the Follies primary competition, the Ice Capades.[28]

The fact he was a paid athlete is one reason so few people have heard of him as a skater. Like John S. Johnson and John Nilsson before him, his professional status kept him from competing in many attention-grabbing national and international competitions like the Olympics, which were for "simon pures"—amateurs—only.

McGowan was a five-sport star at Humboldt High School on St. Paul's west side before moving across town in 1919 to St. Thomas College where he became the star halfback for the Tommies as a freshman. But it was not until the winter of his freshman year that McGowan's transcendent athletic ability became known beyond Minnesota. In January 1920, McGowan represented the Hippodrome Skating Club at the national championships at Saranac Lake, New York. Although he arrived late and missed the first two events, he did well enough in the events of the second day to tie Roy McWhorter of Chicago for the title.[29] Three weeks later, McGowan proved his performance was no fluke by easily winning the international amateur championship at Lake Placid over McWhorter and Eastern United States champion Charles Jewtraw.[30]

McGowan returned to St. Paul from New York a hero and won the Northwest Indoor Championship at the Hippodrome in front of the largest crowd that had ever filled that arena.[31] No less an authority than John S. Johnson raved about McGowan's speed, surmising that within a year he would defeat the reigning professional champion, Bobby McLean.[32]

McGowan never again skated as an amateur. He announced in April that he would return to St. Thomas for the 1920 football season and then turn pro as a skater in December. His announcement shot down the rumor that he would transfer to Notre Dame to play football for Knute Rockne but fueled the other rampant rumor that he had already agreed to race the legendary Norwegian skater Oscar Mathieson, the reigning European champion, for a purse of $25,000.

McGowan quickly proved that Johnson was a shrewd talent evaluator. In a series of elimination matches among the elite American professional skaters in early 1922, McGowan beat them all, including Bobby McLean in a head-to-head four-race match at the Hippodrome.[33] In two years McGowan had gone from local celebrity all-around athlete—St. Paul's Jim Thorpe, said some—to defeating every top speed skater in North America, amateur or pro.

Arriving on the skating scene just after McGowan was Richard "Duke" Donovan, also from St. Paul. Donovan, only a year younger than McGowan, was the first Olympic speed skater from Minnesota. While he did not make the same splash as McGowan with his first national success—a third-place finish in the national amateur meet at New York in 1921—he remained an amateur and was selected for the United States Olympic team for the first Winter Games in 1924 at Chamonix, France.

McGowan was one of the only speed skaters with the versatility to leave speed skating for hockey. Throughout the 1920s McGowan skated on some of the best quasi-amateur teams, including the famous St. Paul Athletic Club team. He then moved up to play professionally from 1926–1930 in Vancouver, Winnipeg, Cleveland and Springfield in the years the NHL was taking shape. He was often considered the fastest skater in hockey.[34]

Dot Franey rivalled McGowan and Donovan as the best skater to emerge from the Hippodrome Skating Club in the 1920s. She was such a famous skater that she had her own ad for Camel cigarettes. In a 1938 color comic-strip ad that ran in newspapers across the country, Dot, short for Dorothy, promoted Camels as the cigarette that all the skaters she knew smoked. The ad noted that she set a world record for 500 meters in 1932 when she was eighteen, won national championships in 1934 and 1936, and in 1937 held eleven speed skating records.

In 1963 Franey joined John Johnson and Ken Bartholomew in the Minnesota Sports Hall of Fame. She was the second woman inducted, following golfer Patty Berg, one of the inaugural inductees in 1958. Franey was a superb athlete whose career underscored the diminishing opportunities for women and girls in mainstream sports in the 1930s.[35]

Franey played in all-star games as a softball and basketball player, was partnered against Byron Nelson in a pro-am event of the St. Paul Open golf tournament in 1936, was a golfing pal of Babe Didrikson, and is reported to have been one of the only women that Mickey Mantle would play golf with in her later life in Dallas.[36]

Franey first appeared in race results in 1929 when, at the age of fourteen, she won the junior girls 220- and 440-yard races at the weekly indoor meet of the Minneapolis Skating Club at the Minneapolis Arena. She may have been inspired to take up skating as many other young athletes were when Minneapolis hosted the national championship on Lake of the Isles that January. Future men's star Don Johnson said that meet, especially watching US champion Alan Potts in his bright-red skating suit, compelled him to take up speed skating.[37]

Within a year Franey was enough of a sensation that a race between Dot and two rivals was the featured entertainment between periods of a St. Paul-Kansas City hockey game at the "Hipp." By 1931 Franey was winning most of her races, including her first national title in the half-mile at the national indoor meet in Chicago. The next year she finished third in the national championship at Oconomowoc, Wisconsin. Her prize? A place on the US women's team that would skate in the 1932 Lake Placid Winter Olympics as a demonstration sport.[38]

No Minnesota men made the speed skating team or the hockey team that year. St. Paul's Jimmy Webster, a former high school football star and the fourth famous product of the Hippodrome club, won the men's national championship in January 1932, which led many to believe he would be named to the US men's team, but that team had been selected a year earlier and was already in training at Lake Placid when he won his title. Webster won a second national title in 1934.

The American men and women did quite well at the Lake Placid Olympics, but there was a catch. Several European nations, including Finland, and world champion Clas Thunberg refused to participate in the games because the races were skated by North American pack-style rules on a shorter track instead of the European style of racing in pairs against the clock. Europeans disdained the rough-and-tumble tactical races, and most chose not to skate that way. The 1932 Olympic races, skated in North America, were the only time that North American rules were used. With the European rules in place again in the 1936 Olympics in Germany, Europeans once again won nearly all the medals. Olympic speed skating added a more extreme version of the old North American-style racing in 1988 with the introduction of short-track speed skating, pack skating on an even shorter rink than was used years earlier in North America.

In the women's demonstration skating races at Lake Placid, only Canadian and US teams raced, which may have diminished Franey's accomplishment of placing third—bronze medal position—in the 1,000 meters. She never got a chance to skate for a gold medal. Women's speed skating was not upgraded to a regular medal sport after its demonstration status in 1932; instead it was eliminated from the Olympic schedule completely. The next time women raced on ice in the Olympics was in 1960 at Squaw Valley.

By 1937 Dot Franey had, as the comic-strip cigarette ad claimed, set eleven speed skating records. Her dominance was clearly noted when a Minneapolis sportswriter wrote facetiously after a January 1936 race that Dorothy must have been mad at herself because she broke only one national record that day.[39]

The timing of Franey's appearance in a Camel ad is not surprising—apart from our current sensibilities about the product she endorsed. She decided to turn pro in late 1937, so was finally able to leverage her athletic skills into income. By that time turning pro as a skater did not mean racing for prizes; it meant strictly skating in ice shows—or endorsing products. Franey became a regular with the burgeoning touring companies. She finally quit touring in ice shows when she established her own regular show at the Adolphus Hotel in Dallas, Texas. She produced and starred in the show on a square of ice in the hotel for fourteen years, becoming a local celebrity. When, in 1960, women were finally allowed to participate in the Olympics as speed skaters, Franey was an active supporter of the skaters and a leader in the organization of Olympic alumni to support young athletes following in their footsteps.

Amateur speed skating was thriving in Minneapolis at the time of Franey's dominance, however, thanks in part to World War I. Tens of thousands of young men returning home from war maintained their brothers' bond through a new organization for veterans only, the American Legion. Many legion posts were active in civic and community affairs, but one post, Lawrence Wennell Post 233 in south Minneapolis, petitioned the park board in December 1928 to create a speed skating track on Powderhorn Lake. For several years the post had sponsored a Fourth of July celebration at Powderhorn Park. Their aim was to improve safety at the Powderhorn rink, where speed skaters and recreational skaters sometimes collided, but the veterans at Wennell also wanted to promote winter sports in area schools.[40]

Interest in speed skating had been increased by the Silver Skate races the *Minneapolis Star* began sponsoring in 1926. Named for the famous novel starring Hans Brinker, the Silver Skate races were a citywide contest that awarded the winner of each age group a pair of high-quality skates, a highly-desired prize to many kids who could afford only strap-on skates. The concluding event, where champions from each playground raced others of their age and gender, were hugely popular—not only in St. Paul and Minneapolis but in Chicago, New York, and other northern cities. The event also featured open races that provided a venue for accomplished skaters to continue to compete even after they had won their skates.

The park board liked the Wennell Post idea and approved its request for a new speed skating track at Powderhorn.[41] It was the first step in the creation of what many American skaters over the next thirty years considered the best racing track in North America. More elite skaters called the Powderhorn ice home in that time than any other rink on the continent.

Until the Legion request, the park board had maintained a speed skating rink only on Lake of the Isles. When the park board received the request from the Wennell Post, it was preparing to host the National Speed Skating Championship on the Lake of the Isles rink in early 1929. That national championship, featuring the best skaters in the country and an attendance that was estimated at twenty thousand, inspired many young skaters in Minneapolis. It was also the coming-out party for an energetic young park board employee, Chet Roan, who would make enormous contributions to the speed skating program in Minneapolis and the nation over the next decade. Within six years, the Augsburg College grad was elected president of the American Skating Union, the national body that oversaw amateur skating.[42]

The Wennell Post's initial request to move the speed skating track from Lake of the Isles to Powderhorn was soon followed by a request for permission to form the Powderhorn Skating Club and to conduct an annual skating event, the 10,000 Lakes Championship at Powderhorn in 1933. That meet became one of the most important skating events in the US, after the national championships.

The Wennell Post was soon joined by other American Legion Posts in the promotion of youth sports and recreation in Minneapolis and in St. Paul. The Great Depression, however, was the trigger for a much deeper commitment of Legion posts throughout Minneapolis to the park system. The decline in tax revenues at the onset of the Depression had a drastic impact on park revenues. A park system that in 1932 operated fifty skating rinks and thirty-eight hockey rinks, sixteen of them lighted, had to cut back to ten skating rinks and nine hockey rinks in 1933. Even those rinks were maintained and supervised only through collaboration with the Civil Works Administration, a work-relief agency.[43]

The American Legion tried to raise money to keep playground recreation programs going, but when fund-raising attempts fell short, some posts organized volunteers to keep playgrounds open.[44] Those volunteer programs and the example of the Wennell Post's growing success with speed skating was an important factor in other Legion posts sponsoring speed skating teams. Within a few years, several Posts—Falldin, Laidlaw, and Bearcat, among others—sponsored teams from different playgrounds.

Minneapolis park superintendent Wirth wrote that the 1933–1934 skating season, at the peak of the Depression, was the best season ever on the lighted speed skating oval on the lake in the bowl of Powderhorn Park.[45] Wirth's assessment was due in part to the national outdoor championship held on the lake in 1934, which was attended by an estimated sixty thousand people over two days. Grandstands were erected around the track where admission was charged to help defray costs, but tens of thousands of people stood on the surrounding hillsides and watched the races for free. The event created excitement that would reverberate through the next thirty years of speed skating.

The 1934 national championship races drew an estimated sixty thousand spectators over two days to Powderhorn Lake in Minneapolis. Minnesota Historical Society.

Not only were the 1934 nationals a triumph for the organizers, but Twin Cities skaters dominated on the track. Jimmy Webster validated his 1932 national championship with a convincing win over a field that included Melvin Johnson, Minneapolis's lone standout from the previous decade and defending national champion who was then skating in the colors of a Detroit club. On the women's side, Dot Franey won easily over defending champion Kit Klein, setting a national record in the 220 along the way. [46]

Future national men's champion, Olympic bronze medalist and St. Thomas College student Leo Freisinger from Chicago, dominated the intermediate boys' races by winning all five events. Other Minneapolitans who performed well in age-group races and would feature on the local sports scene in coming years included Olga Mikulak, Dick Beard, Edna Schwartz, and Louise Herou from the North Commons club, who was runner-up in the juvenile girls category. Herou would go on to become one of the premier female skaters in the country. She would win many senior skating races in addition to playing on the University of Minnesota golf team and becoming a prominent Minneapolis attorney and restaurateur as owner of Charlie's Café Exceptionale.[47]

The triumph of the 1934 nationals was dampened only by the death three days before the event of John S. Johnson, the greatest skater in Minnesota history and a great contributor to the sport as an official and coach after his competing days. Skaters from around the country who were in town for the championships attended his funeral as a group.[48]

No one could have known at the time, but the 1934 national championships at Powderhorn marked a turning point in American speed skating history. Gradually, the organizational support, public interest, and emerging young skaters in Minneapolis would lead to the city's dominance of speed skating for nearly three decades. One of the first elite skaters nurtured by the Powderhorn Skating Club, Marvin Swanson, won the national outdoor title the next three years.

Swanson did not do well in the trials held at Powderhorn for the 1936 Olympic team, however, and failed to make the team. The trials were the first event for which the Powderhorn rink was configured for European-style racing featuring two racers at a time skating against the clock, which was how the Olympic races would be conducted. Proponents of North American pack-style racing always claimed that it was more interesting for fans, but the 1935 Olympic trials at Powderhorn were not a good test of its popularity. Subzero temperatures and howling winds reduced crowds to the hundreds instead of the thousands anticipated. The weather didn't scare off the skaters, however, who returned to Powderhorn in early 1936 to train for the upcoming Games.

Nineteen-thirty-six was an eventful year for Minnesota skating. While no Minnesotans made the Olympic speed skating team, two Minneapolis natives led the figure skating team, Erle Reiter and sixteen-year-old Robin Lee. That was also the year Oscar Johnson became the coach of the Powderhorn Skating Club from which many future Olympians would emerge. It was also the year that another Oscar Johnson, this one from St. Paul, would create the Ice Follies with his boyhood friends Eddie and Roy Shipstead. With many of the top skaters competing in Germany, Marvin Swanson again won the national title—as he would for a third time in 1937 against a full complement of American skaters. Finally, in the Minnesota championships in the junior and juvenile classes, the names of Mary Dolan, Charles Leighton, Don Johnson, and Ken Bartholomew first appeared.[49] It would not be the last time for any of them.

In 1938 Johnson won the national Silver Skate Open championship at Madison Square Garden, and Mary Dolan won the national outdoor title. The next year Bartholomew, still a teenager, won the national outdoor title, while Chuck Leighton won the North American men's championship, with Bartholomew third and Johnson fifth. Mary Dolan was nipped for the North American women's title, finishing a close second. Leighton also won a coveted place on the 1940 Olympic team after training secretly for the trials on Interlachen Lake, in what was then rural Edina, under the guidance of the highly respected coach Joe Collins. Of course the 1940 Games were cancelled after the outbreak of World War II.[50]

Military service began to claim Twin Cities skaters. After losing the 1940 national championship to Leo Freisinger, Ken Bartholomew swept the national and North American championships in 1941 and 1942 against reduced fields of skaters.[51] With his 1942 win, Bartholomew joined John Johnson and Marvin Swanson as one of the only three-time national champions—but he was far from finished. No championships were held from 1943 to 1945 due to war, but when they resumed in 1946, Minneapolis skaters again led the way on the track at Como Lake in St. Paul. Military veteran Bob Fitzgerald had returned from service and beat Bartholomew for the national championship only a few days before graduating from St. Thomas.[52]

In 1947 Ken Bartholomew returned to form and captured his fourth national title as well as a spot on the 1948 Olympic team. The trials for the 1948 team were held at Powderhorn and four of the nine skaters who won places on the team were from Minneapolis. Bartholomew and Fitzgerald were joined by two more Powderhorn skaters, Art Seaman and John Werket.[53] Chuck Leighton and Don Johnson, who had been at the forefront of the Minneapolis skaters that followed Marvin Swanson to the top of the national podium, did not qualify for the team. After finally recovering his strength and speed after a four-year layoff and "infantry legs," Leighton was edged out on the final day of the trials, along with Johnson, by another Minneapolitan, Art Seaman. All four of the Olympic skaters from Powderhorn were not only sponsored by the American Legion, they were members, too.[54]

The top American performers at the 1948 Olympics in St. Moritz were Bartholomew and Fitzgerald, who tied with Norwegian Thomas Bryberg for the silver medal in the 500 meters. The only other Minnesotan to perform on ice in St. Moritz was figure skater John Lettengarver from Minneapolis who placed fourth in the men's event.

John Werket improved on his overall Olympic performance two weeks later in an international competition in Norway against the same skaters he had faced in the Olympics. Werket, a former paratrooper who stood five foot four-and-a-half inches tall, won the overall title. He nearly replicated the feat the next week in Helsinki at the world championships where he finished second overall after a last-second letdown on bad ice in the concluding 10,000-meter event. Given his small stature, it was no wonder that he said upon his return to the United States, "I love that European style of skating. There's no element of chance like there is in our competitive style. The fastest skater wins with no bumps, falls or pockets to bother him." He said upon his return to a large welcoming committee at the Minneapolis train station that he was glad to be "just another 23 year old junior at Augsburg."[55]

While Werket and Fitzgerald stayed in Europe to race, Bartholomew hurried home, skipping the presentation of his silver medal. He didn't hide his disgust with the way he thought the Olympics were mismanaged and unfair. He said that when he finished his 500-meter race against the clock he was told that the four official timers with hand-held watches had his time at 42.7 to 42.9 seconds, but when the final results were announced he was given a time of 43.2 seconds, a tenth of a second behind a Norwegian who was awarded the gold medal. Bartholomew returned home just in time to enter the 10,000 Lakes meet at Powderhorn. He won five of the seven races to capture the championship.[56] The man couldn't pass up a race.

The triumvirate of Werket, Bartholomew, and Fitzgerald appeared set to compete for Minneapolis skating supremacy for some time. The only challenge to that lineup appeared to be a young football star from Minneapolis Roosevelt High School, Gene Sandvig, who ascended through the intermediate ranks. The only real surprise of the 1949 skating season, however, was Ken Bartholomew's second-place finish at the national outdoor meet to Ray Blum, his Olympic teammate from New Jersey. It was only the second time since 1939 that Bartholomew hadn't won that title. He must not have liked the sensation, because after that year he rattled off another eight straight national titles—1950–1957—and ten out of eleven, winning again in 1959 and 1960 when he was forty. It was a level of domination that few in any sport could challenge. The unusual aspect of his story is that despite his domination of American racing, Ken Bartholomew never again qualified for an Olympic team. He was a master tactician and manager of pack-style races and not timid about mixing it up in the pack, but alone against a clock he was not as fearsome.

The 1950 skating season was noteworthy especially for the return of tight competition among three top women skaters in the Twin Cities. Newcomer Janet Koch and veteran Donna Wang from Minneapolis pushed Janice Christopherson, a University of Minnesota student from St. Paul, to the women's national outdoor title.

With the 1951 skating season came preparations again for trials to select a team for the 1952 Olympics in Oslo and with it a surprising new face. Former marine Pat McNamara had only taken up skating after he began studying at the University of Minnesota but promptly suffered injuries that prevented high-level competition. He didn't have the credentials to skate for the high-powered Wennell-Powderhorn team, but Chuck Leighton's former coach, Joe Collins, who was then coaching skaters at Diamond Lake, saw McNamara's potential. When the 1952 Olympic team was chosen, four Minneapolis speedsters were included again: Werket, Fitzgerald, Sandvig, and McNamara. Team managers believed they had the youngest and strongest American Olympic team ever.

Difficulties began when Sandvig was drafted due to the Korean War. Organizers arranged to get Sandvig released from his duty in Germany to travel to Oslo, but he broke a leg in an army football game that fall. Things got worse when Bobby Fitzgerald decided that he really couldn't afford to take time away from work to get in competitive shape. Ken Bartholomew was selected to replace him, but as Ken was packing for Oslo, Fitzgerald changed his mind and said he would go. That left the Olympic team in a pickle. Athletes in the Olympics at that time were not fully subsidized by Olympic funds. Minneapolis had to raise $1,500 for each of the four skaters from the city. When that number was reduced by Sandvig's broken leg, the city raised the $4,500 for the remaining three skaters. So when Fitzgerald retired and Bartholomew replaced him, the cost of the three skaters was still covered. When Fitzgerald reversed course at the last minute, there wasn't time to raise another $1,500 to pay for a fourth Minneapolitan to skate in Oslo. Bartholomew graciously backed out claiming that he really couldn't afford to miss two weeks' pay from his job as a telephone lineman anyway.

John Werket was quite comfortable with the Olympics in Oslo, which had become his second home. He had met his wife in Norway and had trained extensively there. Prior to the Olympics, Werket emphasized the relative importance of skating in Norway and the United States when he said, "In Norway you could send me a letter just addressed to John Werket and I'd get it. In Minneapolis I'm just another guy who works for the railroad and likes to skate."[57]

Minneapolis skaters were shut out in the medal chase in 1952. Ken Henry and Don McDermott finished a surprising 1–2 in the 500 meters, but that was it for American medals. Werket caught a flu bug which made it impossible for him to finish one of his races. With his top competition off in Norway, Ken Bartholomew won his seventh national title at home. Two other Minneapolis skaters participated in the Olympics in 1952 on different ice: University of Minnesota pairs skaters Janet Gerhauser and John Nightingale finished in sixth place.

Little changed in Minneapolis speed skating over the next eight years. Ken Bartholomew was pushed in local races by a raft of old friends and enemies, but he clawed out win after win. He would win the national outdoor meet again and again, and he would narrowly lose in races for places on Olympic teams. The 1956 Olympic speed skating team again included Werket, Sandvig, and McNamara. Although Bartholomew once again failed to make the Olympic team, he claimed that he could still beat anyone in American-style racing, and he proved it by winning national titles in 1955, 1956, and 1957. The only thing that prevented him from winning eleven in a row was Gene Sandvig's national championship in 1958.

One new name, Floyd Bedbury, began to emerge consistently in intermediate, then senior, races in the Twin Cities in the late 1950s. The young skater from St. Paul garnered attention in 1955 when he set an intermediate record at the 10,000 Lakes Championship at Powderhorn, and he kept improving. Of all the talented teen skaters that had won consistently at the weekly races at Powderhorn for many years—Dick Beard, Roger and Earl Mosiman, Ed Suttle, Gary Eikas, and many others—none could break into that elite group of men who had shown promise as teenagers, went off to war, and returned home to dominate skating for nearly two decades. Sandvig had broken through, as had McNamara, but they were the only ones until Floyd Bedbury.

In 1959 Bedbury became the first St. Paul speed skater to make an Olympic team since Duke Donovan in 1924. At the trials in 1959 for the 1960 Games in Squaw Valley, he joined old reliables Werket, McNamara, and Sandvig. For the first time in twenty-eight years, one had to specify men's or women's team when talking about Olympic speed skaters because women were finally allowed to race for Olympic medals in 1960. No Minnesota women made the team, and we can only imagine the stories that might be told about the Olympic achievements of Dot Franey, Louise Herou, Mary Dolan, Donna Wang, Janet Foch, Janice Christopherson, and many others if they had had the chance.

Before the 1960 Games began, both John Werket and Pat McNamara withdrew from the team; they said it was because the facilities at Squaw Valley were inferior. When the competition commenced, Bedbury was the only Twin Cities skater to compete in the Games. Gene Sandvig stood by as an alternate but announced that he would retire after the Games.

Another poor showing by American skaters in 1960 led to pleas to skating authorities in Minnesota and the United States to abandon North American-style racing and to build Olympic-sized facilities. The Minneapolis park board listened and moved the speed skating track to Lake Harriet which could better accommodate the larger Olympic track. That development was met with widespread approval, and Minneapolis secured the Olympic trials in 1963 for the 1964 Olympics. But gone were the days when Twin Cities skaters would win consistently.

By the winter of 1963, Ken Bartholomew had lost his third straight attempt to win another national title and was retiring. Two Twin Cities skaters earned places on the 1964 Olympic team, Tom Gray from Bloomington and eighteen-year-old Minneapolis Marshall high school student Marie Lawler. She was the first female speed skater from the Twin Cities to compete for an official Olympic medal. Their coach was a figure familiar to many longtime fans of speed skating, the once unbeatable Leo Freisinger.

The era of Minneapolis dominance in speed skating really ended with Ken Bartholomew's last national title in 1960, but if anyone had doubts they had to be dispelled when the first Olympic indoor skating arena in the United States was built not in Minneapolis or St. Paul but in West Allis, Wisconsin, in 1964. That arena led to a period of dominance for Wisconsin and Illinois skaters similar to what Minneapolis and St. Paul had once enjoyed.

Of course the Twin Cities have continued to produce Olympic skaters in long-track and now short-track skating, and the John Rose Oval in Roseville, Minnesota, is among the premier rinks in the country. But the sport is different on a short track and a long track. It is largely indoors in controlled temperatures on mirror-smooth artificial ice where skaters wear precision-edged clap skates and sleek head-to-toe suits of material that is manufactured, not grown. Minneapolis is still proud of skating rinks that are among the most beautiful in the country, especially on Lake of the Isles where the city's first speed skating track was built. There at night, under the lights on a vast expanse of lake ice, you can still imagine the whoop and holler of kids with strap-on skates or some old hand-me-downs pretending to stretch to cross the finish line first in front of the tens of thousands who crowded the hillsides around the best ice skating race track in the country at Powderhorn Park, perhaps dreaming of winning a pair of Silver Skates or imagining how fast John Johnson, Everett McGowan, Dot Franey, or Ken Bartholomew really could skate.

## CHAPTER FOUR

# The End of Jim Crow and the Decline of Minnesota Gopher Football

## SHELDON ANDERSON

In the fall of 1961, Ohio State coach Woody Hayes led the Buckeyes to a 6–0 Big Ten record and the conference championship. At the end of November, the Ohio State Faculty Council voted 28–25 to turn down a bid to play in the Rose Bowl, the "granddaddy" of college bowl games. The professors felt that football had become too important at the university, overshadowing its academic mission.

Thousands of students and Buckeye fans took to the streets of Columbus in protest, but to Hayes's credit he did not egg them on. Hayes was scheduled to give a speech at an alumni dinner in Cleveland when he heard the news. "I'm bitter," he said. "The vote deeply disturbs and dismays me. But I cannot question the faculty's sincerity or their right to act. But I seriously question their judgment."[1] The decision stood, and the football team stayed home.

The Rose Bowl committee turned to the Minnesota Gophers who had finished second that season. The Gophers accepted the invitation. Ironically, in the late 1950s the Minnesota faculty had questioned the Big Ten's binding contract with the Rose Bowl, arguing that the weeks of practice before the game were too disruptive to the football players' studies. The Minnesota Faculty Senate Committee on Intercollegiate Athletics voted 108–33 to allow the Gophers to play in their second straight Rose Bowl. The decision was made in part because

DOI: https://doi.org/10.34053/scs2019.tcs.4

the university had received its share of Rose Bowl money in the past, and the faculty did not think it fair to deprive other Big Ten schools of the payout if the Rose Bowl invited a school from another conference.[2]

On January 1, 1962, Sandy Stephens, Minnesota's first African American quarterback, led the Gophers to a decisive 21–3 victory over UCLA, avenging a 17–7 loss to Washington in the Rose Bowl the year before. Stephens was named the game's MVP.

That was the Gophers' second and last Rose Bowl appearance. In 1962 Wisconsin came from behind to beat the Gophers 14–9 at Camp Randall Stadium to win the Big Ten and earn a trip to Pasadena. The Gophers have not been back to the Rose Bowl for over a half-century. Minnesota won a share of the Big Ten football championship in 1967, but Indiana went to the Rose Bowl. That is the last Gopher Big Ten title. All of the other original Big Ten teams have been to the Rose Bowl since 1962.[3] Surely *Time* magazine was not referring to Gopher football in its famous 1973 cover story on Minnesota, calling it "the state that works." After the great Gopher teams of the 1930s and 1960s, one "Minnesota miracle" is how mediocre the Gophers have been for so long.

Why were the Gophers so good before World War II? What contributed to the short-lived resurgence of the Gophers in the fifties and sixties, and why has Minnesota fallen on such hard times since then? The success of early Gopher football is rooted in its tough, home-grown players, and in coach Bernie Bierman. After World War II the Gophers benefitted from discrimination against African American football players in the Jim Crow South, and limited opportunities for northern black players to play key positions at northern schools. No one laments the end of Jim Crow and greater opportunities for black players, but it did have an impact on Gopher football. Of course there were other northern schools that recruited from the segregated South, but the Gophers recruited two of the greatest defensive linemen of their time: Bobby Bell and Carl Eller. And unlike any of the other legacy Big Ten schools, the fall of the Gopher football program can also be traced to Minnesota's progressive political, cultural, and educational tradition; the university's unique urban campus; and competition from the Twin Cities' professional sports.[4]

Early Gopher football teams mirrored Minnesota's predominantly European American ethnic character. The Gophers only had a handful of African American players in the early twentieth century. The best was end Bobby Marshall, who led the Gophers to a 27–2 record and two Big Nine championships from 1904 to 1906. The most famous Jewish players were halfback Sigmund Harris, whose runs helped the Gophers to winning records from 1902 to 1904, and tackle Butch Levy, who starred on Minnesota's championship teams from 1939 to 1941.

The Gophers were mainly a team for Christian white guys, and they were good. In the late 1920s, Bronislau "Bronko" Nagurski helped put Minnesota football on the map. Born in Canada in 1908 to Polish and Ukrainian immigrants, at the age of four Nagurski moved to International Falls, the coldest city on average in the continental United States. He took the Gophers to the Big Ten title in 1927 and finished his career at Minnesota with an 18–4–2 record.

Nagurski began a tradition of fearsome Gopher teams. In the 1930s and early 1940s, the Golden Gophers were one of the powerhouses of college football, led by Minnesota's greatest coach Bernie Bierman. Born in Litchfield, Minnesota, Bierman was an All-American halfback at Minnesota from 1913 to 1915, leading an undefeated team to the Big Ten title in his senior year. After graduating, Bierman took the head coaching job at Montana, followed by a stint at Mississippi A&M (today Mississippi State). Although Bierman posted a so-so .500 record at Montana and at A&M, in 1927 Tulane University offered him the head coaching job. There Bierman turned the Green Wave into a national power. Tulane won three straight Southern Conference championships, going 9–0 in 1929, 8–1 in 1930, and 11–0 in 1931, but lost to the University of Southern California (USC) in the 1932 Rose Bowl.

Bierman returned to Minnesota to coach the Gophers in 1932, and in the next decade he guided Minnesota to four undefeated seasons, six Big Ten championships and five national championships. In those days the Big Ten champs did not have an automatic bid to the Rose Bowl, so the Gopher season ended in the fall. There were only a few African Americans on those championship teams, and none played prominent roles. When Tulane played the Gophers at Memorial Stadium in 1935, and the Texas Longhorns came to Minneapolis a year later, the southern teams refused to play unless the Gophers sat their black players. Bierman acceded to their demands.[5]

Bierman's teams provided a small morale boost for Minnesotans mired in the Great Depression. About a quarter of the state's work force was unemployed in the 1930s, but at least Minnesotans had a winner on Saturdays. Halfback Francis "Pug" Lund, the star of the 1934 national champions, recalled, "We played bruising schedules. Every game was bitter. I suppose the Depression had something to do with it. We were all hungry. We had to work hard to survive, to get an education, and football was just part of it."[6]

Bierman used a single-wing offense in which the center long snapped the ball to the quarterback, and a phalanx of blockers led the runner around the strong side. Bierman rarely used the forward pass. The 1934 national championship team, led by Lund and Butch Larson, averaged 325 yards of offense, all but thirty on the ground.[7]

The Big Ten's hard-nosed style of play and Bierman's relentless running game paid homage to the rough and tumble game that had deep roots in the Midwest. The league reflected the character of the rugged working class industrial states along the Great Lakes. Unlike the Ivy League or the Pacific Coast Conference, even the name Big Ten sounded gritty just like its players, many of them Slavs and Germans, such as Nagurski in the 1920s, and Illinois middle linebackers Ray Nitschke and Dick Butkus in the 1950s and 1960s. Woody Hayes's strategy of "three yards and a cloud of dust" set the tone of league play. He used to say that four things could happen with the forward pass and that three of them were bad: an incomplete pass, an interception, or a sack of the quarterback. Hayes made football into a metaphor for life: "Without winners," he declared, "there wouldn't be any goddam civilization."[8]

When Minneapolis got the Minnesota Vikings in 1961, the franchise took on the foreboding image of Bierman's Gophers. The "Purple People Eaters" gobbled up warm-weather opponents on the "frozen tundra" of the old outdoor Metropolitan Stadium, reaching the Super Bowl four times. The Gophers and the Vikings lost that forbidding, frigid home-field advantage in 1982 when they moved into the hermetically-sealed Metrodome, which was torn down in 2014. The Vikings are now gracious hosts to opponents in their new $1 billion, climate-controlled indoor stadium. The university built a new outdoor stadium on campus, hoping that playing outside would again give them the cold-weather advantage that Bierman's Gophers had at Memorial Stadium.

Bierman guided the Gophers to consecutive undefeated seasons in 1940 and 1941, its last interwar national championships. With All-American Bruce Smith leading the way, the last important victory of Bierman's prewar tenure was a 41–6 drubbing of Wisconsin on November 22, 1941, two weeks before the Japanese attacked Pearl Harbor.

Bierman had joined the Marines during World War I, and he left Minnesota after the 1941 season to serve again in World War II. Dr. George Hauser, a 1918 Minnesota graduate, in the late 1920s became the line coach at Ohio State, where he got his doctor of medicine in 1932. Hauser returned to Minnesota as the team physician and assistant coach. He took over the Gophers for three years during the war, but he could not duplicate Bierman's success. The Gophers finished third once and fourth twice, and after the war Bierman was called back to Memorial Stadium. After a disappointing eighth-place finish in 1945, the Gophers finished over .500 for four straight years but could not finish higher than third in the Big Ten. All-American tackle Leo Nomellini bolstered the offensive and defensive line in the late forties. Nomellini gained All-National Football League (NFL) honors with the San Francisco 49ers on both offense and defense. Future great Vikings' head coach Bud Grant was Nomellini's teammate on those Gopher teams. "We would pull him, we were running the single wing then, and when he'd come around the corner, he would just roar," Grant remembered. "His blocking technique wasn't so great, but he'd just run you over like a truck."[9]

Gopher fans had higher expectations in those days, and Bierman was ushered out after a dismal 1950 season when the team won only one game. Forgetful fans are fickle; Gopher loyalists hung the great coach in effigy and demanded Bierman's sacking.

The fate of Gopher football after World War II had a recurrent link to Ohio State. Gophers turned again to their Big Ten rival for their next coach. Wes Fesler was a Buckeye All-American end in the late 1920s, and was named the Big Ten MVP in 1930. Fesler took the head coaching job at Ohio State in 1947, leading the Buckeyes to the Big Ten title in 1949 and a berth in the 1950 Rose Bowl. Over objections from some Minnesota boosters that former Gopher All-American and Oklahoma coach Bud Wilkinson should return to his alma mater, in 1951 Fesler was hired to return the Gophers to greatness. Fesler had All-American halfback Paul Giel who finished second to Notre Dame's Johnny Lattner in the 1953 Heisman Trophy voting, but the Gophers finished no higher than fifth in the Big Ten under Fesler, and he was fired after the 1953 season. The university began looking for a new coach, the Gophers' fourth in a dozen seasons.

Like Bierman, new Gopher coach Murray Warmath came from a job at Mississippi A&M, but he was a Southerner by birth. Warmath grew up in Humboldt, Tennessee, a town of ten thousand on the western side of the state. In 1930 he enrolled at the University of Tennessee and played for the Volunteers' great coach Bob Neyland. In his first nine seasons at Tennessee, Neyland's teams compiled an amazing 75–7–5 record. Warmath recalled that Neyland's conservative strategy was "defense and the kicking game."[10] Warmath would never deviate from that formula.

After graduating, Warmath joined Neyland's coaching staff. At Tennessee Warmath began his practice of recruiting far from the campus; he went to famous Massilon High School in Ohio, coached by future NFL icon Paul Brown, to find star guard Ed Molinski. Warmath enlisted in the US Navy during World War II, and after the war he returned to Tennessee as an assistant coach under Neyland. In 1949 Warmath left to join the staff of renowned Army coach Red Blaik, which included future Green Bay Packer coach Vince Lombardi. With that pedigree, Mississippi A&M hired Warmath in 1952.[11] Warmath posted a record of 10–6–3 in his two years at A&M. In 1954 Warmath left Starkville for Minneapolis. The Big Ten was arguably the best football conference in the country, and the Gopher job was a plum.

Warmath, like Neyland, Bierman, and Hayes, was a devotee of the running game, field position, and defense. With the great holdover from the Fesler era, All-American halfback Bob McNamara, Warmath's first team went 7–2 overall and 4–2 in the Big Ten for fourth place. It was a remarkable turnaround for the Gophers, but the next season the Gophers sank to eighth. A third-place finish in 1956 saved Warmath's job, but the Gophers won only nine games in the next three seasons with only one win in 1958. Warmath was in the hot seat. After another dismal 2–7 record and a last-place finish in the Big Ten in 1959, disgruntled fans hung Warmath in effigy and threw garbage on the lawn of his home. They were tired of his conservative style which often included punting the ball away on third down.

Warmath realized that the Gophers were getting beat by faster players, and he couldn't find faster players in the Upper Midwest. Warmath went shopping for recruits far from Gopherland. Senator Humphrey and Tennessean Carl Rowan of the *Minneapolis Tribune*—one of the first black reporters on a major newspaper in the country—were frequent visitors to Gopher practices and big supporters of Warmath's recruiting efforts in Pennsylvania and in the South.

As long as they helped him win, Warmath did not care about where his players came from or their ethnicity. He benefitted from other coaches' reluctance to recruit and play African American players in key positions. Hayes kept the number of black players to a minimum and usually played them on the line. Offensive tackle Jim Parker and defensive end Jim Marshall starred at Ohio State in the 1950s and went on to Hall of Fame careers in the NFL. After mediocre seasons in 1966 and 1967, Hayes relented and increased the number of African Americans on the team from three in 1967 to thirteen the next year.[12]

Western Pennsylvania was a natural recruiting ground for Ohio State, but in the late 1950s Hayes declined to go after Uniontown High School star Sandy Stephens because he did not want to start an African American quarterback. Hayes did not recruit blacks to play middle linebacker either, a position considered the brains of the defense. Ten years after Stephens won the Rose Bowl with the Gophers in 1962, Hayes finally started a black quarterback—Cornelius Greene—who led the Buckeyes to four straight Big Ten titles and Rose Bowl appearances.

Uniontown is a working-class community about forty miles south of Pittsburgh, but the name has nothing to do with labor unions. The "town of Union" was founded on July 4, 1776. In the 1790s Fayette County was one of the centers of the Whiskey Rebellion, a failed uprising of farmers against the federal government's excise tax on the production of spirits. The National Highway, also known as Cumberland Road, ran through Uniontown in the early nineteenth century, ushering settlers west on the nation's first federal highway. Coal mining and the steel industry dominated the landscape until the 1950s, when the once prosperous region began an inexorable decline. There was little future there for a young black man like Sandy Stephens.

Rather than follow the National Highway (US Route 40) from Uniontown to Columbus, Stephens detoured north to Minnesota. Halfback Judge Dickson from nearby Clairton, Pennsylvania, had a name and a crunching running style suited for the rugged Big Ten, and Warmath wanted him too. Stephens and Dickson met on their recruiting visit to Minneapolis. Stephens remembered their culture shock: "Judge and I stood in front of the Radisson Hotel in downtown Minneapolis for three hours on a Saturday afternoon. We didn't see one black face." But Stephens and Dickson liked Warmath's straight-shooting style, and they decided to build a winner together at Minnesota.[13]

In those days universities wanted freshmen athletes to acclimate themselves to the rigors of academics and college social life, so they were not allowed to play in varsity games. This is a quaint idea in big time college sports today where some would-be pros do one semester and leave. Stephens admitted that it was a difficult transition from a small town in Pennsylvania to a predominantly white state: "It's tough enough for any kid to go away to school, but if you are black and going to a place like Minnesota with a very small minority population, it's doubly intimidating."[14] But he liked the idea of going to a big city and the Gophers' urban campus:

Even Minnesota was almost too small . . . but I liked everything else about the Twin Cities. . . . The college was kind of in the middle of it and you still had your campus life as well as the cities were near. I'm more of a city boy myself, I like the bright lights of the cities and you can't get enough of them for me.[15]

As a sophomore in 1959, Stephens took control of the Gopher offense, but Minnesota won only two games and finished last in the Big Ten. No one thought that the 1960 edition would be any better. Five of the Gophers' seven losses in 1959 were by a touchdown or less, however, and that year Uniontown running back Bill Munsey followed his buddy Stephens to Minnesota. Gopher boosters helped out by offering some of the players well-paying summer jobs, which today is a violation of NCAA rules.

In the 1960 season opener against twelfth-ranked Nebraska in Lincoln, the three African Americans from Pennsylvania started in the backfield. The Gophers upset the Huskers 26–14 on the way to a Big Ten title and the 1960 National Championship (at that time the Associated Press voted before the bowl games). Minnesota lost one conference game, a shocking 23–14 loss to underdog Purdue in Minneapolis. Nonetheless, the confident national champions went to the Rose Bowl with the rallying cry "Squash Wash," but the Washington Huskies whipped Minnesota 17–7. It was a disappointing finish to an otherwise breakout season.

In 1961 the Gophers were on their way to another Big Ten Championship before suffering a devastating home loss to Wisconsin in the last game of the season, 23–21. Ohio State won the title, but Stephens was named Big Ten MVP and an All-American, the first black quarterback to receive that honor. He guided the Gophers to the victory over UCLA in the 1962 Rose Bowl.

Stephens credited Warmath for the success of the team on and off the field. "He was just the greatest man I ever knew," Stephens said, recalling the abuse Warmath and his family had suffered during the 1959 season. "He never flinched one iota during all the time and is the greatest testimony I've seen of a man under that kind of pressure. He was the greatest role model for our whole team and I think our whole team was helped invaluably by this: watching his character during a horrible time."[16]

Stephens had limited opportunities to play quarterback on a major college football team, and when he left Minnesota, no NFL team would give him a chance to play the position. Cleveland drafted Stephens, but the great Browns running back Jim Brown told Stephens about the realities of race in the

NFL: "Sandy," he said, "if you think you're going to be the quarterback of the Cleveland Browns, you're crazy."[17] Stephens had to go even farther north to play for the Montreal Alouettes and the Toronto Argonauts of the Canadian Football League. After his career was over Stephens returned to live in Minneapolis until his death from a heart attack at the age of fifty-nine. "If you travel around a lot and you get to meet a lot of people from all around," he once said, "I don't think there's no contest. Minnesota is above many, many places. There's still room for improvement, but still, they're heads and tails above almost everywhere I've been anyway."[18]

The Gophers' success in the early 1960s can be attributed to two of the greatest defensive linemen in college football history, both from North Carolina. Ironically, it took a southerner to recruit African Americans from below the Mason-Dixon Line to play football at Minnesota. Segregation directly contributed to the success of Gopher football under Warmath. African Americans could not play at the big segregated football schools like Alabama and Mississippi. The Southwestern Conference had its first black player in 1963, and the Atlantic Coast Conference did not integrate its teams on a regular basis until the late 1960s. In 1967 after the federal government threatened to withhold funding to the southern states, the Southeastern Conference (SEC) broke down, but it took until the late 1970s for Alabama and Mississippi to recruit a significant number of African American players.

Bobby Bell bolstered the Minnesota defense on those championship teams in the early 1960s. Like Stephens, Bell was fortunate to have the football talent to escape a segregated part of the country that held little opportunity for young black men. His home town of Shelby, about thirty miles east of Charlotte, was a thriving cotton, textile, and farming town in the first half of the century, but by the 1950s the local economy was struggling. Bell was one of twenty-six students in the graduating class at his segregated high school and the star quarterback on the six-man football team.

Warmath's old friend, North Carolina head coach Jim Tatum, alerted Warmath to Bell, who declined offers to play at North Carolina A&T, an all-black school. "I wanted to go to a big school," Bell recalled. "I had those big eyes, but everybody else around there said, 'No, you can't do that.'"[19] Bell played quarterback, halfback, and end on the 1959 Gopher freshman team, but with Stephens firmly at the helm of the varsity, Warmath moved Bell to defensive tackle for the 1960 season. It was a smart move; Bell became a two-time All-American and Big Ten MVP, and in 1962 he won the Outland Trophy, awarded

Star quarterback Sandy Stephens (15 in the back row) and defensive line standout Bobby Bell (78 in the front row) led the Gophers to the 1960 National Championship. Minnesota Historical Society.

to the country's best lineman. Bell's record at Minnesota was 22–6–1. He went on to a distinguished career with the Kansas City Chiefs, becoming the first outside linebacker to be elected to the Pro Football Hall of Fame. Warmath declared, "I never played with or coached a player any better than Bobby Bell."[20]

The other defensive lineman was Carl Eller, who grew up in Winston-Salem, about one hundred miles northeast of Shelby. Winston-Salem is best known for Hanes underwear and Wake Forest University. Eller and Bell wreaked havoc on opposing backfields in the 1961 season. Minnesota's defense held UCLA to a measly field goal in the 1962 Rose Bowl. Eller also received All-American honors and was runner-up in the 1963 Outland Trophy voting. After college "Moose" had fifteen outstanding seasons for the Minnesota Vikings. He was the NFL Most Valuable Defensive Lineman twice and was elected to the Pro Football Hall of Fame in 2004.

Sandy Stephens graduated in the spring of 1962, but with Bell and Eller leading the defense that fall, the Gophers went 6–2–1, finishing second in the

Big Ten. The Gophers shut out their opponents five times that season and only allowed a touchdown in two other games. Minnesota was on pace to win another Big Ten title but suffered yet another demoralizing season-ending loss to Wisconsin at Camp Randall, 14–9. A dubious roughing-the-passer penalty on Bell nullified a Gopher interception at midfield and kept the Badgers' game-winning touchdown drive going. Warmath got an unsportsmanlike conduct penalty on the play, putting the ball on the Gopher thirteen-yard line. The Badgers scored with 1:37 left in the game.

In those days Minnesotans were passionate about their team; some angry Gopher fans ran onto the field and punched out Wisconsin band members. A week later Bell happened to meet President John F. Kennedy at the annual Army-Navy game. "I'm standing there nervous, because I'm shaking hands with the president," Bell remembered. "He told me that he watched the play, and he said, 'You really got robbed in the Wisconsin game. That was a bad call. Bad call.'"[21]

Warmath never got over the loss. "He talked about it all the time," Bell recalled, "about how they stole the game from us." Eller said the coach was heartbroken:

> That game plagued Murray Warmath until his dying days. He never forgave those guys for that because it was a bad call, and he held onto that. I was there with him in the end. That was one of the things that haunted him the rest of his life. It was a horrible call.[22]

Bell went to the pros the next season. Eller could not make up for all of the graduations, and the Gophers ended up 3–6 in 1963, falling to ninth in the Big Ten. The Gophers finally beat Wisconsin 14–0 at Memorial Stadium, but that was little consolation for the previous late-season defeats to the Badgers. It was only the Gophers' second conference win and had no impact on the standings. The Gophers went 17–19–2 from 1963 to 1966, and once again Gopher fans were calling for Warmath's head.

Two more All-Big Ten linemen from the South led the Gophers to their last Big Ten title in 1967, saving Warmath's job. John Williams from Jackson, Mississippi, anchored the offensive line, while tackle McKinley Boston from Elizabeth City, North Carolina, spearheaded the defense. "I was told by black players who were ahead of me that Coach Warmath was very fair," Boston recalled. "I learned quickly that was indeed true. He treated all of us—black and white—honestly and as individuals."[23] The team got steadily worse in the next four years, however, and a sixth-place conference finish in 1971 ended Warmath's eighteen-year career as coach of the Gophers. His final record with Minnesota was 87–78–7.

The Gophers began a half-century slide into mediocrity. In 1971 the university brought back Giel to head the athletic department, and McNamara spearheaded fundraising efforts, but the former All-Americans could not turn the Gophers to gold again. Attendance at Gopher games dwindled, and the team became a Saturday afternoon afterthought. After the 1967 season and until the Big Ten split into two divisions in 2011, the Gophers never finished higher than third. Thirty times the Gophers finished in the bottom half of the conference. Jerry Kill finally coached the Gophers to second place in the Western Division in 2014, but the team went 2–6 in 2015. No other original Big Ten football team has fallen as far as the Gophers in the last half century.

What explains this dismal record? Only a few other former major college football powerhouses—among them Army and Southern Methodist—rival the Gophers' demise. For one, the Gophers' decline coincided with the integration of southern football teams. In the immediate postwar years, there was some relaxation in the policy of segregated southern college football teams playing against integrated northern teams, but after the Supreme Court's monumental 1954 *Brown v. Board of Education* decision, the South hunkered down against the federal government's gradual dismantlement of Jim Crow. As the *Jackson Daily News* put it, "Being a little bit integrated is like being a little bit pregnant."[24] In November 1955 Georgia Tech was invited to play in the Sugar Bowl against Pittsburgh, but the administration declined the bid because Pitt had a black player, Bobby Grier. Georgia governor Marvin Griffin declared that "the South stands at Armageddon. The battle is joined. We cannot make the slightest concession to the enemy in this dark and lamentable hour of struggle.... One break in the dike and the relentless seas will rush in and destroy us." Georgia Tech students protested the decision not to go to the Sugar Bowl, and the Board of Regents relented. Southern football fans wanted to see their teams play the best, and by 1965 most schools had lifted the ban on playing integrated northern teams, albeit away from home.[25]

In the 1960s Coach Bear Bryant made Alabama into one of the best football teams in the country. Alabama won the 1961 National Championship, a year before James Meredith showed up at Mississippi to integrate the university.

Bryant was able to take his segregated team to two more national championships in the early 1960s, but Alabama fans became disgruntled with mediocre records and bowl losses later in the decade. Without playing integrated teams on a regular basis, Alabama's claim to national prominence was suspect, so Bryant made the bold move to invite USC to a game in Alabama.

On September 12, 1970, the Crimson Tide played the Trojans at Birmingham's Legion Field. It was a groundbreaking meeting for the state that symbolized Jim Crow. In 1950 Birmingham had passed a law banning whites from playing blacks "in any game of cards, dice, dominoes, checkers, baseball, softball, football, basketball, or similar games."[26] *Los Angeles Times* columnist Jim Murray, who had baited the segregationist schools for years, wrote that "the bedsheet-and-burning cross conference is coming out in the daylight of the twentieth century." Behind fullback Sam "Bam" Cunningham's 135 yards, USC trounced Alabama 42–21. The story is often told that because of the resounding defeat, Bryant decided to recruit more black players, but he had already begun to do that before the USC game. Alabama and Bear Bryant did not lead SEC integration. Other SEC schools such as Kentucky and Tennessee had integrated their teams in 1967. Bear Bryant and Alabama were latecomers to recruiting black players. In 1971 John Mitchell was the first black player to make it on the field for the Crimson Tide.[27]

Today most southern African Americans stay home to play in a part of the country where college football is a religion. As one Southern writer observed in reference to the Civil War and the federal onslaught of Jim Crow, "The South had come by way of football to think at last in terms of causes won, not lost."[28] The gain of the universities south of the Mason-Dixon Line was Minnesota's loss. The Gophers could no longer compete for the Bells and Ellers.

Minnesota's traditional dedication to higher education also has had something to do with the Gopher's feeble record, although faculties have long lost the kind of power over intercollegiate athletics that the Ohio State professors exercised in 1961. Big time college football has done an end run around the academic side of university life. Players can stay eligible by taking the minimum of soft courses, game schedules pay no attention to academic calendars, and university leaders would not think of turning down the money offered to play in a big bowl game. Minnesota fans do not go apoplectic about losing seasons, however, reducing the pressure on coaches to recruit players regardless of their academic abilities. Minnesotans have kept big-time sports in perspective, and the state's reputation for relatively clean politics carries over into Gopher sports.

Some Minnesota coaches *have* played fast and loose with NCAA rules, but the university has *repeatedly* punished its sports programs for violations. Other schools have willfully ignored such transgressions. Minnesota has had several academic scandals, mostly having to do with the basketball program. The most notable indiscretion was a tutor who wrote hundreds of papers for Gopher Coach Clem Haskins's basketball players, resulting in the NCAA's vacating the Minnesota's 1997 NCAA Final Four appearance. The university also had what was called the "General College," a remedial course of study that kept many Gopher athletes in school and progressing toward a degree. But with less than a third of the General College students getting a degree within six years, the university abolished it in 2005.

Nonetheless, the university has maintained relatively high academic standards for its sports programs, football included. Early on Bernie Bierman set the tone for Gopher student athletes. Dale Warner, a Gopher halfback in the late 1940s, remembered, "Without good grades, he banished you off the squad. The conference lost some good athletes because of poor marks—and they'd go play in the Big Eight. The Big Eight would take them."[29] Oklahoma coach Bud Wilkinson recruited Minnesota players to Norman whether or not they had the necessary academic credentials.

Warmath was a stickler for academics as well. Stephens admired him for looking beyond the gridiron: "Coach Warmath gave us opportunities not just on the football field, but in the classroom and later life that we would not have otherwise had. I will always be in debt to him."[30] When Bobby Bell left Shelby to play for Warmath at Minnesota, Bell promised his father that he would get his college degree. Bell's segregated high school could not prepare him for college, and although Bell worked hard, he did not graduate with his class in 1963. Bell finally fulfilled his promise fifty-two years later. Jerry Kill, the Gopher football coach in 2015, remarked that "Bobby approached getting that degree like he did football. In my opinion, this may be the most rewarding thing he's done in his life." As Bell walked in the graduation ceremony, he concurred: "It's the top of the pyramid, man."[31]

Another reason for the lack of the community's focus on the Gopher football program was the arrival of pro sports in the early 1960s. No other original Big Ten team other than Northwestern has to compete for attention from the four major pro sports—the NFL, the National Basketball League (NBA), Major League Baseball (MLB), and the National Hockey League (NHL). Football is among the royalty of Minnesota sports, but it is not king.

Minnesotans love basketball, baseball, and ice hockey too. In 1967 the NHL-expansion Minnesota North Stars took even more attention away from Gopher football in the hockey crazy state, and a new NBA franchise—the Minnesota Timberwolves—began play in 1989. When Major League Soccer (MLS) came to St. Paul in 2017, the Twin Cities became one of only a handful of US cities with every major men's professional sport. The Women's National Basketball Association Minnesota Lynx won four professional championships in the 2010s and established a firm fan base.

Football fans also have other games to attend on Saturday afternoons. The Twin Cities has four private colleges that play high caliber Division-III football, and one playing Division-II. One team in the Minnesota Intercollegiate Athletic Conference—St. John's University—has won four Division-III football championships. Former St. John's coach John Gagliardi is a Minnesota legend, having won more games (489) than any other coach in NCAA history.

As an urban campus, the Gophers also have to compete with other Twin City cultural and recreational attractions. Minneapolis is home to the Walker Art Center, the Minneapolis Institute of Art, and the renowned Guthrie Theater. The Twin Cities music scene is vibrant too, from the Minnesota Orchestra to the late Prince, a north Minneapolis native.

Minnesota winters are long, and from September on people know when spending a nice fall Saturday afternoon outdoors that it might be their last. Minnesotans are fanatic about boating, fishing, and hunting, and on autumn weekends the highways are clogged with cars on the hajj north. People crave getting on the water to catch a walleye, northern, or the big bad muskie. The state issues the most fishing licenses per capita in the country. Hunters take about 150,000 deer a year, and Minnesota and surrounding states are considered the best places in the country to hunt grouse and pheasant. The Twin Cities also has the most urban park land per capita in the country and a chain of several clean, swimmable lakes. On a warm fall day, Twin Citians are as likely to go hiking, biking, or boating as they are to go to a Gopher football game.

The Gophers became part of the downtown scene in an ill-advised departure from Memorial Stadium in 1982. The on-campus stadium was built in 1924 in honor of the fallen in World War I. The charged atmosphere of Saturday autumn games on the Minnesota campus ended when the Gophers began to play indoors in the sterile downtown Metrodome, a cheap ($55 million), multi-use, artificial-turf stadium that was built for the Minnesota Vikings and the Minnesota Twins. Stephens reflected on driving through the campus after Memorial Stadium was torn down:

> It seems odd now. I still think I'm in the wrong city when I go by that corner... because there should be a stadium there.... [On game day] it would be nothing but maroon and gold up the whole University Avenue.... You'd hear that band playing and we'd be ready. We couldn't get off the bus fast enough. Like I say, we had the greatest fans in the world.[32]

If Cleveland's Municipal Stadium was "The Mistake on the Lake," the Metrodome was Minnesota's "Mistake on the Lakes." Under the weight of snow, the Metrodome roof collapsed five times before it was finally demolished in 2014. The downtown stadium offered no place to tailgate, a big tradition among football fans. The Gophers now play in a new on-campus stadium a block away from the old site of Memorial Stadium, but there is little space to party there either. The team has struggled to regain its fan base. In the early 1960s, the Gophers averaged sixty-five thousand fans a game. Although the metropolitan area is much larger today, few games attract more than fifty thousand spectators, usually for home games against Wisconsin and Iowa, whose fans travel in droves to Minneapolis for the interstate derby.

Minnesotans have become accustomed to finishing second. Unlike the fans of Ohio State, Alabama, USC, and other college football juggernauts, Minnesota partisans dare not think about national championships. The younger generation has no memory of the Gophers' glory days anyway. Maybe there is something to Garrison Keillor's line that in Lake Wobegon "all the children are above average." It seems that Minnesota Gopher football fans are okay with that.

## CHAPTER FIVE

# From the Cedar-Riverside Marines to the Purple People Eaters

## Professional Football in the Twin Cities

### DICK DAHL

When it came time for the management committee of the Twin Cities' newly awarded National Football League (NFL) franchise to pick a team nickname in September 1960, they decided on one they hoped would capture a mythic cultural identity that would resonate with Minnesotans. Team officials had reportedly bandied about a variety of names—the Chippewas, the Miners, the Voyageurs—but chose the Vikings at the urging of general manager Bert Rose. Rose recommended the nickname to the team's board of directors because "it represented both an aggressive person with the will to win and the Nordic tradition in the northern Midwest."[1] The press guide for the team's inaugural season the following year expanded on the idea: "Certainly the Nordic Vikings were a fearless race. Following many years of victories in the British Isles and France, under Eric the Red, they sailed in open boats across the North Atlantic seeking new people to conquer. Their entire history is punctuated with the aggressive desire and will to win."

Minnesotans are a notoriously mild-mannered people, so opting for a name that conjures a violent band of rapacious pillagers might seem odd. It is nevertheless true, however, that the Viking is part of Minnesota's Scandinavian cultural identity. In large part this is due to a persistent legend that the Vikings

DOI: https://doi.org/10.34053/scs2019.tcs.5

made their way to present-day Minnesota some 130 years before Christopher Columbus arrived on the shores of the New World. That legend is a product of the so-called Kensington Rune Stone, a large rock bearing chiseled inscriptions of an ancient Norse language, discovered (supposedly) by a Swedish immigrant farmer near the central-Minnesota town of Kensington in 1898. The tale told by the inscriptions describes the Vikings as missionaries who came to the area in 1362 only to be massacred by Indians. Its authenticity has been widely debunked, but the myth has lived on. In his book *Myths of the Rune Stone: Viking Martyrs and the Birthplace of America*, David M. Krueger argues that belief in the authenticity of the rune stone is a form of civil religion that Scandinavian immigrants have used to identify themselves as a select people whose forebears were the first true white Americans. "Immigrants from Sweden and Norway used the inscribed stone to anchor their presence in the Minnesota landscape and the narrative of American history," Krueger wrote. "They could simultaneously dwell in their new environment while maintaining a mythical connection to their homeland."[2]

The naming of the new professional football franchise in Minnesota was noteworthy in another respect: it was the first time that a sports franchise in the United States was named after a state instead of a city. The Minnesota Twins baseball team started play first in 1961, but the Vikings' naming decision came first. The unofficial original name of the baseball franchise, the Twin Cities Twins, followed the Vikings' lead and changed to the Minnesota Twins. Given its longstanding tradition of collective civic spirit—from local creamery cooperatives to the Democratic-Farmer-Labor Party—Minnesota would seem to be a perfect candidate to be the first state to have its name connected to a sports franchise.

Relations between Minneapolis and St. Paul, however, have not always been so harmonious. In 1890 the two cities engaged in a vicious fight over the US Census, arresting and kidnapping each other's census takers in an effort to maintain a population advantage.[3] The cities shared some deep-seated enmity in other ways. St. Paul, the older of the two, began as a transportation hub but became overshadowed by Minneapolis and its lumber and flour-milling industrial base. In the twentieth century, the gap between the cities widened as Minneapolis grew into a center for national and international corporations while St. Paul's economy remained focused on local and regional consumers.[4] The two cities had old sports rivalries—the Minneapolis Millers and the St. Paul Saints in minor league baseball's American Association, the hockey Millers and Saints in various minor leagues, and the annual high-school championship football game between Minneapolis and St. Paul.

The Millers and the Saints had a rivalry so intense that fans sometimes fought in the stands. And when the prospect of a major league baseball franchise seemed near in the 1950s, each city built its own stadium in an effort to lure it instead of working together. Thus, proclaiming the Vikings to be a team for the entire state may have been a politic maneuver by forward-thinking leaders to circumvent differences between the two cities and achieve civic accord.

The Vikings played their first game in Bloomington's Metropolitan Stadium on September 17, 1961, a surprising 37–13 victory over the Chicago Bears, thanks in large part to the work of rookie quarterback Francis Tarkenton, a future Hall of Famer who came off the bench to throw three touchdown passes. The Vikings would win only two more games that year, but they played before capacity crowds who were excited to be rooting for their very own NFL team. The crowds kept coming as the team's fortunes improved in coming years, and the Vikings evolved into one of the league's premier franchises.

But the story of professional football in the Twin Cities really originated long before the creation of the Minnesota Vikings. In fact, Minneapolis had a team—the Marines—that was a charter member of the NFL in the 1920s, and several semipro teams had been playing in the area since shortly after the turn of the century.[5] The first recorded football game of any kind in Minnesota took place at Hamline University in St. Paul on September 30, 1882, when the host team lost to the University of Minnesota, 4–0. (The only scoring allowed in the rules of that time were one point per touchdown.) By that time football had become established at many eastern colleges and universities, and its popularity was spreading westward. Various "athletic associations" around the country also began to embrace football, and perhaps inevitably, the first elements of professionalization began to appear. The first recorded instance of player payment in the United States occurred on November 12, 1892, in Pennsylvania, when the Allegheny Athletic Association (AAA) team openly paid William (Pudge) Heffelfinger $500 to play in a game against the Pittsburgh Athletic Club. By 1896 the entire AAA team played for pay.[6]

Along with its increasing popularity, the sport had begun to draw attention for its extreme violence. The most successful teams were ones with the most brute power—the ball was advanced via a technique known as "mass play," in which the entire offensive team would move together as one, while the defense was forced to respond in kind. One particular play, the flying wedge, was particularly brutal: ten of the eleven players would form a V-shaped wedge, with the ball carrier following closely behind and then leaping over them. The defenses were forced to counter the leaping ball carrier with a leaper of their own. In December, 1905, the *Cincinnati Commercial Tribune* claimed that twenty-five people had been killed that year while playing football and another 168 seriously injured, and calls for reform led to the creation the following year of the National Intercollegiate Athletic Association (which was later named the National Collegiate Athletic Association) to govern college sports.[7]

In the Twin Cities area, the first semipro football league got its start in 1907 with the creation of the Sunday Football League of Minnesota. The league had six teams—the Deans and the Ramblers from Minneapolis, the National Guards from St. Paul, the Stillwater Football Team, the Deephaven Beavers, and the New Prague Seals. The league ostensibly committed itself to clean play and equitable sharing. Ticket revenues were to be divided equally between competing teams and then distributed to players after expenses.[8]

One of the founders of the league, Bobby Marshall, was a remarkable figure in Minnesota sports history. An African American, Marshall was a sports star at Minneapolis Central High School, where he excelled at football and other sports as well as academics. He went to the University of Minnesota where he became the first African American to play football in the Big Nine (later, the Big Ten) Conference, while being named to the All-America team and earning a law degree. After graduating in 1907, Marshall sought to combine development of a law practice with his work in the fledgling football league, where he was the coach and star player of the Minneapolis Deans. An end at the University of Minnesota, Marshall played quarterback for the Deans (in all likelihood, he was the game's first black quarterback) and led them to dominance and a reputation as one of the best teams in the area. The Sunday Football League lasted for three years, disbanding in 1909.[9]

Meanwhile, another team that initially formed in 1905 had risen to prominence as an independent club and would go on to lay claim in the 1920s as the first truly professional Twin Cities football team when it became a charter member of the fledgling NFL. This was the Minneapolis Marines.[10] At the beginning, the Marines were a team of mostly working-class teenagers from the Cedar-Riverside neighborhood (near the site of the Vikings' present home, US Bank Stadium), but they quickly built a reputation as a formidable independent squad. In 1910 the thirty-year-old Marshall joined the Marines, switching from quarterback to end, and the Marines rose in prominence playing other independent teams from the area and the Upper Midwest, at one time winning thirty-four consecutive games.

Within the Twin Cities, the Marines' dominance was challenged by a south Minneapolis team called the Beavers (the former Deephaven Beavers from the Sunday Football League), whose roster was dominated by former players from the University of St. Thomas in St. Paul. For five years—from 1910 to 1914—the two squads played an unofficial "Minneapolis championship game." The Marines won the first contest, 6–0, but then were upset by the Beavers the next two years, 6–0 and 7–3, prompting the Marines to make major changes toward increased professionalization. They hired their first full-time coach, Ossie Solem, who had graduated in 1912 from the University of Minnesota, where he played end for the Gophers football team. Solem introduced the team to the complex new single-wing offensive system that Minnesota had used, and the next two years the Marines overpowered the Beavers in their annual match, 33–0 and 48–0. Solem coached the Marines until 1920, its final year before joining the league that would become the NFL, compiling a record of forty-four wins, seven losses, and three ties. Solem went on to enjoy a long and successful college football coaching career at Drake, Iowa, and Syracuse.[11]

Marshall also did some football coaching, serving as head coach at his old *alma mater* Minneapolis Central in 1907, leading it to a city championship, and as an assistant coach at Minnesota—in both instances as the first black coach at those schools. By 1909 Marshall decided to drop coaching and focus on playing football and baseball—he was a star player on a semipro baseball team called the St. Paul Colored Gophers—and developing a law practice. By 1911, however, Marshall gave up on law—in part due to his heavy commitment to sports, and in part due to limited opportunities in a racially divided climate. He took a civil-service job as a grain inspector for the State of Minnesota, a job he would hold for the next thirty-nine years until retirement, while still playing sports into his forties. He continued to play for the Marines for most of the next thirteen years, including the team's entry into the American Professional Football Association at the age of forty-one. The following year, the APFA adopted a new name: the National Football League.[12]

Although the Minneapolis Marines hold the distinction of being a charter member of the NFL, a full account of professional football in the Twin Cities must include another Minnesota professional team, the Duluth Kelleys, which

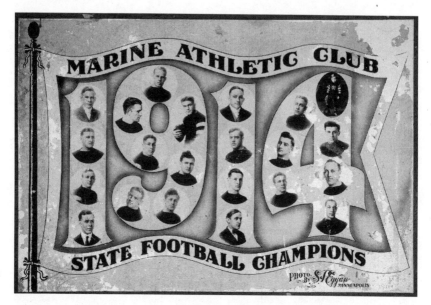

The Minneapolis Marines were the Twin Cities' first professional football club, featuring African American Bobby Marshall (lower right), who had starred with the Gophers. Minnesota Historical Society.

joined the NFL in 1923 and changed its name to the Eskimos in 1926, because there is a direct link between the Kelleys/Eskimos and the Vikings.[13] The Kelleys were sponsored by Kelley Hardware of Duluth, a longtime supporter of amateur and semipro sports teams in the area. Four investors, including the manager of the store's sporting-goods department, Marshall C. Gebert, put up $250 each to meet the league's $1,000 entry fee. Gebert served as coach and filled the initial sixteen-man roster with former semipro players from the Duluth-Superior area. The Kelleys compiled a 4–3 record (including a 9–0 victory over the Minneapolis Marines) in their inaugural season, but the team faced serious financial problems—mostly because the team's home field, Athletic Park, was a venue of very poor quality with limited seating capacity and because attendance was meager. In response to this dire financial situation, team members contributed their own money to keep the team afloat in 1924. The team needed someone to be its general manager, and in 1924 a Duluth produce company owner named Ole Haugsrud volunteered to fill that role as the team's secretary-treasurer. Other teams in the league were also financially strapped, and several dropped out—including the Minneapolis Marines after the 1924 season after compiling a four-year record of 4–17–3 in the NFL. In 1925 forty-five-year-old Bobby Marshall joined the Kelleys.[14]

That year the Kelleys played only three games (losing each one), in large part because increasingly financially strapped teams did not want to face the expense of traveling to Duluth, the league's most far-flung franchise, and the team considered disbanding. But then the team and league received a saving grace when Haugsrud landed perhaps the greatest football player in the country at the time, Ernie Nevers, to come to Duluth. A native of Willow River, Minnesota, Nevers was a childhood friend of Haugsrud and attended Stanford, where he played fullback and was named to the 1925 All-America team. Haugsrud offered his old friend a lucrative deal: a personal-services contract with Haugsrud that would pay him $15,000 for the season plus 25 percent of the gate. He then renamed the team "Ernie Nevers' Eskimos" and turned it into a traveling squad. After the Eskimos played their first game of the 1926 season in Duluth, they never again played in the Port City. Despite having only a tiny roster to keep costs down—at times only thirteen Eskimos were suited for games—the team was successful, going 6–5–3, and drawing sizeable crowds. In 1927, however, the wear and tear had taken its toll and the Eskimos won only one game. In 1928 Haugsrud decided to take the year off and suspended operations indefinitely.

The NFL greatly missed their star attraction, Nevers, and made an arrangement with Haugsrud so Nevers would return to the field. Haugsrud sold the team to buyers in New Jersey and then took a job with the Chicago Cardinals, bringing Nevers with him as part of the personal-services contract. Nevers continued to be a major attraction playing for the Cardinals, and the move by Haugsrud was cited by legendary Chicago Bears owner and head coach George Halas as one that may have saved the NFL. Under Halas's influence, the other owners in the league agreed to a deal stating that if the NFL ever had another franchise in Minnesota, Haugsrud would have the first crack at purchasing it. Three decades later, he would.[15]

During the prosperous 1950s, the popularity of pro football skyrocketed. Americans had more money, more security, and more leisure time than ever before, and they had a new device—the television—that was tailor made for viewing football. Clearly, there was ample demand for the creation of new franchises, and a group of local businessmen headed by entrepreneur Max Winter mounted an effort to land one in the Twin Cities. Winter, an Austrian Jew who moved to the United States in 1914 with his mother when he was ten,

played basketball at Hamline on a scholarship and then became a successful businessman in Minneapolis. He co-owned the 620 Club in downtown
Minneapolis (later the site of Moby Dick's bar) before turning his attention
to sports. He became a well-known boxing promoter and president of the
Minneapolis Lakers team in the National Basketball Association.

In the mid-1950s, Winter and like-minded entrepreneurs in other cities
were pushing the NFL to create expansion franchises, but the league was ham-
strung by a rule that required any expansion to gain the unanimous consent of
all owners, and by decade's end, none had been awarded. Perhaps inevitably,
the American Football League (AFL) arose to compete with the NFL, and
Winter and his partners joined it as a charter member of the new six-team
league (along with Dallas, Denver, Houston, Los Angeles, and New York). The
first meeting of the new AFL was held on August 14, 1959. Two weeks later,
Chicago Bears owner George Halas and Pittsburgh Steelers owner Art Rooney,
principals on an NFL expansion committee a year earlier, jointly announced
that the league would finally be expanding. Although no specific cities were
mentioned, it was generally considered that Dallas and Houston—both already
on the AFL roster—were the frontrunners (the announcement prompted
AFL Commissioner Lamar Hunt to find two replacement franchises: Boston
and Buffalo).

By November of that year it had become clear that Minneapolis-St.
Paul's fortunes as a potential NFL expansion city had risen. The NFL's
Chicago Cardinals had been drawing poorly for years and had begun to eye
Minneapolis-St. Paul for a possible move. In the fall of 1959, the Minneapolis
Star and Tribune Company endeavored to influence a potential Cardinals
move to Minnesota by, in effect, sponsoring two regular-season home games
for the Cardinals at Metropolitan Stadium. Sports columnist Sid Hartman and
Minneapolis Chamber of Commerce executive director Gerald Moore had
traveled to Chicago to arrange the deal, guaranteeing the Cardinals at least
a $125,000 gate. The games were successful, one drawing a capacity crowd of
26,625 and another for 20,112. Soon, Hartman and *Minneapolis Star* sports editor
Charles Johnson began writing articles about NFL expansion committee chairman Halas's growing interest in Minneapolis-St. Paul. Halas perceived the Twin
Cities as a desirable market for an expansion team, and sentiment in the Twin
Cities began shifting away from the AFL toward the NFL. On October 11, NFL
commissioner Bert Bell died of a heart attack and was replaced by Los Angeles
Rams general manager Pete Rozelle, who made the historic announcement of

Minneapolis-St. Paul's successful bid a few months later, on January 28, 1960. Rozelle said expansion franchises had been awarded to Dallas for that season and Minneapolis-St. Paul for 1961.[16]

Halas was reported to have guaranteed the Minneapolis-St. Paul group a franchise. While he saw it as an area that was prime for an NFL franchise, he also saw it as an opportunity to reward Haugsrud for the role he had played thirty years earlier when he brought star player Ernie Nevers into the fledgling NFL—a move credited by many as one that saved the league.[17] The old agreement with Haugsrud was that he would have an ownership stake if the NFL returned to Minnesota. So when Winter and his partners Bill Boyer and H. P. Skoglund got the NFL franchise, Haugsrud was added to the group. He put up $60,000 of the $600,000 expansion fee and became a 10 percent owner.

On January 29, the day following Rozelle's announcement, *Tribune* columnist Sid Hartman quoted Halas as saying that "nothing can keep the Twin Cities from having pro football in 1961 if they sell 25,000 season tickets and have a stadium to seat 35,000 to 40,000." He also said that the additional year to prepare would mean that they should field a team that would be better than Dallas.

*The Lakers' relocation to Los Angeles in 1960 briefly left the Twin Cities without a major professional sports franchise.* However, the word that pro football was coming to Minnesota, coming on the heels of the Washington Senators' major league baseball team's move, cemented the Twin Cities' place in professional sports. For sports lovers in the Upper Midwest, the area's emergence into the two professional sports leagues was a godsend. Minneapolis and St. Paul had frequently fought each other over the decades; it was a long overdue opportunity for officials from each city to finally work together.

Bert Rose, who had been the public relations director for Pete Rozelle with the Los Angeles Rams, was hired as the team's first general manager. The first item of business for both the Vikings (and the Twins) was to significantly expand the seating capacity of Metropolitan Stadium to at least forty thousand. The second task was to assemble a roster of players that might be at least somewhat competitive. In that regard the Vikings may have had a slight advantage over the Dallas Cowboys, who began play in 1960 without the benefit of taking part in the college football draft. In 1960 each of the twelve established NFL teams created lists of eleven players from which the Cowboys picked three. In late December 1960, the draft of college players for the following season was conducted, and among their picks, the Vikings obtained several top-rated players, including Tarkenton, Tulane running back Tommy Mason, and University of Pittsburgh defensive back Ed Sharockman. Given that advantage, the league made the expansion pool more restrictive for the Vikings; each team created lists of eight players, instead of eleven, from which the Vikings could pick. In addition, the Vikings swung a deal with the New York Giants to obtain the veteran quarterback they so sorely needed, in the person of George Shaw. In exchange for Shaw, the Giants got the Vikings' top draft pick for 1962.

The first head coach for the Vikings was Norm Van Brocklin, a former star quarterback who had led the NFL in passing three times during the 1950s. He ended his career by guiding the Philadelphia Eagles to victory over the Green Bay Packers in the 1960 championship game, 17–13, and then announced his retirement. Van Brocklin had understood that he would then become the Eagles head coach, replacing the retiring Buck Shaw, but when the Eagles instead named Nick Skorich to the job, Minnesota made Van Brocklin an offer, which he accepted.

The Vikings took the field for the first time on August 5, 1961, for an exhibition game against the Dallas Cowboys at Howard Wood Field in Sioux Falls, South Dakota. The Vikings lost that game 38–13 before a crowd of 4,954. When they launched the regular season with a home game on September 17, Metropolitan Stadium had been retrofitted to expand the seating capacity. The stadium, of course, had been built as a baseball facility, so making changes to accommodate football presented a challenge. The playing field itself ran from third base to the right-field fence, barely leaving enough room for end zones. The stadium held about thirty thousand for baseball, and to provide the additional ten thousand seats that were required for football, the team simply moved in large, wooden bleachers on one side of the field, extending from baseball's left field to center field. In 1965 the Vikings built permanent, double-decker stands in left field in exchange for reduced rent, expanding the capacity to more than forty-six thousand. The original plan called for building the double-decker stands so that they could be moved toward the football field, but that part of the project was never realized.

Van Brocklin coached the Vikings for the first six years of the team's existence, achieving only one winning season (8–5–1 in 1964) and compiling an overall record of 29–51–4. Van Brocklin, known as "The Dutchman," had a fiery reputation, oftentimes losing his temper and screaming at players and referees alike. He also had an ongoing contentious relationship with the team's starting quarterback, Tarkenton. Van Brocklin did not like Tarkenton's penchant for "scrambling" to evade pass rushers instead of staying in the pocket. The feud led to Tarkenton's ultimate demand for a trade after the 1966 season, and on February 11, 1967, Van Brocklin announced that he was resigning, later explaining that he felt he had lost control of the team. The Vikings had been negotiating with the New York Giants on a deal involving Tarkenton, and on March 7 both teams announced that it had been consummated: Tarkenton would go to New York in exchange for two first-round draft picks and two second-round picks.

Van Brocklin's exit paved the way for the Vikings to replace him with the coach they had wanted from the beginning of the team's creation: Bud Grant, a native Wisconsite who had already attained legendary status for his coaching successes in the Canadian Football League (CFL). Over the course of ten seasons as head coach of the Winnipeg Blue Bombers, Grant's teams won four CFL championships and compiled a record of 122–66–3. The signing of Grant on March 10, 1967, marked the beginning of the Vikings' most glorious period in the NFL. In 1967 the Vikings compiled a record of only 3–8–3, but over the course of an eleven-season span starting in 1968, the Vikings won ten Central Division titles and made four trips to the Super Bowl.

The Vikings' emergence as a formidable NFL power from the frozen North Country captured the national imagination as a team that actually did conjure images of Norse warriors. Many of the Vikings games were played in sub-freezing and even subzero temperatures, but Grant—himself wearing only a light jacket for those games—forbade the employment of sideline heaters or the use of gloves or sleeves by players. The Vikings fans relished their new national reputation as singularly tough and hardy people. The Vikings' success and the national reputation the team and region were acquiring coincided with other cultural developments that elevated Minnesota's national stature. The *Mary Tyler Moore* show, fictionally based in Minneapolis, began an eight-year run in 1970 as one of the most popular comedies in TV history. In 1973 *Time* magazine ran a cover story (with governor Wendell Anderson holding a northern pike on a stringer) titled, "The Good Life in Minnesota." The article focused on the accomplishments of the state's progressive government at the time but also lauded the state's citizens as being unusually civic-minded souls who believed in hard work and shared sacrifice. Minnesota enjoyed significant adulation in the 1970s, and the Minnesota Vikings were a big part of it.

The beginning of the Vikings' eleven-year period of dominance, 1968, was also a time of tremendous social and political upheaval in the United States. The Vietnam War hit its peak, with some 543,000 troops committed there, and in the US opposition to the war also escalated to new levels, culminating in riots at the Democratic National Convention. It was also the year when presidential candidate Robert Kennedy and civil-rights leader Martin Luther King were assassinated. King's assassination on April 4 escalated civil unrest that was already well underway around the country, including in Minneapolis-St. Paul. In July 1967 violence broke out in north Minneapolis along Plymouth Avenue, and 150 members of the National Guard were called in to restore order. The impact of the event was a general reactionary public shift to the right, leading to the political rise of former Minneapolis police detective Charles Stenvig, who ran for mayor as an independent on a law-and-order platform. Vowing to "take the handcuffs off the police (and stop) racial militants," Stenvig was elected in 1969. According to reports at the time, "Although Stenvig denies that his political strategy included appealing to white racism, his law-and-order rhetoric likely appealed, even if indirectly, to the racist vote."[18]

For the NFL, integration was slow in coming. Although NFL teams started signing black players in the 1950s, they also employed quotas limiting their numbers on league rosters. Roosevelt Grier, for example, when a star defensive lineman for the New York Giants in the late 1950s, stated, "We knew only six black guys would make the team no matter how good they were."[19] The 1961 Vikings had six black players, which remained a typical number for the time. (The Green Bay Packers had five, and the Chicago Bears six, whereas the Washington Redskins would not sign their first black player until the following year.) By 1968 the number of black Vikings had increased to eight—including three who would soon gain fame as members of "the Purple People Eaters," the superb defensive core of the team. These were Carl Eller, Alan Page, and Jim Marshall, who along with defensive tackle Gary Larson, manned the defensive line of a team that won the Central Division title with a record of 8–6. In their first playoff game ever, the Vikings lost to the Baltimore Colts (five black players), 24–14.

The following year the Vikings (now with nine African American players) emerged as the top NFL team with a 12–2 record. After dispatching the Los Angeles Rams and the Cleveland Browns in the playoffs, they went to Super Bowl IV as thirteen-point favorites to defeat the AFL-champion Kansas City Chiefs. The previous year the New York Jets (with thirteen African American players) had executed one of the biggest upsets in sports history with a victory over the heavily favored Colts, but many sports fans considered that win a fluke and expected the Vikings to win easily. Instead the Chiefs overpowered the Vikings in every aspect of the game—and did so with a roster that was nearly half African American (twenty-three of fifty-two players). The Chiefs' victory over the Vikings was a watershed event for the advancement of African Americans in professional football. NFL teams realized that with their unofficial racial quotas, they were losing talent to the AFL (whose teams were far less likely to restrict the numbers of African Americans). The Vikings, like all other NFL teams, began to sign increasing numbers of African Americans.

Among the team's first black players, Page went on to make a significant impact on Minnesota life after his playing days. Page had come to the Vikings as a first-round draft choice out of Notre Dame, where he was an All-American, in 1967. For much of his eleven-year tenure with the Vikings he was recognized as perhaps the best defensive tackle in the league. He played on all four Vikings Super Bowl teams during that time and in 1971 achieved the rare honor of being named the NFL's Most Valuable Player, only the second defensive player ever to achieve that distinction. During his playing days, Page began taking classes at the University of Minnesota Law School, where he received his doctor of law in 1978. He played four more years with the Chicago Bears before retiring. He began his legal career in the Minneapolis law firm of Lindquist and Vennum in 1979 after the football season and stayed there until 1985 (four years after his retirement from football), when he was named as a special assistant attorney general. Soon thereafter he was named an assistant attorney general. In 1992 he was elected as an associate justice on the Minnesota Supreme Court, the first African American to serve on the court. He stepped down from the court in August 2015, when he reached the mandatory retirement age of seventy. Page and his wife, Diane, continue to serve Minnesota, however, through the Page Education Association, which they founded in 1988. The Foundation awards Page Grants to Minnesota minority students who attend Minnesota postsecondary schools and agree to mentoring projects with young children. Since its creation, the Page Education Association has provided 6,500 grants to 4,200 students.[20]

Although the Vikings were consistently successful on the field, it had become apparent by the early 1970s that Metropolitan Stadium was an inadequate facility. When the NFL and AFL merged in 1966, the NFL declared that stadiums in the league had to seat at least fifty thousand people. The Met seated 48,700 for football, the smallest capacity in the NFL. So with the Vikings' Met Stadium use agreements set to expire in 1975, discussions began in the Twin Cities about building a new stadium. In 1971 the Metropolitan Council came up with a plan to expand and remodel Met Stadium, calling upon the city of Minneapolis to again use its credit (as it had in the initial construction of the stadium) to enable the commission to borrow money to do the job. However, when the Met Council announced the plan, old animosities between Minneapolis and Bloomington arose anew.

Situating Met Stadium in Bloomington was initially seen as a compromise between government leaders in Minneapolis and St. Paul who saw the suburb as a "neutral site" that would reduce the longstanding friction between the two cities. When the stadium was built in 1955, Bloomington still had actual farmland within its borders and had a population of only ten thousand. After the stadium became a major league facility in 1961, Bloomington experienced a huge commercial boom, mostly along the I-494 freeway corridor, and Minneapolis officials became upset that Bloomington was not, in their opinion, shouldering its share of stadium upkeep. Thus when plans for an expanded Met Stadium were announced in 1972, Minneapolis government leaders responded by saying they were tired of dealing with Bloomington and announced their intention to build a domed stadium in downtown Minneapolis. Plans were announced for a sixty-five-thousand-seat stadium priced at $49 million.

Minneapolis was not alone in wooing the Vikings, however. Bloomington and the adjacent suburb of Richfield came forward with a joint proposal to either expand and renovate Met Stadium or build a new stadium adjacent to the Met. The University of Minnesota made improvements to its sixty-six-thousand-seat Memorial Stadium in an apparent effort to attract the Vikings, and St. Paul made a late entry in the stadium competition with plans for a $60-million, eighty-thousand-seat stadium near the Minnesota State Fairgrounds. The Vikings' five-man Board of Directors assessed the varying options and failed to achieve unanimity. Haugsrud and St. Paul newspaper publisher Bernie Ridder voted to stay in Bloomington, either with a new or revamped Met Stadium. Winter and insurance executive H. P. Skoglund favored Minneapolis. That left President E. W. Boyer with the deciding vote, and he cast it for Minneapolis.

The Minneapolis City Council had commissioned a feasibility report which concluded that the project could be financed completely out of revenues, with no burden on taxpayers. Furthermore, the downtown stadium project received significant backing—and financial support—from the business community. For many years one of the striking characteristics of Minneapolis civic leadership has been the degree to which the private sector has helped government in meeting public needs. The relationship dates to the late 1930s, when the Internal Revenue Service adopted a law to provide tax breaks to corporations who give at least five percent of their income to charity. Few businesses around the country took advantage of the new law, but in Minneapolis Gene Nelson Dayton, owner of Dayton's department store, and John Cowles Sr., owner of Minneapolis's morning and afternoon newspapers, immediately took advantage and others followed their lead.[21] In 1976 the practice became more formalized when the Minneapolis Chamber of Commerce created the Five Percent Club. By the time discussions of a downtown stadium grew serious in the early 1970s, the business community had already paid for and built a number of downtown buildings and amenities to benefit the public—Orchestra Hall, the Guthrie Theater, the Nicollet Mall, and the downtown Skyway system. Several corporations lined up to underwrite part of the stadium cost and provide a significant business guarantee against any losses that might result.

The public, however, was unconvinced. Influenced by stories of how taxpayers in other cities had been left to foot the bill as the result of failed stadium-financing projects, significant public opposition to the stadium grew. Polls showed that nearly two-thirds of Minneapolitans opposed the new stadium. Nevertheless, the project appeared to be in place and the Vikings were ready to move—until, that is, Minneapolis's antiestablishment mayor, Stenvig, stepped in. Although Stenvig had at one time voiced support for the stadium, he bowed to political pressure from his constituents, called for a funding referendum, and the plan died.[22]

For the next several years, the stadium wrangling continued with no clear solutions, leading Governor Wendell Anderson to state his concern, in 1975, that both the Vikings and Twins might leave the state as a result. That same year the Vikings named Mike Lynn as the team's new general manager, replacing Jim Finks, and Lynn spoke of his strong support for a new stadium on the Met Stadium site. He also made veiled threats that the team might leave Minnesota if they did not get it. Over the next two years, the state legislature got in on the act, putting together a revenue bonding package to finance a stadium. A new public agency, the Metropolitan Sports Facilities Commission, was created with an immediate charge of selecting the stadium site. Again, multiple proposals came forward, and in the end the finalists were downtown Minneapolis and the Bloomington Met Stadium site. In December 1978 the commission voted 4–3 to make the Metrodome a reality in downtown Minneapolis. Ground was broken a year later, and the Vikings began play there in 1982.

In playing their games indoors, the Vikings sacrificed one of the greatest home-field advantages in the NFL. While playing at Met Stadium, opposing teams—especially from warmer climes—were oftentimes unaccustomed to the frequent frigid weather and frozen turf. But in the sterile, temperature-controlled Metrodome, the Vikings played in a venue type to which all teams were accustomed. In moving into the Metrodome, the Vikings also harmed themselves financially with a strange financial arrangement the team consummated with its general manager, Mike Lynn.

Lynn had joined the Vikings in 1974 at the age of thirty-eight, despite the fact that he had no experience in professional football. Up to that time, Lynn's work experience consisted of various retail jobs and management of a movie theater. Max Winter was impressed by a personal letter that Lynn had sent him, however, and took him on as a personal assistant. The general manager at the time, Jim Finks, resigned at the end of the 1974 season, reportedly due to a dispute with Winter, and in 1975 Winter named Lynn as the team's new GM.

Lynn would serve as the team's GM for the next fifteen years, during which time the Vikings had ten winning seasons and six Central Division titles, but the team was no longer as consistently dominant as it had been prior to his tenure. Lynn would be known as the architect of one of the worst trades in team—and perhaps NFL—history when the Vikings sent five players and seven draft choices to the Dallas Cowboys in 1989 for veteran star running back Herschel Walker, a transaction that helped the Cowboys win three Super Bowls, while Walker—his peak years behind him—failed to produce for the Vikings.

The failed trade is part of Lynn's legacy, but so is a lucrative deal that he cut with Winter that diverted millions of dollars of revenue into Lynn's pocket. Although Winter was enamored of Lynn initially, differences had grown between them after Lynn became general manager because Lynn favored a new open-air stadium in Bloomington, while Winter wanted the team to move into a Minneapolis domed stadium. Backers of the downtown dome were aware of Lynn's position and pressured Winter to harness Lynn and bring him on target for Minneapolis and under its tight $55 million budget. Even though he favored the open-air stadium, Lynn agreed to get behind the push for the domed stadium. And in so doing, he pressured Winter to agree to a contract that would enrich him. In the run-up to the construction of the Metrodome, the Vikings announced that they would pay for construction of the facility's one hundred luxury suites themselves in order to keep the project under budget. Lynn was named as the president of a subsidiary company that would manage the suites, and as part of his compensation, his contract provided him not only 10 percent of luxury-suite revenue for Vikings games but for all Metrodome events for as long as the stadium would stand. Over the course of three decades, until his death in 2012, Lynn made an estimated $14–$20 million on the deal.[23]

During the Vikings' thirty-four years playing in the Metrodome, they were essentially a slightly above-average team. They had a composite regular-season record of 282–243 while winning eight division titles. In playoff games they went 10–18. Grant closed out his coaching career with three seasons in the Metrodome, compiling a losing record. He was followed by Jerry Burns, who coached the Vikings for six years, going 52–43 in the regular season and 3–3 in the playoffs. Burns was replaced by Dennis Green, the second African American to be named as a head coach in the NFL. Green coached the Vikings for ten years and was quite successful, his teams making the playoffs eight times. His best season in Minnesota was 1998, when the Vikings, led by African American quarterback Randall Cunningham, compiled the best record in the NFL at 15–1 and led the league in scoring. They were within one game of advancing to their fifth Super Bowl, but lost the NFC championship game to the Atlanta Falcons, 30–27 in overtime after placekicker Gary Anderson, who had not missed a field-goal attempt all season, missed a relatively easy thirty-eight-yard kick late in regulation play. The Vikings would play seventeen more seasons in the Metrodome, winning only four more Central Division championships and compiling a record of 140 wins and 143 losses.

Mostly mediocre on the field, the Vikings were sometimes notorious off it, developing a reputation for an unusually high number of off-the-field mis-behaviors. In 2012, the *St. Paul Pioneer Press* reported that since 2000 the Vikings ranked first in the NFL in the number of players who had been arrested or cited.[24] The problems were particularly acute during the four years, 2002–2005, when Mike Tice was the head coach, compiling a record of thirty-three wins and thirty-four losses. In early 2005 Tice himself was fined $100,000 for scalping Super Bowl tickets, and that fall four players were charged with lewd and disorderly conduct for their participation in a drunken sex party on a boat on Lake Minnetonka, an incident that came to be known as the "Love Boat" scandal.[25] Tice was fired after the 2005 season, but the problem of poor off-field behavior by Vikings players continued. Between 2010 and 2015, no other franchise had more reported player arrests than the Vikings, with eighteen. Star running back Adrian Peterson was arrested twice—first in Houston in 2013 for pushing a police officer in a bar and resisting arrest and again in 2014 for child abuse.

The Vikings played their last game in the Metrodome on December 29, 2013. The following two years, they played their home games in the University of Minnesota's TCF Bank Stadium, while their new home, US Bank Stadium, was being built on the Metrodome site. While the Metrodome was broadly criticized as a cheaply built, inferior facility (its Teflon roof collapsed five times during its lifespan), the new stadium spared no expense. The fixed-roof stadium's overall budget was estimated at $1.061 billion, with $348 million from the state of Minnesota, $150 million from the city of Minneapolis, and $551 million from the team and private contributions. The Vikings played their first game in the new stadium on September 18, 2016, a 17–14 victory over the Green Bay Packers. At season's end, the Vikings finished with eight wins and eight losses.

The story of professional football in the Twin Cities is a long one, extending from the pre-World War I years to today. The differences between then and now are, of course, profound. The initial semipro teams in the Twin Cities area were young men who played for the (oftentimes violent) fun of it, charging spectators nominal amounts to help subsidize expenses, while today the game is played by millionaires. When the Twin Cities joined the modern NFL with the creation of the Minnesota Vikings in 1960, it marked a significant step in the region's emergence as a national center. Minnesotans grew rightfully proud of the Vikings, not only for their success on an oftentimes frozen field but also for the cultural identity that the Vikings helped to create for the state and its people. The myth of Nordic hardiness has diminished since the Vikings began playing their games indoors in 1982, but the passion for the team and the game has not.

## CHAPTER SIX

# Just for Kicks

## *The World's Game Comes to the Twin Cities*

TOM TAYLOR

It may not be the day that soccer made it in the Twin Cities but it is certainly the day I got hooked on the world's game. It was a bright, steamy day at the old Metropolitan Stadium, the former home of the Minnesota Twins in the near southern Minneapolis suburb of Bloomington. It was June 1978. I was with a few of my college buddies sitting high up in the third deck along the first-base line. Tickets and beer were cheap. The stadium was packed. There was a hip, young vibe. Late in the game with the score tied, the Minnesota Kicks pushed the ball up the right side of the field. A long cross floated across the pitch from our right winger. Several Kicks attackers leaped for the ball to no avail; the ball carried across the goal mouth just past the left goal post. "Damn," I muttered, "another missed chance." Then, miraculously, just as the ball was inches off the infield dirt of the third base area, an orange-clad missile launched itself. The floppy haired head of Alan Willey, the Kicks' lanky English forward, flew toward the ball, risking a mouth full of dirt or much worse and deflected the seemingly errant cross into the near corner. It was one of the coolest, bravest athletic moves I had ever seen. The crowd went crazy, and I became a soccer fan. "The artful dodger," as a Twin Cities columnist nicknamed him, had won me and many other Minnesotans over to the world's most popular sport.[1]

There had not been much opportunity to be a soccer fan in Minnesota before the Kicks arrived in 1976. Until the Kicks transformed the Twin Cities' soccer landscape, the game was largely recreational. Organized soccer dates

DOI: https://doi.org/10.34053/scs2019.tcs.6

back to the late nineteenth century when immigrant communities carried their love of the game with them. German, English, Norwegian, Polish, and Serbian teams regularly played in men's leagues. "The game in Minnesota started, as in other States," noted a *Spalding Soccer Guide* for 1917–18, "through a number of old country boys getting together."[2] The first mention of soccer in the local papers was in 1906 when the *Minneapolis Tribune* announced the upcoming game between the Minnehaha Thistles and the Minneapolis Hibernians. The paper promised that it would be a "fast and exciting game."[3] No results were subsequently published. Some teams occasionally traveled to Chicago or other Midwest towns for tournaments. The Shaw Cup, the local Twin Cities' highest soccer prize, started in 1888 and was regularly won in the early years by the Thistles, a team of largely British heritage. Their top rival was the local Norwegian team, the Vikings.

The University of Minnesota has had a team for almost one hundred years, with club soccer starting in the 1910s, but it has never competed as a men's Division-I program. The first teams were led by three exchange students from Shanghai—two brothers, Wen Huen Pan and Wen Ping Pan, and their friend Yih Kum Kwong. They were the first Chinese students at the University and were described as "very skilled on the ball."[4] Women's soccer has been a D-1 sport at Minnesota since 1993.

While undoubtedly these games were fiercely contested and winners brayed about their success, soccer remained below the public radar for most of the twentieth century. An organized men's league started in 1952 when the Northwest Kickers of Minneapolis and four other teams officially registered with the US Soccer Association.[5] In 1968 many of these adult teams established the Minnesota Junior Soccer Association, a companion league for younger players.

By the early 1970s, soccer was beginning to find a foundation in the Twin Cities. In the 1960s a few Twin Cities high schools sponsored club soccer, and in 1974 it became an official boys' sport. Many high school teachers scrambled to learn the basics and became the first coaches. One of those early players later recalled, "There was such a low level of knowledge about soccer that [our] athletic director wasn't sure what to order for uniforms. We played one year in jerseys that were actually for girls' softball or something."[6] Bloomington Lincoln won the inaugural boys' soccer title. Six years later girls' soccer crowned its first champion, Bloomington Jefferson. The sport was growing and in the mid-1970s it skyrocketed.

# The Kicks Era (1976–1981)

The Minnesota Kicks were a phenomenon that, unfortunately, lasted only six short years. In 1976 they moved to Bloomington from Denver at a time when attendance and financial problems with many of the North American Soccer League (NASL) teams led to the league's failure and the collapse of the team that was a major force on the Twin Cities sports scene. The Kicks drew legions of fans, averaging over thirty thousand per game at their height, and became *the* thing for hordes of young people in the Twin Cities. Ian Plenderleith, a British soccer writer, recently maintained that the Kicks were the coolest team in the old NASL.[7] Tickets were $2.50 for general admission and the parking was free. It was likely that the cheap tickets and the ability to tailgate in the massive Metropolitan Stadium lots before the game, more than the quality of the soccer itself, created the Kick's mystique. Longtime *Minneapolis StarTribune* columnist Patrick Reusse recently remembered those halcyon days of the Kicks and summarized the reasons for success: "Forty years later, if you want to know the key to the Kick's immediate success, it was this: free parking."[8] Many fans never left the parking lot and the party scene, but some did go in to the Met and the world's game began to take hold, albeit grudgingly. One fan quipped, "This is a heck of a game, but there should be more baskets."[9]

The Kicks started at a propitious time. The NASL had been a semipro operation for several years, but in the mid-1970s it began to take roots in cities across the United States. Between 1973 and 1975 it expanded from nine to twenty teams. More importantly, the league attracted international stars, some of the game's biggest names. Brazilian soccer star Pele, arguably the greatest player to ever kick a ball, signed with the New York Cosmos in 1975. So too did German 1974 World Cup hero Franz "the Kaiser" Beckenbauer, maybe the best defender ever to put on cleats. Giorgio Chinaglia, an accomplished Italian striker and an even larger personality, joined him soon after. British legend George Best and Dutchman Johan Cruyff, the man later credited with developing Barcelona's unique soccer style in the 1980s, joined the Los Angeles Aztecs.

The Kicks benefited from the interest that these international superstars brought to the league, but they also did play good soccer. In their inaugural year, they played in the league's championship game at the Kingdome in Seattle. They lost to Toronto 3–1. but made the playoffs in each of their six years in the league. English players made up nearly half of the initial roster. Alan Willey, whose header converted me and many other Twin Citians to the world's game, made his way to Minnesota from Middlesbrough Football Club (FC) in Yorkshire. Willey's journey to Minnesota was typical of many young players at the time. He had risen early in the ranks of Middlesbrough, signing as an apprentice at age seventeen and making periodic appearances with the first team within the year. Freddie Goodwin, the first coach of the Kicks, had made a bit of a name for himself in English soccer before injuries compelled him to take up coaching.

Like many, Goodwin saw the emergence of the NASL as a new, if largely unknown, opportunity. Once he had made the jump across the pond, he used his connections to scout and recruit players from England. He convinced Willey's coach at Middlesbrough that playing in Minnesota during England's off season would be a good way for the young striker to stay in shape and develop. Besides, English soccer was rather stodgy at the time. Young players like Willey were expected to dutifully wait their turn, ride the bench, and (if you were an apprentice) clean the stadium after the home games. Some players like goalie Geoff Barnett had played for storied English teams like Everton and Arsenal; perhaps sensing their careers at the top of English football were ending, they saw Minnesota as a way to continue to make a living with the game they loved.

Willey had never heard of Minnesota, but playing in Minnesota offered a chance for him to make his own way. For two years Willey led the vagabond life of a young soccer player, shuffling between the fall to spring English season and the summer NASL campaigns. In 1978 the Kicks bought out Willey's contract in England, and he became a full-time player in the United States. He finished his career as the leading scorer for the Kicks and the second leading scorer in NASL history with 129 goals in 238 games. The vagabond wound up never leaving Minnesota. Willey became the color commentator for many of the NASL's Minnesota Union games and is a fixture in the Twin Cities soccer scene today.

Maybe the best player on that Kicks team was Patrick 'Ace' Ntsoelengoe, an incredibly creative midfielder from South Africa whose ability to pass made life easy for Willey, Merrick, and the other Kicks attackers. In 2010 BBC Sports hailed him as "perhaps the best player you never saw."[10] This was likely the case because while the Kicks were fan favorites in the Twin Cities, the NASL days are remembered for the star-studded Cosmos team of Pele, Beckenbauer, and Chinaglia. The national media paid scant attention to teams not located on the coasts. It is also because Ntsoelengoe played during apartheid in South Africa, and the country was banned from all international competitions including the

African Cup and World Cup. South Africa's loss was Minnesota's gain, as the lack of international opportunities was likely the reason that Ntsoelengoe flew under the international radar and was available to a fledging franchise like the Kicks. For Goodwin, Ntsoelengoe, Willey, and other players and coaches from around the world, soccer in Minnesota offered a fresh start.

August 14, 1978, was without a doubt, the high point of the Kicks' six-year run in the NASL. On that night Willey, Ntsoelengoe, and the rest of the team took on the Cosmos in the semifinals of the NASL cup. Almost forty-six thousand raucous fans, enjoying copious cans of Hamms, "the Land of Sky Blue Waters" beer sold in the stadium on that sweltering night, crammed into the Met. And even before they settled in, less than a minute into the match, Charlie George, who had signed with the Kicks that year from Arsenal, found the back of the net, and the Cosmos goalie, Erol Yasin, was injured on the play. Soon afterward a sloppy Cosmos defense led to an own goal and the rout was on. Down 3–0 at halftime, the Cosmos rallied for an early goal in the second half, but the Kicks quickly calmed the fans' nerves with a goal from Ntsoelengoe and five from 'the Artful Dodger.' The Kicks annihilated the Cosmos 9–2.[11]

The NASL playoff system was not based on aggregate scores the way most home-and-away matches are now played in soccer competitions, and

Minnesota Kicks manhandle Cosmos great Pele at Metropolitan Stadium. Minnesota Historical Society.

the Cosmos defeated the Kicks 4–0 in the return match in front of over sixty thousand fans at Giants' Stadium. The series went to a mini playoff game on the same night. That ended in a tie, and the Cosmos advanced with a 2–1 win in the shootout. The narrow win allowed the Cosmos to go through and eventually win the Cup. Interestingly, and perhaps reflective of the general lack of knowledge about the league at that time, a report on the first game in the *Chicago Tribune* noted that the Cosmos would have to win the return match by eight goals to advance.[12]

The Kicks survived for a few more years, but the glory days of the NASL and professional soccer in Minnesota had reached their apogee. The aging stars of the Cosmos and Aztecs moved on, and the league lost its most recognized players and the media attention they garnered. Overexpansion and too many struggling franchises diluted the quality of play and the financial resources of the league. National television networks picked up some signature games in the 1970s, but the league failed to establish itself in the critical national media markets. The Kicks' attendance ebbed, dropping from over thirty-five thousand a game to half that number by 1980. A year later the team folded. A Kicks indoor team played until 1984.

## Soccer in the Twin Cities After the Kicks

The brief explosion of Kicks' soccer has had a long-term impact on the development of the sport in the Twin Cities. Not only did it fuel a new passion for the game in schools and clubs across the region but former Kicks players, like Alan Willey, Alan Merrick, and several others, stayed in town and helped build soccer at many levels. Merrick moved on to coach the Kick's indoor team and eventually started a highly successful soccer academy. He continues to coach high school soccer in a St. Paul suburb. Willey, as noted earlier, is now on the microphone for United's games. In many, many ways, the solid growth of soccer in Minnesota in the last decades has built on both the enthusiasm and visibility that the Kicks brought in those years and on the coaches and players who came to the Twin Cities and never left.

The 1980s were a down time on the Twin Cities soccer front. In the early 1980s, Met Stadium was torn down. Professional soccer disappeared for more than a decade, but the foundation of enthusiasm for the sport established in those years did not die; it simply began to find new outlets and as a result, develop strong grassroots structures and support that are responsible for the strength of the sport in the area today. Most importantly soccer took off at the club and high school levels.

Soccer had been introduced as a high school boys' sport in the 1960s, and by the late 1970s it was firmly established among almost all metropolitan schools and was spreading to larger cities around the state. In 1980 the boys' tournament expanded from a four-team to an eight-team affair, and girls' programs began to flourish. In 1986 the tournament moved into the Metrodome and attendance averaged over ten thousand for the finals. Paralleling the growth in schools was the growth in club teams, and soccer began to become a year-round sport for many in the Twin Cities.

This slow but steady growth of soccer at the high school and club levels exploded into two coming-of-age events in 1989. The first was the coronation of Briana Scurry as a major force in Metro women's soccer. The second was the success of a club team in St. Paul, the Blackhawks, which created a new family of soccer and new stars from the area that have significantly carried the Twin Cities into its current glory days.

In 1989 Scurry led her suburban Anoka High School soccer team to the state title, and she was later named the Minnesota female athlete of the year. It would be the first of many accolades for one of the most accomplished Twin Cities' women athletes ever. But if she had had her way, she may have never played the game. Her first love growing up in the northern Minneapolis suburb of Dayton was football—American football. In the 1980s girls were not allowed to play football, so her mom found Briana a soccer team. Until Briana showed up it was an all-boys team, but she wanted a challenge, and girls' soccer was still very much in its initial growing stages. The coach of the team, afraid to have his only girl get hurt, put her in goal.

Scurry rankled at being a goalie, at least for a while. In her early high school years, she played forward before returning to the nets. Anoka High was sure glad she did. "I learned that I could control the game from goal," she later told *Sports Illustrated for Kids*.[13] At the University of Massachusetts and later with the national team for much of the 1990s, she certainly did just that. In 1993 she was voted the national collegiate goalkeeper of the year and by the next year was a regular on the national team. Over thirteen seasons she had 173 appearances for the national team, a record for keepers at the time that Hope Solo eclipsed in the 2010s. She finished her national career with an amazing record of 133–12–14 and seventy-one shutouts. Scurry was, according to her national team coach, Tony DiCicco, "the best in the world. That's the truth."[14] She helped the United States take third at the 1995 World Cup. Scurry played every minute for the gold medal Olympic team of 1996, and in 1999 at the World Cup in Los Angles she made "the save."

The 1999 World Cup tournament is usually remembered for Brandy Chastain's clutch left-footed penalty kick shot and shirt tossing celebration that ended the championship match against China, but it was Scurry who had to make the save that opened the door for Chastain's heroics. With the game tied after regulation and overtime, it went to a penalty shootout. Five players on each team got a shot against the goalie. Penalty situations strongly favor the shooter, and both teams had made their first two penalty kicks when the third Chinese player set the ball down. Years later Scurry recalled changing her routine and actually looking at the player as she set the ball down. "At that moment," she remembered, "I knew I was going to make the save."[15] Confident, she read the shooter's intention, got a good hop forward, dove left and solidly blocked the attempt. The United States did not miss any attempts and were crowned the World Champions.

Some say Scurry got too much of a hop off the line and that in that moment of crowning glory she cheated. Goalies are supposed to stay on the goal line until the shooter hits the ball. Almost all goalies try to get a bit of a jump to get their momentum going forward to cut down the shooter's angle and to be better prepared to parry a shot away. Bill Dwyre, sports editor for the *Los Angeles Times*, wrote after the game, "There is also no questioning the fact that the US cheated to win." Scurry admitted it but said, "Everybody does it. It's only cheating if you get caught."[16] Ethicists can debate it, but Scurry's job was to save the shot; it was up to the referee to determine if she had done it fairly. The referee's whistle was silent. Scurry was a hero.

Scurry played on US World Cup and Olympic teams for another nine years. She also was a central figure in the fledging Women's United Soccer Association, the first women's pro league in the United States. In 2010 she suffered a bad concussion that eventually forced her to retire. She has continued to advocate for women athletes and to speak about the dangers of concussions.

The other event that began to bring a fresh infusion of soccer energy to the Twin Cities in the late 1980s was the establishment of the Blaine Soccer Complex and its feature event: the USA Cup. In 1987 Governor Rudy Perpich signed legislation authorizing the establishment of the Minnesota Amateur Sports Commission. As part of that effort, over $14 million was appropriated to build a signature complex for amateur sports. The Blaine Complex, north of St. Paul, opened in 1990 with facilities for all kinds of sports, including over twenty soccer fields.

That year it hosted a fledging soccer tournament, the USA Cup, sponsored by the Minneapolis-based Schwan's food company.

The Schwan's USA Cup is an international amateur soccer tournament that was started in 1985 by the Sons of Norway, a fraternal society in the Twin Cities dedicated to preserving the area's Scandinavian heritage.[17] The organization's goal was to model a very popular youth international soccer tournament held annually in Oslo, the Norwegian Cup, which is the largest youth soccer tournament in the world. In 1985, sixty-nine teams, including eleven international teams, participated in the Schwan's Cup. Today the annual summer gathering hosts over 1,100 teams for boys and girls from ages ten to nineteen. Teams from nineteen US states and almost twenty countries, and over fifteen thousand players, gather for the tournament in Blaine annually; it is now the largest soccer tournament in the Western Hemisphere.[18] In 2016, 2,524 games were played during the nine-day tournament.

Perhaps the most memorable game in USA Cup history, certainly from the Twin Cities' perspective, was the 1989 game between the St. Paul Blackhawks and the U19-level Moscow Dynamo. It did not carry the legendary significance of the 1980 "Miracle on Ice" between the United States and the Soviet Union, but it was nonetheless a game of David and Goliath. David won. In the semifinals the Blackhawks somehow beat Haarlam, a team that had demolished their opponents by sixteen or seventeen goals. In the finals the Blackhawks upset Dynamo in the U19- soccer version of the "Miracle on the Pitch."

That Blackhawks team went on to even bigger things in the next year when they won the U19 Boys national championship in Virginia, defeating a team from San Francisco 2–0 behind two goals from Manny Lagos. Lagos and Tony Sanneh were the top players on that team. They represented the growing success of Twin City players on the national and international stage.

Sanneh, the son of a Gambian father, grew up in St. Paul and went on to become a second team All-American right back at the University of Wisconsin-Milwaukee. A fifteen-year professional career followed, including a five-year period in Germany and a very successful run with the USA national team. He played every minute for the United States in the 2002 World Cup. His whipping cross assist of Brain McBride's game winner header led to a huge upset win over Portugal; this victory remains one of the highlights of US Men's World Cup history.

After the "Miracle on the Pitch," Manny Lagos joined Sanneh at UW-Milwaukee. Like Sanneh, Lagos enjoyed a great collegiate career, earning first team All-American Honors in 1991. In 1992 he played in the Olympics and later earned three international caps. After playing for his father for a few years with the Minnesota Thunder in the early 1990s, Manny made the jump to the remerging Major League Soccer (MLS). Injuries crippled his promising career, and after ten years trying to get healthy, he finally retired.

Manny Lagos is the son of a local Twin Cities soccer legend, Buzz Lagos. Buzz was the coach of the St. Paul Blackhawks during their best years. It is safe to say that after the departure of the Minnesota Kicks, Buzz Lagos saved soccer in the area. Buzz grew up in New Jersey. He ran cross country and played lots of basketball and baseball but never touched a soccer ball until he wound up in graduate school at the University of Minnesota. There he started kicking the ball around with student friends. After graduate school he got into coaching his kids, eventually leading them to the only national youth men's soccer championship for a Twin Cities team.[19]

After Manny Lagos joined Tony Sanneh at the UW-Milwaukee, Buzz looked for ways to continue to develop soccer in the Twin Cities. In 1990 he established the Minnesota Thunder. An amateur club for the first several years, the Thunder went on to a long, successful run in the US Interregional Soccer League (USISL), including an A-league championship in 1999. In 2005 Buzz retired from the Thunder and passed on the reins of the Thunder to his son Manny who had just retired from the Columbus Crew. Manny eventually took over the coaching duties of the Thunder, later repackaged as the Stars FC and led them to a NASL (now the second division) title in 2011.

After Buzz left the Thunder in 2005, he returned to his youth coaching roots and has spent the last decade helping young immigrants find opportunities for assimilation and soccer coaching at Higher Ground Academy, a charter school on Marshall Avenue in St. Paul. St. Paul was a hotbed of baseball talent, the breeding ground for Dave Winfield, Paul Molitor, Jack Morris, and Joe Mauer. Buzz Lagos helped put soccer firmly on the city's sports map.

Tony Sanneh has returned home as well. In 2003, while playing in Germany, he established the Tony Sanneh Foundation, a nonprofit dedicated to helping inner-city youth lead healthy, productive adult lives. In 2009 he retired and returned to St. Paul to manage and direct the foundation full-time. Naturally soccer is a major part of the foundation's efforts. Each summer the foundation runs dozens of free soccer clinics throughout the Metro region. It also sponsors life coaches in Twin City high schools (seven in St. Paul and one in Minneapolis) to ensure that those youths get not only coaching in sports but preparation in life. Sanneh has also helped establish initiatives to work with earthquake-devastated areas of Haiti and travels globally as part of a US State Department initiative to demonstrate the power of sports to bring people together.

## The Present and Future State of Soccer in the Twin Cities

As the Twin Cities' population has diversified, especially with an influx of immigrants from Asia, Africa, and Latin America, the number of players entering the national and international stage has slowly grown. Fuad Ibrahim, born in Ethiopia and raised in the Minneapolis suburb of Richfield, became the second-youngest player ever signed by a Major League Soccer (MLS) squad. For five years he was a fixture on US youth squads, but for a variety of reasons it did not work out, and Ibrahim has since bounced around Europe looking for a club and playing time. In a slight twist on the typical immigrant story in which the young person comes to the United States and becomes a mainstay on the national team, Ibrahim has played internationally for Ethiopia, the land he left as a young boy.

It should be noted that one of the most successful Twin Cities players emigrated from Canada, which is not known for soccer. Teal Bunbury, a Canadian-born forward, spent his formative soccer years in Prior Lake, Minnesota, and started his club play with Apple Valley Juventus before attending Shattuck-St. Mary's High School. After graduation he went on to have a storied collegiate career at Akron University, capped by winning the Hermann Award given to the best collegiate player in the nation in 2009. While an ACL injury seems to have derailed his US national team career, he remains a key member of the New England Revolution lineup in the highest levels of US soccer, today the MLS.

The Minnesota Thunder Academy, a US Development Academy, is proving to be a good preparation ground for a number of emerging Twin Cities players. The US soccer federation established these academies to speed the development of players for national teams. Many of the Academy's players are sons of immigrants and are bringing international styles to the game. Perhaps the most prized player to come out of the Academy is Mukwelle Akale. A diminutive midfielder, he has been consistently called the best US player in his age group, and he is now working his way up the professional ranks with Villarreal in Spain. Some think he may get a look for the US national team.

Mukwelle's father, Ralph Akale, a coach at the Academy, tells a story about when his son was thirteen and anxious for more competition than his youth team could offer, Ralph brought him and another couple of friends to Powderhorn Park where a group of Somali men were playing their regular Saturday summer pickup game. Predictably, the elders initially scoffed when the father insisted the boys be able to join. But by the end, Ralph notes, "they were arguing over who got to have the boys on the team."[20] Mukwelle has gone on to international recognition, Jackson Yuiell recently was named a Pac-12 first team selection at UCLA, and Jack Miler now plays at Harvard. All have been called in to national camps and both Akale and Yuiell were on the 2016 U-20 squad.[21]

Academies across the country are central to taking young players to the level of skill that can potentially open doors to college and even international play, but these boys' stories also highlight another critical aspect for the growth of soccer in the Twin Cities: the public parks. Pickup games now spread across the grass of many pitches in the renowned parks' system. Club soccer games for kids of all ages now pack the cities' fields as soon as the snow melts. Today there are around 138 clubs and over seventy thousand youth players (ages thirteen–nineteen) registered in the Minnesota Youth Soccer Association. Interestingly, given Minnesota's justified reputation as a hockey state, more kids are signed up for soccer teams than hockey teams by a wide margin.[22]

Leagues once dominated by teams composed of British, Norwegians, or Germans are now significantly comprised of players of diverse, global ethnicities. According to one estimate, there are now at least fifteen Latino leagues in the area, each with at least thirty teams at different age groups and skill levels. Oromo immigrants from Ethiopia and Kenya now hold a soccer tournament each summer at St. Paul's Central High School.[23]

The growing importance of soccer in the Twin Cities is reflected in the changing nature of its many parks. In the summer of 2016, the Minneapolis park board undertook an extensive review of its fields. Some plans were to reduce the number of baseball diamonds throughout the city in favor of creating more soccer space. In part, the board has argued it needs its parks "to match changing demographics and cultural preferences."[24]

# Back in the Big Time: The Minnesota United

The Minnesota Thunder struggled financially, and by 2011 a new team, a third-division United States League (USL) team that eventually became known as Minnesota United FC began play in Blaine. That year the team won the USL championship and began to build a loyal foundation of support. As the United built that base in the 2010s, they caught the attention of the expansion-minded MLS, and in 2015 they were awarded a franchise.

The United's move to first-division status was not without controversy. As the MLS started to contemplate expansion to the Twin Cities, United owner Bill McGuire first reached out to the Vikings ownership for possible co-ownership deals. But as those initial negotiations fractured around majority control and other issues, McGuire decided to go it without them. Instead he turned to the Pohlad family, owners of the Minnesota Twins, and his friend Glen Taylor, owner of the Minnesota Timberwolves. Together they put forth an attractive package that the MLS readily endorsed.

Becoming the owner of an MLS franchise was probably a bit of a surprise even to McGuire. Before buying the United he had little interest in soccer and wound up purchasing the struggling club more as a favor to the cities that had become his home. But like many converts, the more he watched, the more he became enamored with the sport and within a few years had made the significant commitment to bring Minnesota soccer back to the elite level.

Figuring out where they would actually play then became the next challenge. The Blaine Complex had served the soccer community for a long time, but the stadium was small and far from the urban core for fans. The new Vikings stadium was a possibility but the MLS wanted soccer-specific venues, and United owners worried about perceptions of not filling a massive football stadium. The MLS wanted downtown stadiums that matched their demographic and image. Initially, a site by the old farmers market on the north side of downtown Minneapolis was attractive, but after much wrangling, a site off of I-94 in St. Paul was picked. Designers imagined a twenty-thousand-seat soccer-only facility nestled amidst an urban village in the underdeveloped Snelling-Midway area. Allianz Field opened for the 2019 season.

The United began MLS play in 2017 at the Minnesota Gophers' TCF Bank Stadium. Their roster had a sprinkling of players that were MLS capable. Stephano Pinho, a Brazilian striker and USL golden boot winner for the most goals in the league, was added to the roster. Damion Lowe, a draftee of the

Seattle Sounders, was acquired on loan. In 2018 the club signed their first designated player, Darwin Quintero, a veteran of the Mexican League. Team captain
Francisco Calvo is playing for Costa Rica in the 2018 World Cup Finals. To
bolster their tradition of uniting the Twin Cities' long but somewhat fractured
soccer history, the United brought back stars and leaders from the past. Alan
Willey and Buzz Lagos do work as commentators for the team.

Many issues continue to swirl around the Twin Cities' professional franchise, but soccer is now a significant part of the local landscape at all levels.
From its very modest, largely European immigrant roots in the first half of the
twentieth century, soccer has taken on the character of its global attractions
in the metro area. Players of all ethnicities and all ages gather on sunny days in
the area's many parks, throw a few cones down for goals, and roll out a ball.
Boys and girls compete in major tournaments for club, school, and country.
Those glory days of Alan Willey headers at the Met may be a distant memory,
but soccer is firmly entrenched in the Twin Cities.

## CHAPTER SEVEN

# The State of Basketball

*Minnesota's Storied Hardcourt History*

SHELDON ANDERSON AND DAVID C. SMITH

*The State High School basketball tournament back then had a bigger impact on the state of Minnesota than a Lakers' championship.*[1]

—Minneapolis Star Tribune *sports columnist Pat Reusse*

In 2009 the Library of Congress listed *Hoosiers* (1986) on its National Film Registry. Many critics consider the film, nominated for two Academy Awards, to be one of the best sports movies ever made. The film loosely follows the Cinderella season of tiny Milan High School on its way to winning the 1954 Indiana State High School Basketball Tournament.

*Hoosiers* solidified Indiana's reputation as the heart of small town basketball, but the film could have been made in Minnesota, which has its own "Hoosiers" story. In 1960 the Flying Dutchmen of little Edgerton High School, with a graduating class of thirty-one, beat Chisholm and then Richfield—a big Minneapolis suburban powerhouse—to reach the finals of the Minnesota State High School basketball tournament against Austin, the home of Hormel Foods and its most famous product—Spam. Fourteen years earlier Coach Ole Berven's Packers had crushed another small town, Lynd (population 292), 63–31, in the final. Austin was the heavy favorite, having won the title in 1958 and finishing third in 1959. Nineteen thousand fans jammed the University of Minnesota's Williams Arena for the championship game, four thousand more than the capacity of Butler University's Hinkle Fieldhouse where Milan won its title.

DOI: https://doi.org/10.34053/scs2019.tcs.7

In the most memorable upset in Minnesota boys' basketball tournament history, the Flying Dutchmen won easily, 72–61. Edgerton finished the season with a perfect 27–0 record and is the smallest town ever to win the unified championship. An Edgerton student penned this poem:

> Ove Berven's famous Austin team
> Came out on the floor with lots of steam
> The boiler soon cooled
> The fire went out
> Of Edgerton's championship
> There was no doubt.[2]

Minnesota is known today as "The State of Hockey," but after World War II, few high schools outside of the Iron Range and the Twin Cities had a hockey team. Gopher hockey was an afterthought, and the National Hockey League (NHL) had not expanded beyond its original six teams.

The land of snow, cold, and water was, in fact, a hotbed of basketball, with direct connections to basketball's inventor James Naismith. Minnesota's early love affair with basketball ran from Springfield, Massachusetts, through Hamline University in St. Paul and Carleton College in Northfield. The first intercollegiate basketball game in history was played in St. Paul in 1895. Hamline University Athletic Director Raymond Kaighn, who had played in Naismith's first basketball games in Springfield, organized a game with the Minnesota State School of Agriculture. Each team had nine players on the court, and dribbling was prohibited. Minnesota won the game, 9–3.

Naismith's roommate Max Exner also played in the Springfield games. In 1892 Exner enrolled at Carleton College in Northfield, Minnesota, about forty miles south of the Twin Cities. Today Carleton is considered one of the best liberal arts colleges in the country, but Northfield is better known for the James-Younger Gang's robbery and shootout at the First National Bank in 1876. Exner was hired to teach physical education at the school and promoted basketball on the campus.[3] Future Hamline NCAA Hall of Fame coach Joe Hutton Sr. learned his trade at Carleton, as did Ozzie Cowles, who later became head coach at Michigan and Minnesota.

In 1913 the first Minnesota boys' state basketball tournament was held at Carleton. According to a Minnesota State High School League (MSHSL) history, "The first tournaments drew little public attention or even newspaper publicity. Attendance was largely limited to the few students of the College who dropped in for brief moments between classes. By 1922, the final year the tournament was held at Carleton, attendance had grown rapidly and larger quarters were essential."[4]

The tournament moved to Kenwood Armory in Minneapolis in 1923. The beautiful castle-like building sat on a swamp near the Lake of the Isles, however, and it was slowly sinking into the muck. The tournament had to be moved to the Municipal Auditoriums in Minneapolis and St. Paul, and then to the University of Minnesota fieldhouse before finding a home at the Gophers' Williams Arena in 1945, where the popularity of the game skyrocketed.

"The Barn," as Williams is affectionately known, opened in 1928 and is still regarded as one of the most famous basketball venues in the country. Renovated in 1950, Williams housed hockey at one end and basketball—with its distinctive raised court—on the other. Over nineteen thousand fans could cram into the Barn, the largest seating capacity of any basketball arena in the world at the time.[5] The court was shortened for the high school tournament; the basket supports were extended, fan-shaped backboards installed, and the lines repainted.

Until the early 1970s, Minnesota's three-day boys' high school basketball tournament drew more fans than any other tournament in the country. Only Gopher football games across University Avenue at Memorial Stadium drew more fans for one game. The basketball tournament was the most coveted ticket in Minnesota. In 1956 mail-in ticket demand for the championship rounds exceeded supply by about ten percent, even though the tournament was to be televised for the first time.[6] Fans even sat in the aisles, much to the consternation of the fire marshal.

Basketball in Minnesota was a white man's sport, but then in 1950 African Americans comprised only 0.5 percent of the state's population.[7] Until 1947 there were no known African Americans who played in the state boys basketball tournament.[8] One of the first great African American players on the Twin Cities basketball scene was the Minneapolis Lakers' Elgin Baylor, whose vertical dipsy doodle, flashy style was a sensation in the white winter flatland. Just how much people identified with their ethnicity in those days is borne out in the "All-Nations Basketball Tournament" that was held at the Pillsbury House in south Minneapolis. On March 17, 1943, the *Star Tribune* reported, "The Negroes surprised the Russians, 32 to 22; the Norse outlasted the Jews, 38 to 33, and the Swedes edged the Irish (on St. Patrick's night), 38–37." Other teams in the tournament included the "Poles," the "Bohemians," the "Finns," and the "Germans."[9]

Even after the National Basketball Association (NBA) integrated in 1950 and Texas Western University beat an all-white Kentucky team in the 1966 NCAA Championship, the prevailing national image of boys' basketball in middle America featured white basketball players from rural towns. Three teams epitomized the college game, all from the middle of the country: Kentucky, Indiana, and Kansas. Wilt Chamberlain's stint at Kansas from 1956 to 1958 did not fundamentally change the notion that African Americans played hoops for fun (the Harlem Globetrotters), while whites played the serious game.

*Hoosiers* confirmed this nostalgic trope of white farm boys shooting at netless rims on bare patches of Indiana earth. Screenwriter Anthony Pizzo and director David Anspaugh grew up in rural Indiana and included such a scene depicting Bobby Plump, the Milan player who made the winning shot to upset Muncie Central in the championship game.

Fifteen years later Purdue University's slender guard Rick Mount carried on the tradition, shooting his way to 35.4 points a game in his senior year and Big Ten MVP honors. Mount was arguably the best shooter of his time, launching bombs from way beyond what is today the three-point line. No Hollywood movie has ever been made of NBA Hall of Famer Oscar Robertson's historic back-to-back Indiana state titles with Crispus Attucks High School in Indianapolis, the first all-black high school in the country to win an integrated tournament.[10]

The shooting and passing game became a hallmark of the rural Midwestern game; dribbling on icy outdoor playgrounds or on makeshift dirt courts was dicey anyway. In the conservative heartland, behind-the-back-dribbling or a behind-the-back pass was considered "hot dogging"—just a little too much mustard.[11] According to legend, in 1946 Lynd High School's Casper Fisher threw the state tournament's first ever behind-the-back pass.[12] Even the MSHSL's "Sportsman's Creed" hinted at a particular style of decorous play, and the didactic purpose of sports: "[The player] lives clean and plays hard. He plays for the love of the game. He wins without boasting, he loses without excuses, and he never quits." As for the fan, "He never boos a player or official."[13]

Minnesota basketball was a coach's, not a player's, game. In efforts to speed up play and counter the huge advantage of having a big center, in the 1930s the jump ball after a basket was eliminated. In a 1941 poll, however, Minnesota high school coaches favored bringing back the jump ball to slow down the game and "give the kids a breather. . . . It's too hard on young growing bodies." Most players bought into the conservative style. Pat Rogers was on the 1931 championship Glencoe team that beat Chisholm in the final, 15–14. Glencoe took one shot beyond the free throw line. "There was discipline in those days," Rogers noted.[14]

Before Edgerton, another "Hoosier" story in Gopherland played out at the Kenwood Armory in 1926 when the little southern Minnesota town of Gaylord beat Gilbert 13–9. After the game Gaylord fans passed the hat in the stands to raise funds to send the team to the national tournament at the University of Chicago. Fargo (North Dakota) High School ended Gaylord's run in Chicago, 25–20. Gaylord did not get back to the state tournament until 1969, and never won another game in the unified tournament.[15]

The small-town teams were naturally in awe of the bigger schools in the state, and especially those from the Twin Cities. But Edgerton played in District 8, which had its own powerhouse in Luverne. "Any team in the southwest corner that beat Luverne in anything," noted sports journalist Pat Reusse, "was for real."[16] Earlier in the year, the Cardinals were involved in one of the most infamous games in Minnesota high school basketball history. Luverne was up five on Windom with two minutes to go when Windom coach Jed Dommeyer jumped up from his bench and stole the ball from a Cardinal player. "I don't know why I did it," a dumbfounded Dommeyer deadpanned.[17] In the last game of the regular season the Flying Dutchman whipped Luverne, sending notice to the region that Edgerton was the team to beat.

Given the names on Edgerton's team, one could imagine that Leroy Graphenteen, Dean Verdoes, Dean Veenhof, and Larry Schoolmeester had just come over on the boat from Amsterdam clad in blue Dutchman's pants. Edgerton was coached by twenty-three-year old Richie Olson, who had played basketball at Mountain Iron High School on the Iron Range and then at Macalester College in St. Paul. Olson immediately felt at home in a small town like Edgerton: "My first impression was that I liked it because there wasn't a single stoplight." The young coach joked that his players used to say that the only difference between them was that "I drank coffee and they drank milk."[18]

Edgerton won District 8 and then ran up against the Region 2 defending champion Mankato, a small city with a population twenty times that of Edgerton. Before the game, reserve guard Daryl Stevens noticed that the Mankato players were leaping far above the rim to lay in the ball. "They had socks that stayed up, and nice warmups." Stevens worried. "I looked down at our socks and our old Converse shoes. I asked Dean, 'How are we going to beat these guys?'" Olson agreed that his team's uniforms were "pretty ratty," but the Flying Dutchman paid no mind to their wardrobe and soared past Mankato 73–44 and then beat Mountain Lake 61–55 in the final for a ticket to the Twin Cities.[19]

In the first round of the tournament the Flying Dutchmen drew Region 7 champ Chisholm, a perennial Iron Range power. The northern Chisholm has nothing to do with the famous trail but was named after Archibald Chisholm, an early explorer and investor in the Mesabi Range. Chisholm is probably best known for Archibald "Moonlight" Graham," who had a cup of coffee with the New York Giants in 1905 before practicing medicine in Chisholm. The memory of Doc Graham was resurrected from obscurity by Burt Lancaster's portrayal in the 1989 hit movie *Field of Dreams*.

"I think probably our team was the only people who thought we had a chance to win," recalled Dean Verdoes, but Edgerton disposed of Chisholm 65–54.[20] Edgerton's toughest game of the tournament was the semifinal against the number-one-rated Richfield Spartans, a team loaded with great athletes such as Bill Davis, who later starred in basketball and baseball at Minnesota, and had a brief career in the major leagues. Five of the Richfield players went on to play varsity sports with the Gophers. The reception the Spartans got as they came on the court was as though most of the nineteen thousand fans were from Athens. "The boos started to come," recalled Davis. "And it became very apparent there that Edgerton was the crowd favorite. We were the bad guys—we were the big school."[21]

The closely contested game went into overtime. Both Verdoes and Veenhof fouled out, forcing Olson to use Stevens and then Schoolmeester, who seldom played. Schoolmeester was sitting on the far end of the bench when Olson barked, "Schoolie, get in there." A shocked Schoolmeester recalled, "I didn't have time to get nervous." With sharpshooter Darrell Kreun leading the way, Edgerton eked out the win, 63–60. Years later Davis conceded that no one would remember if Richfield had won, but he was still not over that defeat: "I'd take a state championship and kind of fade into the sunset to say that we did win in 1960."[22]

The Williams Arena fans embraced the little team from southwest Minnesota; when Austin stepped on the court for the Saturday night final, they were jeered as well. Edgerton completed its improbable season by cruising to victory. "There was one division," boasted Stevens years later. "Little guys take on the big guys. We beat them all."[23]

There was no dramatic last second shot like Bobby Plump's in any of Edgerton's games in the tournament. Edgerton's overtime win against Richfield came at the free-throw line, where the Flying Dutchman hit thirty-five of forty-three free throws. Richie Olson said that was no fluke: "They shoot baskets from morning 'til night most of the year, they're in the gym on Saturdays, they stay after practice, we do shoot quite a few free throws. Every time I take a break and they're tired in practice they don't rest, they shoot free throws."[24] Reusse, who grew up in nearby Fulda, cracked that Edgerton had great shooters because "the parents wouldn't let them go to movies, no dances, because of the Dutch Reformed Church."[25]

Not wanting to create a ruckus in Edgerton on the Sabbath, the team did not return home from Minneapolis until Monday. They were met by small-town crowds all along their route home. Virtually the whole town of Edgerton showed up for the downtown celebration at which a Dutch Reformed pastor jokingly swore in Richie Olson: "You are no longer a Norwegian. You are now a Dutchman."[26]

At midcentury Minnesota had top notch college and professional teams, although they never had the popularity of the Minnesota boys' high school basketball tournament. Once again Hamline put its stamp on college basketball history. From 1940 to 1960, coach Joe Hutton Sr. led the Pipers to twelve National Association of Intercollegiate Basketball (NAIB) National Tournaments, winning three (1942, 1949, and 1951). Hutton mentored three of the four coaches in the Class AA semifinals of the 1972 High School Basketball Tournament, although some of them had deviated from his conservative style. When the Gophers went from averaging fifty-three points a game in 1949 to seventy-three points in 1953, Hutton lamented, "I guess all of us—even Ozzie [Cowles] at Minnesota—are falling victim to the general trend of basketball. Everybody thinks only of offense today."[27]

While Hamline was dominating NAIB basketball, the Minneapolis Lakers were piling up NBA championships (see chapter 8). Few basketball fans know why the Los Angeles Lakers' colors are blue (gradually becoming more purplish over the years) and yellow. At its inception in 1947, the Lakers paid homage to the large Scandinavian population in the Minneapolis by donning the colors of the Swedish flag. The Lakers were the NBA's first dynasty. Much to the chagrin of the Lakers' rival Boston Celtics, which has won seventeen NBA championships, the Lakers' franchise claims sixteen titles, including the ones in Minneapolis. The championship banners that hang at the Los Angeles Lakers' Staples Center make no mention of the five titles won in the city where there actually *are* lakes.

Center George Mikan was the force behind the Laker dynasty, and although he was an Illinois native, he began a tradition of great Minnesota big men, such as Kevin McHale from Hibbing, Mark Olberding from Melrose, Randy Breuer from Lake City, Ben Coleman from Minneapolis North, and Mark Landsberger from Mounds View, all of whom played in the NBA. At the NBA's fiftieth Anniversary celebration in 1997, McHale was named as one of the best fifty NBA players of all time.

Minnesota was not a Big Ten basketball power in the first few decades after World War II, but the Gophers and Hamline were feeders for the Lakers. Among the former Gophers who played for the Lakers were future Minnesota Viking head coach Bud Grant and guard Myer "Whitey" Skoog, who as older Minnesotans have it, invented the jump shot (of course there are many others who claim that distinction). Johnny Kundla coached the Lakers during their championship run. When the team left for Los Angeles, Kundla led the Gophers from 1959 to 1968.

Hamline alumnus and NBA Hall of Famer Vern Mikkelsen teamed with Mikan to win four NBA titles in the 1950s. A native of Fresno, California, Mikkelsen fit right into the Minnesota scene when his father, a Lutheran minister, moved the family to Askov. A Hamline recruiter had a flat tire in Askov on the way to see another player and found the strapping Mikkelson working in a neighbor's rutabaga field: "Back in those days," recalled Mikkelson, "my parents didn't have a lot of money. So my Lutheran father . . . overlooked the fact that Hamline was a Methodist school."[28] A six-time NBA All-Star, Mikkelsen is considered the first power forward in the game, as well as perhaps the most physical; he holds the NBA record for fouling out of the most games.

Piper alumni Jim Fritsche, Joe Hutton Jr., and Howie Schultz also played on those Laker championship teams. Schultz is one of the few pros to receive a pension from two different pro sports—the NBA and Major League Baseball (MLB). He is a little-known footnote in MLB history. Wally Pipp is forever remembered as the injured player who was replaced at first base by the New York Yankee "Ironman" Lou Gehrig. Schultz was playing first for the Brooklyn Dodgers before Jackie Robinson took his spot at the beginning of the 1947 season. Schultz never got his job back either.

A decade after Edgerton beat Austin, the glory days of Minnesota High School basketball ended when the tournament split into two divisions (today four). Before 1970 fifteen small schools in the lowest division today had won the state championship, and twelve had finished second. Nonetheless, high school principals, athletic directors, and coaches lobbied for more berths in the state tournament. The 486 members of the MSHSL voted overwhelmingly to create two tournaments. In 1970, the last year of one tournament in the Barn, attendance averaged over eighteen thousand for the championship rounds.[29] Since then the numbers have been in steady decline. The *Star Tribune*'s long-time sports columnist Sid Hartman griped that high school officials had turned the tournament into a "non-event."[30] The Indiana high school basketball tournament, which went to divisions in 1998, has suffered the same drop in attendance.

As the relative interest in boys' high school basketball and the Gopher men has waned, Minnesota women's basketball has flourished, returning to the game's glory days of the early twentieth century. Minnesota girls' basketball was a popular game from 1900 to 1940; about 350 high schools—mostly in rural Minnesota—had girls' teams.[31]

Before World War II, however, conservatives were in high dudgeon about the declining morality of women. Successful in passing Prohibition in 1919, they also succeeded in restricting sex on the silver screen with the Hayes Code of 1934. The spectacle of girls and women playing men's sports was also anathema to the guardians of traditional gender roles; sweating was for the working classes and men, not for women of higher standing. Competition was unladylike and dangerous for the fairer sex. These self-appointed purveyors of prim and proper Victorian values claimed—without any evidence—that strenuous exercise for women would damage their reproductive organs (they should have told that to working class women who toiled to the bone). In 1925, *The Journal of the American Medical Association* warned:

> Our young girls, in this age of feminine freedom, are also overdoing athletics. A girl should not be coddled because she is menstruating, but common sense . . . at such a period should be exercised. How many of a basket ball [sic] team of girls, scheduled to compete with another team on a given day, are beginning or in the midst of this feminine function, in which the uterus is physiologically congested and temporarily abnormally heavy and hence, liable to displacement by the inexcusable strenuosity and roughness of this particular game?[32]

Following this lead, Belle Plain High School ended girls' basketball in 1926. One teacher warned that players such as Marie Keeler would not be able to bear children "with all that bouncing around." Keeler had eleven hale and hearty kids.[33]

Cheerleading was the more desired contribution to the boys' basketball games. The MSHSL sponsored cheerleading clinics for girls, which were to "improve skills and abilities and emphasize the responsibility of cheerleaders for sportsmanship and crowd control."[34]

After the formation of the National Amateur Athletic Federation— Women's Division (NAAF-WD) in 1923, inter-high school sports for girls was replaced by the Girls' Athletic Association (GAA), which was an intramural recreational program of sports within the schools. Colleges did the same with the creation of the Women's Athletic Association.[35]

There were sports such as swimming, golf, and tennis that were, according to the NAAF-WD, "competition of the right kind." Emotional games like basketball, it was argued, would compromise a girl's modesty and good character. The International Olympic Committee (IOC) was of the same mind and did not allow women's track and field until 1928. The NAAF-WD lodged official protests against women's Olympic track and field, but the events were on the program again at the 1932 Los Angeles Olympics. The NAAF-WD was particularly influential in Minnesota; in 1938 the Minnesota Department of Education recommended the elimination of girls' sports, and the number of schools playing girls' sports dropped from ninety-two in 1939 to thirty-eight a year later. The department found that "this represents a decided change for the better."[36]

Some smaller Minnesota towns held on to their high school teams, but most of those were gone by World War II. One of the most heartbreaking stories of girls' basketball was the demise of the Grand Meadow High School team, which won ninety-four games in a row from 1929 to 1939. Grand Meadow is a small community not far from Austin and the Iowa border. The Grand Meadow Superlarks played "Iowa rules," in which three players play on the offensive side of the court and three on the defensive side.[37]

Mae Harvey Gross, one of the Grand Meadow players, remembered her disappointment when the sport was eliminated: "I was mad. They told us we could be cheerleaders for the boys and that's what made us mad. I did it, but they didn't go hog wild on cheerleading then. I would've rather played basketball. It was good exercise and we had good coaches." One of the 2018 Superlark players, Isabelle Olson, reflected on the changes in women's sports. "That would suck to not be able to play sport,' she said, "and 30 years [without girls sports] is a long time." Skylar Cotton, another Grand Meadow cager, added, "It pushes us harder to know that they accomplished so much."[38]

The MSHSL did not sanction a girls' track and field meet until 1972 and finally held its first official basketball tournament (in two divisions) in 1976, the same year women's basketball was introduced into the Montreal Olympics. Federal Title IX legislation in 1972, which barred gender discrimination in public schools, was the impetus for the return of girls' sports. An integrated team from St. Paul Central High School won the first title in the top division (AA). One of the Pioneer players was Teresa Tierney, the mother of famed Minnesota Twins baseball player Joe Mauer. By 2004 Minnesota had 418 girls' teams and over thirteen thousand players.[39]

Janet Karvonen from New York Mills was the first Minnesota girl to capture the imagination of sports fans and inspire young girls to play the game. New York Mills is a little community of about 1,200 people 170 miles northwest of the Twin Cities. Founded by Finns in the last half of the nineteenth century, the majestic white pines of the lake region supplied the town's lumber mills. A Finnish-language newspaper—the *Amerikan Uutiset*—was published until 2000. Today New York Mills is best known as the home of Lund Boats, whose boats can be seen on almost every one of the state's ten-thousand-plus lakes.

Karvonen carried the New York Mills Eagles to three straight Class A state championships from 1977 to 1979. As a ninth-grader, she made fourteen of sixteen shots to crush Buhl in the final, 68–43. She was named US National High School Player of the Year.[40] Thanks in large part to Karvonen and New York Mills, attendance at the girls' tourney steadily increased from thirty-four thousand in 1976 to fifty-nine thousand in 1979, going from one-third to two-thirds of the boys' attendance totals.[41] For years Karvonen has run one of the most popular summer basketball camps in the state.

In 1997 the MSHSL changed the girls' tournament to four divisions, once again ending the David and Goliath matchups that had so fascinated Minnesota basketball fans. Media attention switched to the top division, where Twin City schools have dominated. St. Paul Central has garnered four championships, while Minneapolis North coach Faith Johnson Patterson guided the Polars to the championship game in eight of nine years from 1998 to 2005, winning five titles.[42]

The number of Minnesota basketball players in NCAA Division-I and the Women's National Basketball Association (WNBA) attests to the quality of the women's game in the state. Tayler Hill from Minneapolis South High School is Minnesota's all-time leading scorer, and she was named to the All-Big Ten team in her last two years at Ohio State University, averaging 21.1 points in her senior year. The Washington Mystics made her the fourth overall pick in the 2013 WNBA draft.

Minnesota center Janel McCarville (from Stevens Point, Wisconsin) holds the Gophers' record for double-doubles and was the WNBA's first overall pick in the 2005 draft. In 2013 the New York Liberty traded her to the Minnesota Lynx, where she contributed to the team's second championship in three years.

It was McCarville's teammate at the University of Minnesota, however, who became the face of women's basketball in the state. Lindsay Whalen burst on the high school basketball scene at Hutchinson High School in 1996, winning all-conference honors four times, and four-time state honorable mention honors.

A twist of fate in fifth-grade put Whalen on the basketball court in the first place. "If it wasn't for her friend Emily Inglis, it might never have happened," remembers Hutchinson coach Andy Rostberg. "Lindsay might have stayed a hockey player." When Inglis's team found itself short players for a weekend tournament, her father said they would have to forfeit. Inglis offered to call Lindsay. "She's a hockey player," her father replied. Emily asked Lindsay anyway, and she agreed. "Why not? I'll play."[43]

Rostberg was stunned at Whalen's gutsy play: "Lindsay got out there and started stealing the ball and making layups, dishing passes for layups and making shots. She was a holy terror." Rostberg said that even at that young age, Whalen was putting fans in the stands:

> Two years later, when she was in the seventh grade, they were putting extra bleachers in the junior high gym for the townspeople who wanted to see her play. . . . [In high school] we would have doubleheaders, with the girls playing at 6 o'clock and the boys at 8. During Lindsay's career here, it got to be that the gym was full for the girls game and then a good share of the crowd would leave.

Soon the athletic director switched some girls' games to eight o'clock to keep the fans in the stands.[44] Gopher coaches took notice of the shooting and passing skills of the five foot nine guard and offered her a scholarship.

Hutchinson High School star Lindsay Whalen brought the Gopher women to national prominence and won four WNBA titles with the Minnesota Lynx. Courtesy of the *Hutchinson (Minnesota) Leader.*

Whalen and the Gopher women rescued Minnesota basketball from mediocre records and repeated scandals on the men's side. The high point of Gopher men's basketball came in the mid-1960s, when Don Yates from Uniontown, Pennsylvania, North Carolinian Lou Hudson, and army veteran Archie Clark played at Williams Arena. Yates came from the same town as Gopher All-American quarterback Sandy Stephens. Yates, Hudson, and Clark were the first African Americans to receive basketball scholarships at Minnesota. Clark also played on the Gophers' 1964 NCAA championship baseball team. Both Hudson and Clark had long NBA careers and gained several All-Star honors.

Coach Bill Musselman arrived at the University of Minnesota in 1971, bringing along an entertaining Globetrotter-like show before the game and a stifling defensive, slow-down style. His Ashland (Ohio) University teams had led the nation in defense in 1968–69 (33.9 ppg), in large part due to Musselman's reluctance to shoot the ball. The pregame show was a sensation, and attendance ballooned to a point that the fire marshal had to crack down on fans sitting in the aisles.

In his first year, Musselmen led the Gophers to the Big Ten title. The championship was tainted, however, by a brawl with Ohio State at Williams, during which some Gopher players kicked the head of prone Buckeye center Luke Witte, leaving him with a serious eye injury. Some observers blamed Musselman for his belligerent, aggressive coaching style. Musselman had a sign in the Gopher locker room that read, "Defeat is worse than death because you have to live with defeat."[45] Musselman left for the American Basketball Association (ABA) in 1975, and the NCAA subsequently discovered over one hundred rule violations.

One of the players on that Gopher championship team that year was arguably the greatest athlete ever to come out of Minnesota, St. Paul Central High School star Dave Winfield. Winfield went to Minnesota on a baseball scholarship, but Musselman discovered him playing intramural basketball at the Barn for the "Soulful Strutters." Winfield took Musselman's offer of a full scholarship (his baseball scholarship was partial) and played both sports.

Winfield was part of an improbable cluster of great baseball players to come out of St. Paul, three of them Hall of Famers: Winfield, Paul Molitor, and Jack Morris. If three-time batting champion and 2009 MVP Joe Mauer had remained a catcher throughout his career, that St. Paulite would have been a shoe-in to make it to Cooperstown as well.

On the mound and in the outfield, Winfield led the Gophers to the 1973 NCAA baseball tournament. In the semifinal against defending champion USC, Winfield pitched the Gophers to a 7–0 lead after eight innings, striking out fifteen. After giving up a couple of runs in the ninth, Winfield was relieved, and the Trojans rallied to hand Minnesota a devastating 8–7 defeat. "I have played in a lot of memorable big games during my career," Winfield said. "World Series games, league championship games, All-Star Games, all kinds. But I will never forget that game against USC. Never."[46] Winfield was drafted by four teams in three different sports—the Utah Stars of the ABA, the NBA's Atlanta Hawks, the Minnesota Vikings, and the San Diego Padres. Winfield chose baseball and had a brilliant twenty-two-year career.

Jim Dutcher took over the Gopher basketball program from Musselman, but on a road trip to play Wisconsin in 1986, three Gopher players were accused of raping a Madison woman. Although they were acquitted, this and other NCAA infractions forced Dutcher out. Former NBA player Clem Haskins coached the Gophers to several deep NCAA tournament runs in the 1990s, but it was revealed that a tutor had written hundreds of papers for Minnesota players. Haskins was gone. In 2016, after several Gopher players were found on a sex tape, one *Star Tribune* journalist wrote, "What is most amazing about the state of the Gophers [men's] basketball program is that the public seems to have become numb to both failure and scandal."[47]

Just as she did in fifth grade, Lindsay Whalen came to save the day in Gopherland. In her first year at Minnesota, the Gophers averaged about one thousand fans, but by her senior year, in 2004, attendance had jumped to nearly ten thousand a game. Demand for tickets was so strong that the Gopher women moved from a smaller campus arena to the Barn.

Minnesota finished last in the Big Ten (1–15) in Whalen's first season, but in 2001–02 Minnesota tied for second (11–5) and received an NCAA tournament berth. Whalen took the Gophers to another second-place finish in 2002–3 and a spot in the Sweet Sixteen. In her senior year, Minnesota won twenty-five games and made it to the NCAA semifinals.

The Gophers and Whalen were the darlings of the Final Four in New Orleans. Terry McFarland, the president of the Gopher Fast Break Club, was exuberant about the team's reception: "The fans from Minnesota are so pumped up. Everywhere they go, people are telling them they're supporting Minnesota," McFarland said. "This isn't just a Minnesota thing. It's almost a national thing— the coaches, the fans from other schools, the people from New Orleans. So it feels like our town, almost."[48]

Sally Jenkins of the *Washington Post* gushed in her praise of the diminutive Gopher guard, who had broken her hand playing against Ohio State a month and a half earlier:

> I've caught a case of Whalen worship. I'm just another idiot like all the rest at the Women's Final Four who can't take their eyes off Minnesota's broken-handed star guard, Lindsay Whalen, a kid with a slipstream glide to the basket and tendrils of wheat-colored hair that won't be tamed by a headband, and a habit of taking absurdly improbable shots, most of which go in. She has a plastic cast on her shooting hand and various other dings because she hits the floor more often than a mop. And she's the most fun I've had in years."[49]

One eleven-year old Minnesota boy agreed and wanted to marry her. "It's not every day you get proposed to," Whalen quipped.[50]

The Gophers lost in the semifinals to eventual champion UConn, 67–58. Whalen averaged 20.2 points a game in her four years at Minnesota, and as of 2018 was the Gophers second all-time leading scorer. She was a three-time All-American and a two-time Naismith Award finalist. In 2004 the *Star Tribune* named Whalen Sportsperson of the Year, the first woman to win the award.

Whalen capitalized on an opportunity to play professional basketball that Janet Karvonen did not have. Whalen was well aware of the opportunities she had that her predecessors did not:

> Being able to play professional basketball is something I never could have dreamed of when I was a kid, so to be out on the court doing what I love, and, getting paid for it—sometimes I have to pinch myself. . . . Girls youth basketball has taken off since the league's inception twelve years ago and that was great to see. It is pretty neat to think that my daughter could one day grow up dreaming of playing professional basketball."[51]

The Connecticut Sun picked Whalen with the fourth overall pick in the 2004 WNBA draft. Minnesota fans were obviously disappointed that Whalen got away. In the early days of the NBA, the league tried to generate interest by giving teams the rights to college players in their region. For example, Vern Mikkelson played with the Lakers, Bob Cousy from Holy Cross ended up with the Boston Celtics, and University of Cincinnati star Oscar Robertson was drafted by the Cincinnati Royals. For five years Whalen toiled far away from her roots, not only with the Sun but in the off-season with teams in Prague and Ekaterinburg, Russia, infamously remembered as the site of the execution of Tsar Nicholas II and his family by the Bolsheviks in 1918.

In 2010 Whalen was traded to the Lynx, and for a third time she lifted the spirits of Minnesota basketball fans and fans of Minnesota professional sports in general. Minnesota has had less success than any other city with *all* of the major men's professional sports, winning only seven championships, and none in the last three decades. The Minneapolis Lakers' dynasty ended in 1954, and the Minnesota Twins won two World Series in 1987 and 1991. The Lakers' successor, the Minnesota Timberwolves, has been the worst NBA franchise since it entered the league in 1989. In thirty seasons from 1989 to 2019, the Wolves made the playoffs only nine times, losing in the first round eight times and reaching the conference finals once. As of 2017 its regular season winning percentage was a dismal .391.

After a mediocre 13–21 record in her first season, Whalen and the Lynx swept Atlanta 3–0 to win the 2011 WNBA championship. The Lynx reached the finals in five of the next six years, winning three more championships. In that time Whalen won four WNBA All-Star team honors.

In 2017 the Minneapolis Target Center underwent renovation, forcing the Lynx to play their home games of the finals against the Los Angeles Sparks at Williams Arena. Lynx owner Glen Taylor pumped almost $1 million to install temporary air conditioning in the Barn. Back in her old haunts, Whalen scored seventeen points (eight in the fourth quarter) and had eight assists to lead the Lynx to an 85–76 win in the fifth and deciding game. In her high school, college, and professional career, Whalen was known for diving on the floor for loose balls. As one journalist commented after the Lynx won that game, "Whalen left it on the floor three times Wednesday, literally."[52] "That's the Wheezy F. Whalen that we know," Lynx guard Seimone Augustus joked afterward. "She's tough. She's been waiting for this moment."[53]

Another signature moment for Whalen came in the spring of 2018 when she was named to coach the Gophers. "I feel like this was supposed to happen all along. . . . I hope I'm the coach here for 30 years. But, no matter what, I'll always be a Gopher."[54] Longtime UConn coach Geno Auriemma, who coached Whalen on two US Olympic teams, predicted that Whalen would succeed in this role just as she had at all levels of her playing career: "Lindsay being from

Minnesota, being in that community all those years as a pro, she earned the respect of everyone in the basketball world up there."[55] In 1895 the Hamline men wrote the first chapter of the remarkable story of Minnesota basketball. The Lakers and Edgerton left their mark in midcentury, and today Whalen and her Gopher and Lynx women are adding exciting new pages.

## CHAPTER EIGHT

# The Minneapolis Lakers

## *The First NBA Dynasty*

### STEW THORNLEY

The prosperity in the United States following the Depression and World War II created transformation in significant and subtle ways. Returning veterans and a renewed economy—bolstered by materials once again available for other uses after wartime rationing—created the production of automobiles, the construction of highways, and the ensuing flight of residents from cities to suburbs.

Metropolitan areas changed dramatically during this time; Minneapolis was typical in some ways, opportunistic in others. The sports scene was a landscape that brought the chance for a city considered an outpost on the national sports map to an emerging status at a higher level. Minneapolis had minor league teams in baseball and hockey, although it had achieved greater notoriety for its championship football teams at the University of Minnesota in the 1930s and early 1940s.

It was a city tied to its history; the mighty St. Anthony Falls, the only ones on the Mississippi River, were once a sacred place for original inhabitants and later the source of power that created the most vital milling district in America. The Gateway at the foot of the bridge that connected downtown and southeast Minneapolis had long been a welcoming entry. A triangular area, formed by the beginning of Nicollet and Hennepin Avenues and known as Bridge Square, had a pavilion on the site of what had once been its first city hall. In a 2015 letter to the editor of the *Minneapolis Star Tribune*, an old-timer wrote, "In the 1930s, '40s and '50s, downtown Minneapolis was a visual delight of funky neon, questionable enterprises with small doors, and merchandisers who expressed

DOI: https://doi.org/10.34053/scs2019.tcs.8

individual taste both outside and in. Hennepin Avenue had music, rhythm, color and many rooflines."[1]

Minneapolis had overcome the corruption in government common to American cities before and after the turn of the twentieth century. A pair of successful strikes in the 1930s had broken the city's stronghold as an anti-union center. Scratching the surface, however, revealed ethnic divisions, none more significant (if not as apparent) as prejudice against Jews. Carey McWilliams, in the article "Minneapolis: The Curious Twin," wrote, "One might even say, with a measure of justification, that Minneapolis is the capitol [sic] of anti-Semitism in the United States."[2] A crusading new mayor, Hubert Humphrey, responded with fair employment acts and the creation of the forerunner of the city's human rights commission.

By this time some of Minneapolis's Jewish citizens were creating their own enterprise. Restaurateur Max Winter, movie-house mogul Ben Berger, ice-show promoter Morris Chalfen, and young newspaperman Sid Hartman (who in 2019 was still churning out columns in the *Minneapolis Star Tribune* at the age of ninety-nine) were the principals in what became professional basketball's first dynasty.[3] Hartman was part of a group that arranged for a game between two teams from the National Basketball League (NBL) to be played in Minneapolis as a test of the city's interest.[4]

With a strong connection to northern industry, the NBL began in 1937, when mostly Midwest company teams joined with independents in the region to create an organization that focused on signing top players coming out of college. The NBL teams used high school gyms and small auditoriums for their games, had a loyal if not large following of fans, and was considered the premier pro league in existence at the end of World War II. After the war the NBL had a challenger in the new Basketball Association of America (BAA), created by a group of arena owners in larger Eastern cities who were looking for additional events to fill their buildings.[5]

The NBL exhibition game in Minneapolis in December 1946 pitted teams from two midsize Wisconsin cities, Oshkosh and Sheboygan, and drew more than five thousand fans; it was enough to encourage Berger and Chalfen to purchase the NBL Detroit Gems and move them to Minneapolis to become the Lakers in 1947.

The Gems had finished 4–40 in Detroit, so it was probably a good thing that none of the Gems' players made the transition to the Lakers. General Manager Max Winter could fill the roster with new players. Winter was co-owner of the

620 Club restaurant, a popular Hennepin Avenue hangout for everyone from sports fans to mobsters to regular folks.

Hartman, however, claims credit for building the Lakers in his dual role as newspaper reporter and basketball executive. For decades Hartman had been low key about his connection with the team, concerned about the perception of a conflict of interest of a newspaper employee helping with the operation of a sports team covered by his paper. Eventually he explained that this was the norm at the time. In a 1989 interview Hartman reflected on how the newspaper business had changed:

> Every guy at our newspaper had a public-relations job with one of the teams. We weren't doing anything behind their backs. The paper knew exactly what we were doing. Charlie Johnson [Hartman's editor] assigned all of these jobs to us. You can't do that anymore—it's considered a conflict of interest now. Back in those days, though, it was allowed because you didn't make much money at the paper; we could add a little to our incomes by working with one of the teams. It was a different world back then.[6]

Feeling unburdened after this explanation, Hartman became more open about his role in building a dynasty. In his 1997 autobiography, *Sid: The Sports Legends, the Inside Scoops, and the Close Personal Friends*, Hartman wrote, "Berger wanted me to quit the paper and run the Lakers as the general manager." When Hartman refused to leave the newspaper, "Chalfen and Berger then realized they'd need someone to run the business side and, a month before the start of the 1947–48 season, brought in Max Winter as the general manager. . . . Max would take care of the business end of the Lakers, and I was in charge of the basketball. Max would be the spokesman and promote the team. I remained in charge of getting the players."[7]

Has Hartman overstated his involvement with the Lakers? Bud Grant, a member of the Pro Football Hall of Fame after many successful years coaching the Minnesota Vikings, played for the Lakers and was quoted by his biographer, Bill McGrane, as saying, "Sid ran the operation, lock, stock, and barrel. He negotiated contracts, signed players, and ran the club."[8] Others, including John Kundla, the Lakers' first coach, scoffed at the idea and said Winter was in charge.

Regardless of who the mastermind was, the Lakers formed a strong team. Minneapolis signed the thirty-one-year-old Kundla as coach. Kundla, who had played at the University of Minnesota and was part of the 1937 Gophers team that tied for the Big Ten championship, left his job coaching St. Thomas College in St. Paul to join the Lakers. His first players were Tony Jaros and Don "Swede" Carlson, acquired in a trade from the Chicago Stags of the BAA. Jaros and Carlson had played for Minneapolis Edison High School and the Gophers. A prize was the signing of Jim Pollard to his first professional contract. Pollard had been a star at Stanford and then played in the Coast Guard and for Amateur Athletic Union teams.

A bigger prize was on its way—George Mikan. At six-feet-ten, tall enough to be considered a giant at the time, Mikan developed his skills at DePaul University and became a dominant player in the pro ranks. He led the Chicago Gears to the NBL title in 1946–47, but the Gears abandoned the league to join a new organization, the Professional Basketball League of America, the following year. The League of America folded less than a month into the 1947–48 season, leaving the Gears without a league and Mikan without a team. In the disbursement of the players from the League of America, the Lakers wound up with Mikan, transforming them from a good to a great team.

Minneapolis had won three of its first four games before Mikan joined them and did not take off right away after that, losing four of their next five; however, the team now had a dominant nucleus, and the Lakers won thirty-nine of their final fifty games to easily win their division. Mikan's presence made the difference. In January 1948 he set a league record for points in a game, scoring forty-one in a win over the Rochester (New York) Royals. Records kept falling, including the 1,195 points Mikan scored in fifty-six games, for an average of 21.3.

Minneapolis was able to handle any team in the NBL and in February went outside the league to test itself against the Harlem Globetrotters. The Globetrotters are still world famous for their combination of basketball and comedy, but they initially played serious ball after their formation in 1927. The Globetrotters' story also provides insights into the game's segregated history along with the significance of independent barnstorming teams even as professional leagues were being formed. Many teams eschewed the formal organizations and were successful in setting their own schedules—not that all-black teams such as the Globetrotters, New York Rens, and Washington Bears, would have been welcomed into leagues with all-white teams.

One event that brought teams together was the World Professional Basketball Tournament in Chicago. NBL teams often won the tournament, but the Globetrotters, Rens, and Bears also claimed titles (winning three of the first five) during the tournament's history from 1939 to 1948. The Globetrotters were the most entertaining team in the sport but were determined to show that they could beat the best teams in a real game. The Globetrotters were led by center Reece "Goose" Tatum and ball-handling whiz Marques Haynes.

Winter and Globetrotters owner Abe Saperstein arranged for a game at Chicago Stadium February 19, 1948, as a preliminary to a BAA game between the Chicago Stags and the New York Knicks. The enduring popularity of the Globetrotters, as well as a chance to see George Mikan, a DePaul grad, drew a crowd of 17,823, a record for Chicago Stadium. The Globetrotters extended their winning streak to 104 games, but it took a buzzer-beating shot to defeat Minneapolis 61–59. Over the years some of the Lakers maintained they did not take the game too seriously and were saving their best efforts for league opponents rather than the Globetrotters. This may be sour grapes on their part and may have been true in later meetings with the Globetrotters; however, at this time the Globetrotters could compete with any team in the country.

The teams met twice the following season, splitting the pair, and five more times over the next nine years with the Lakers winning each of those games. Integration of professional leagues meant the Globetrotters could no longer get the greatest black players; they were and still are a great show, but their years of being among the best basketball teams ended.

The Lakers finished the 1947–48 NBL season with a 43–17 record and won their first two playoff rounds against the Oshkosh All-Stars and Tri-Cities Blackhawks (a team representing Davenport, Iowa, and the Illinois cities of Moline and Rock Island). The Lakers' championship series against Rochester had to wait, though, as Minneapolis accepted an invitation to play in the World Professional Tournament, which was in its tenth and final year. The Lakers won all three games to take the tournament, the final one against the New York Rens as Mikan scored forty points.

The Lakers had one day to rest before opening their best-of-five NBL title series with Rochester at the Minneapolis Armory (the Minneapolis Auditorium, their normal home, was under contract every spring for the Sportman's Show, and the Lakers had to find another floor for the playoffs).

The Armory was jammed as the Lakers took the first two games. The series shifted to Rochester for the remaining games, and the Royals stayed alive with a 74–60 win despite Mikan's thirty-two points. In game four the Lakers grabbed an early lead and held it the entire game. Mikan scored twenty-seven, and Pollard added nineteen, as Minneapolis, with a 75–65 win, took the NBL championship in its first year in the league.

The Lakers' first year in the NBL was also their last. The BAA had completed its second year of operations and continued to control the large population centers and big arenas. However, the NBL teams, especially the Lakers, Royals, and Fort Wayne (now Detroit) Zollner Pistons, were better than the BAA teams. Maurice Podoloff, president of the BAA, raided the NBL and convinced Rochester, Fort Wayne, and the Indianapolis Kautskys (who would change their name to the Jets) to jump to the BAA.

The Lakers had little interest in making such a move originally but decided that if the other top NBL teams were going to break ranks, they would join them. Clinging to life after the raid, the decimated NBL tried to fill the gap by adding new teams, including a collection of New York Rens past their prime who formed a team representing Dayton, Ohio. But the defections, and particularly the loss of top gate attractions such as Mikan and Pollard, had left the NBL on life support.

The Lakers continued to stand out in the new league. A 117–89 win over the Providence Steamrollers set a team record for points in a game. Soon after, Mikan tied the BAA record with forty-seven points in a game and topped that with forty-eight in a win over Washington in January 1949. His record did not last long; a couple weeks later Joe Fulks of the Philadelphia Warriors scored sixty-four. Fulks and Mikan battled the rest of the season for the scoring lead, with Mikan emerging as the league champion with 28.3 points per game. Seven times during the season Mikan scored more than forty points in a game. Twice he topped fifty.

As for the team, the Lakers were unable to shake Rochester. Minneapolis finished with a 44–16 record, for second place in the Western Division, one game behind the Royals. In the playoffs, though, the Lakers got by Rochester and advanced to the championship series against the Washington Capitals, coached by Red Auerbach. Minneapolis took the first three games, but Washington won the next two. Game six was at the St. Paul Auditorium. Mikan, playing with a cast after chipping a bone in his right hand, scored twenty-nine points to lead the Lakers to a 77–56 win and the BAA title.

Although decimated, the NBL carried on, and following the 1948–49 season, the league signed en masse the graduating starters of the University of Kentucky team that had won the National Collegiate Athletic Association title. These players formed a new franchise known as the Indianapolis Olympians (several of the team's stars had played on the 1948 Olympic team). This coup by

Dick Garmaker of the Minneapolis Lakers drives past George Yardley of the Detroit Pistons.
Minnesota Historical Society.

the NBL helped pave the way for a merger with the BAA before the 1949–50 season. There was only one dominant league in the professional basketball world now, and it took a new name—the National Basketball Association (NBA).

The Lakers, coming off two straight league championships, got even stronger with the addition of a pair of future Hall of Famers. One was a guard from the University of Texas, Slater "Dugie" Martin. An outstanding playmaker, Martin is sometimes credited as developing the point guard position. The other was six-foot, seven-inch Vern Mikkelsen, a Minnesota native who played at Hamline University in St. Paul and led his team to the National Association of Intercollegiate Basketball title.

Mikkelsen got little playing time as an understudy to Mikan for the first third of the season. But on Christmas, playing against Fort Wayne, coach John Kundla acted on a hunch he hoped would allow the Lakers to receive maximum benefit from both big men. Kundla conceived the idea of a double-pivot offense, putting Mikkelsen at forward. The result was basketball's first power forward. Mikkelsen's role was to rebound, set screens, and pick up what Mikan and Pollard did not do.

Pollard, Mikan, and Mikkelsen gave the Lakers the most formidable front line in the game. The Lakers finished the regular season with a 51–17 record, tied with Rochester for first place in the Central Division, forcing a tie-breaker playoff game in Rochester. The Royals led by six points with three minutes to play, but the Lakers battled back to tie the score. With three seconds left Tony Jaros let fly with a long set shot that dropped through the basket to give Minneapolis a 78–76 win.

In the playoffs, the Lakers swept through the preliminary playoff rounds and earned another berth in the finals, in which they met player-coach Al Cervi and the Syracuse Nationals, led by Dolph Schayes, an outstanding rebounder and scorer. The series opened in Syracuse, and the Nationals had a 66–64 lead with barely a minute left in the first game. Future hall-of-fame Minnesota Vikings head coach Bud Grant tied the game with a long shot. He then got the rebound after a Cervi miss and flung a pass to Bob Harrison, who connected with a forty-foot set shot to win the game as time expired.

Syracuse won the second game, and the series shifted to Minneapolis. With the Auditorium and Armory both occupied with other events, the Lakers played the next two games at the St. Paul Auditorium and won both for a three-games-to-one lead in the series. Syracuse, back on its home court, won game five. By this time the Minneapolis Auditorium was available again, and the Lakers felt at home in the sixth game. It turned into one of the wildest affairs ever seen in the playoffs up to that point, but it was a game that epitomized the style of play prevalent at that time.

Fights and fouls dominated the game. Four Lakers fouled out in the fourth quarter. But Mikan and Pollard came through. Pollard scored sixteen points and had ten assists, some to Mikan, who scored forty. Minneapolis won 110–75 to take the series and the title. In three years of existence, the Lakers had won three championships in three different leagues.

The NBA integrated in 1950–51. In the college draft, the Boston Celtics took Chuck Cooper of Duquesne, the first African American to be drafted. The Capitols selected Earl Lloyd of West Virginia State, who was the first African American to play in an NBA game. The New York Knicks lured Nat "Sweetwater" Clifton away from the Harlem Globetrotters, becoming the first African American to sign an NBA contract.

The Lakers remained all-white for many years, but they remained one of the NBA's top teams. The team rarely lost, especially at home. Fort Wayne coach Murray Mendenhall found a way to give his team a better chance to win in a game in Minneapolis on November 22, 1950. He slowed down—some would say stopped—the action. The Pistons got the opening tap and did nothing. Larry Foust stood at midcourt with the ball on his hip. An occasional pass and a less-occasional flurry of action produced a few points. At halftime the Lakers led 13–11.

The second half was even sleepier. Minneapolis had an 18–17 lead when Fort Wayne inbounded with nine seconds left. Foust took a pass and put one over Mikan and into the basket to give the Pistons a 19–18 win, the lowest-scoring game in NBA history.

Not surprisingly the fans were unhappy, and the Minneapolis press blasted Mendenhall for his tactics. Charlie Johnson called the game a "sports tragedy." However, *Minneapolis Tribune* columnist Dick Cullum defended the stall as Fort Wayne's best chance to win: "Therefore, it cannot be criticized for using it. It is a low conception of sports to say that a team's first duty is to give you a lot of senseless action instead of earnest competition." Cullum also saw the game as a remarkable study in basketball tactics that "in a way, may have been the best basketball game played by the pros in Minneapolis."

League President Maurice Podoloff did not see it that way, and he immediately summoned the coaches and officials. Local lore has it that the NBA responded to the game by quickly implementing the twenty-four-second shot clock. Some Minnesotans even claim the clock was introduced during the 1950–51 season, within a few weeks of the game. However, the shot clock was not introduced until nearly four years later. Still, some maintain that the 19–18 game was an impetus for it, although that is probably not the case. Stalling toward the end of close games remained a problem. Even without a shot clock in the NBA, a full-game stall never occurred again. It is possible Podoloff made it known there would be dire consequences for such tactics, even if no rule prohibited them.

The loss of a 19–18 game did not hurt the Lakers, but an injury to George Mikan near the end of the regular season did. Mikan led the league with 28.4 points per game but was hobbled during the playoffs with a broken bone in his ankle. The Lakers still beat Indianapolis in the opening round but lost to Rochester, which went on to beat the Knicks for the NBA title.

Despite being dethroned, the Lakers were still the best team in basketball during this time and demonstrated it by winning the next three NBA titles. The Lakers continued to battle the Rochester Royals during the regular season and sometimes in the playoffs. Each time, Minneapolis came out on top and made it to the championship round.

In early 1952 Mikan scored sixty-one points in a double-overtime win against Rochester, coming within two points of Joe Fulks's NBA record. The Royals beat out the Lakers by a game in the Western Division, but in the play-offs Minneapolis beat Rochester to make it back to the finals against the New York Knicks. The series went the limit, and at the Minneapolis Auditorium, the Lakers won the decisive seventh game to return to the championship ranks.

The Lakers and Knicks met again in the NBA finals in 1953; this time the Minneapolis finished off New York in five games, winning the final three in Madison Square Garden and then celebrating their championship at the Copacabana. Mikan said that the 1953 title was the "sweetest" of all," and that he planned to play five more years.

Whitey Skoog was a talented multi-sport athlete from Brainerd, Minnesota, and a star for the Gophers. Minnesota legend has it that he "invented" the jump shot. Skoog averaged only fourteen minutes per game during the regular season, but he came alive in the playoffs, breaking down the defense and doubling his regular season points per game. New York coach Joe Lapchick said of Skoog, "There's the fellow who beat us. We had no way of stopping him."[9]

Minneapolis was the site of another unusual game in March 1954. Colleges were considering raising the height of the basket, so the NBA decided to try it in a game between the Milwaukee Hawks and Lakers, raising the hoop from ten to twelve feet. Advocates of the higher basket wanted to negate the advantage of the games big men, but others were skeptical. "Seems to me the higher basket will hurt the little fellow more than the tall one," wrote Dick Cullum in the *Minneapolis Tribune*. Minneapolis beat the Hawks 65–63, but the Lakers did not think much of the higher baskets. "It didn't help the smaller guy," said Mikkelsen. "It helped me, the big, strong rebounder, because it gave me another tenth of a second to get set after a shot." Clyde Lovellette, a future Hall of Famer who was in his first year with the Lakers as an understudy to Mikan, added, "It kills tip-ins." And the fans did seem to miss the underbasket action. According to Pollard, it took some time for the Lakers to get the higher baskets out of their system: "It screwed us up for a week or so."[10]

The Lakers lost their next two games but won their regular-season finale, finishing two games ahead of the Royals for the division title. Minneapolis beat Rochester in the playoffs and met the Syracuse Nationals in the finals. This series went the full seven games. Playing in the Minneapolis Auditorium, the Lakers got off to a fast start and beat the Nationals 87–80 for their sixth league championship in their seven years of existence. The title was the last for the Minneapolis Lakers, in large part because Mikan retired after the 1953–54 season. The "five more years" he projected for himself a year before did not happen.

Mikan had 11,764 points in his career, over 3,700 more than Joe Fulks, the player with the second-highest total. In eight years Mikan played on seven championship teams (six with the Lakers, one with the Chicago Gears). He missed only two games for the Lakers. In the 458 regular-season games Mikan played for Minneapolis, he was the team's leading scorer 348 times. In 1950 the Associated Press voted Mikan the greatest basketball player of the first half of the twentieth century. Bud Grant, who played with and coached many great athletes, still maintained that "George Mikan is the greatest competitor I've ever seen in sports."[11]

After his playing career was over, Mikan stayed on with the Lakers as general manager, having purchased the stock of Max Winter, who left to concentrate on getting a professional football team for the Twin Cities (a quest that would be successful). In 1967 Mikan became the first commissioner of the American Basketball Association (ABA).

The Lakers finally integrated during this period, signing Bob Williams, who had played one season at Florida A & M before entering the air force and playing basketball for armed services all-star teams. Williams was the leading scorer on the US team that won the gold medal in the Pan American Games in March 1955. Done with his military commitment by this time, Williams was recruited by many colleges, including Kentucky. Because of his skin color, however, the school's board of regents would not allow him entry. Williams told *Star Tribune* reporter Curt Brown in 2004 that Kentucky coach Adolph Rupp wanted to at least make sure he would not attend another college, so Rupp called Sid Hartman in Minneapolis and suggested that the Lakers sign Williams. In a 2015 *Star Tribune* column, Hartman wrote, "In those days we had a negotiation list, we put Williams on our list, just beating New York, and I signed him."[12] Williams played two years for Minneapolis, although he was cut early in each of those seasons and each time joined the Harlem Globetrotters.

Without Mikan, the Lakers struggled. A year later Pollard retired, and Minneapolis had its first losing record. The Lakers were so bad in the early part of the 1955–56 season that rumors started that Mikan would return to the court. In January it happened and drew a crowd of more than 7,100. Mikan's presence helped the Lakers at the gate and in the standings, although the team finished with a 33–39 record.

In the draft after that season, the Lakers thought they had a chance to get Bill Russell, a center from the University of San Francisco who was seen as the top player entering pro ball. The Rochester Royals, who had the first pick in the draft, passed on Russell; the Royals already had a center and also may have been scared off by Russell's public statement that he would want a $25,000 salary to play in the NBA. (The Harlem Globetrotters had reportedly offered Russell a similar salary to tour with them.)

The St. Louis Hawks, which had the second pick, were also put off by Russell's demands. Another concern for the Hawks, the last all-white team in the league, was how Russell would be accepted in St. Louis. Minneapolis, with the next pick, was ready to take Russell; however, the Hawks foiled that by trading their draft pick to the Boston Celtics, who drafted Russell. Many consider him to be the greatest NBA player of all time.

How close had the Lakers come to getting Russell? The year before, the Lakers and Hawks had tied for the second-worst record in the league, but the Lakers defeated the Hawks in a tie-breaker playoff game. Had they lost that game, they would have drafted ahead of the Hawks and would have been able to select Russell. Hartman also reports that a trade the Lakers almost made in February 1956 would probably have assured them the opportunity to draft Russell. The Lakers were set to trade Vern Mikkelsen to the Celtics for former University of Kentucky greats Cliff Hagan, Frank Ramsey, and Lou Tsioropoulos, all of whom were in the service at the time and would have not been available until the following season.

Hartman theorizes that, with Mikkelsen gone, the Lakers would have finished last and gotten the first pick in the draft. But Lakers owner Ben Berger was talked out of making the trade, and the dynasty that Hartman claims may have been created had the Lakers obtained Russell, along with Tsioropoulos and future Hall of Famers Hagan and Ramsey, never happened. Hartman added that, because of this, he decided to end his involvement with the team. "It was at that time that I had to decide whether to stay with the newspaper or go full time with the Lakers. When Berger called off the Mikkelsen deal, I told him, 'I'm done. Get somebody else to run the team.' I finished out the rest of the season and then I was gone."[13] John Kundla was skeptical of this story, as he was with Hartman's claims of running the Lakers. Kundla claimed that the Lakers would not have parted with Mikkelsen.[14]

With Mikan again retired, the Lakers had another losing record in 1956–57, but a bigger issue was the future of the team in Minneapolis. A pair of St. Louis businessmen, including former Cardinals shortstop Marty Marion, made an offer to buy the Lakers with the plan to move them to Kansas City. However, a civic effort in Minneapolis produced enough money to match the offer, and a syndicate of more than one hundred companies and individuals bought the Lakers. Bob Short, a local attorney, trucking magnate, and political maverick, was elected president.

The Lakers remained in Minneapolis, but the new organizational structure had its problems. Mikkelsen said this was the point at which the franchise began to fall apart: "With over 100 investors, it was not a good deal. We had 100 bosses, and a half-dozen of these guys were constantly telling us what we should do and how we should do it. These were people who had never been closer to a locker room than walking by one when they were in high school."[15] Another change for the Lakers in 1957–58 was that, for the first time, Kundla would not be on the bench. Tired of the stress and travel, he became general manager, and George Mikan took over as coach.

Regardless of who was directing the team, the Lakers were bad. They lost their first seven games of the season. In January, with the team at 9–30, Short fired Mikan and brought Kundla back as coach. Minneapolis finished with the worst record in the league, which got them the top pick in the draft. Elgin Baylor, who had just led Seattle University to the NCAA title game, was clearly the best player available, but he was a junior and had the option of returning to Seattle or signing a pro contract. (Baylor was eligible for the draft as a junior because he had sat out a year after transferring from the College of Idaho.)

Using the draft choice on Baylor was risky, since he might go back to school instead of signing with the Lakers. But Short took the chance and was able to sign him. "If he had turned me down," Short said, "I would have been out of business. The club would have gone bankrupt."[16]

Before Baylor arrived, attendance at Laker games had plummeted. The NBA placed the Lakers under financial probation, meaning that if they could not average gate receipts of $6,600 per home game, the league would have the right to take over the franchise for $150,000. But the league never had the opportunity. In Baylor's debut with the team, he scored a game-high twenty-five points—including the first eight Laker points—to lead Minneapolis to victory over the Cincinnati (formerly Rochester) Royals. He helped the Lakers win more games and drew fans just to see him. As crowds grew at the Minneapolis Auditorium, the NBA lifted its probation on the Lakers midway through the season.

With the increased fan interest in Baylor, Short may have regretted his decision to play more games at neutral sites. Teams sometimes moved a home game to another city if they received enough of a guarantee in receipts to do so. A couple of the alternate-site games were south of the Mason-Dixon Line. The Lakers had three blacks—Baylor, Boo Ellis, and Ed Fleming—who were not allowed at hotels that the Lakers had booked. Short insisted that the Lakers stay together on the road, and the entire team found lodging that allowed blacks.

In Charleston, West Virginia, however, Baylor became upset when he was refused service at a restaurant; as a result, he refused to dress for the Lakers' game that evening against Cincinnati. Without Baylor, the Lakers lost to the Royals, 95–91. The Charleston American Business Club, which had sponsored the game and had counted on Baylor as a gate attraction, asked Podoloff to discipline Baylor and the Lakers. Podoloff, however, sided with the Lakers, and Short stood behind Baylor. "That shows there's a guy who believes in principle," said Short of Baylor. "I don't argue with principle."[17]

Mikkelsen, however, thought Baylor should have played, pointing out that the white players had agreed to stay in lesser accommodations so the entire team could be at the same hotel. Mikkelsen thought someone had "got to him," implying that a person or group had convinced Baylor not to play as a means of calling attention to civil-rights issues.[18]

Baylor was the reason for the Lakers' resurgence in 1958–59. He scored fifty-five points in one game, averaged 24.9 for the season, and was named Rookie of the Year. Minneapolis improved its record from 19–53 to 33–39, good enough for second place in the Western Division although still sixteen games behind the St. Louis Hawks.

The Hawks and Boston Celtics had met in the NBA finals the past two seasons, and it was expected they would do so again in 1959. However, the Lakers upset the Hawks in the playoffs. Kundla explained later he did not need any inspirational speeches during the series against the Hawks. He said Short came into the locker room at halftime and promised gifts for the players if they won. "One night it was blazers; the next night it was a new set of tires," said Kundla. "I didn't have to say much after that. The guys would almost knock me down getting out of the locker room and back onto the court."[19]

It was going to take more than speeches and gifts for the Lakers in the finals against Boston, which had won its last eighteen games against Minneapolis, including a 173–139 drubbing little more than a month before. The Russell-led Celtics kept the streak going, sweeping the final round for their first of eight straight NBA titles.

Two days after the final game, Kundla left the Lakers to become the coach of the Minnesota Gophers. Short tried to get Mikkelsen to become a player-coach but was turned down. Mikkelsen also retired after ten seasons. Short instead hired John Castellani, who had been Baylor's coach at Seattle University. Short also wanted to get away from the Minneapolis Auditorium as the team's primary home, hoping that in 1959–60 a renovated Minneapolis Armory would avoid scheduling conflicts. (It did not.)

Baylor was outstanding again, scoring fifty-two points in the season opener and three weeks later setting a new NBA record with sixty-four points in a 136–113 win over the Celtics, the first Minneapolis victory against Boston since March of 1957. The Lakers struggled, however, and early in 1960 Castellani resigned as coach. Jim Pollard, back in the Twin Cities after having coached at LaSalle College for three years, was hired to coach the Lakers the rest of the season.

Pollard may have wished he had stayed away after what happened a couple of weeks later. On Sunday, January 17, the Lakers lost in St. Louis and arrived at the airport around five thirty p.m. Their DC-3, a converted World War II cargo plane that Short had purchased for the team, was waiting for them, but an ice storm had grounded all flights. Pilot Vern Ullman, a retired Marine flyer who had seen action in both World War II and the Korean War, and copilot Harold Gifford checked the weather as the players waited in an airport dining area. The storm subsided somewhat over the next few hours, the players boarded the plane, and finally the decision was made to go. At eight thirty p.m. Ullman lifted the plane off the ground.

Soon after takeoff, the lights inside the cabin went out. The plane's two generators had failed, and the battery was drained of its remaining power immediately. The power outage left the crew with no guidance instruments except for a magnetic compass, which was erratic. They were without heat, defrosters, lights, or a radio, which precluded an attempt at returning to the St. Louis airport. Ullman pointed the aircraft in the general vicinity of Minneapolis and tried to climb above the storm to pick up the North Star.

Nearly five hours after taking off, the plane had escaped the storm. But it had also drifted off course, and with the gauges dead, Ullman and Gifford had no way of knowing how much fuel was left. "We thought we better find a place to land," said Gifford. Through the blowing snow they could see the lights of a town—Carroll, Iowa—below. They first flew past the water tower, hoping to find the name of the city. Snow had obliterated most of the name, and all the crew could make out were the final letters, "O-L-L." They then began buzzing the town in desperate search of an airport. Ullman dropped the plane down and followed a blacktop road, hoping it would lead to an airstrip. With the strong winds creating a ground blizzard, as well as the visibility problems caused by the iced-over windshield, Ullman did not realize that the road had curved and they were approaching a grove of trees. He finally spotted the danger and pulled back on the control column; the plane shot upward, narrowly missing the trees.

Ullman turned the plane around and followed the road back into town. Unknown to the pilots (including Jim Holznagle, a pilot present for an orientation flight) was that the townspeople were aware of their plight and were doing what they could to help. "We found out later that someone with a gasoline truck was trying to get our attention to have us follow him to the airport," said Gifford.[20]

Eva Olofson, Ullman's wife, was on the flight. Years later she said that she had received a letter from one of the residents who wrote that the police knew there was a plane in trouble and were telling people to turn their lights on to help the pilots see the town better. "I do recall the city lighting up like a Christmas tree, and it really helped."[21]

The pilots gave up hope of finding an airport and looked for other options. They considered putting the plane down on the highway, but then they spotted a cornfield on a farm north of the city. Because of the wet weather the previous fall, the field's owner, Hilbert Steffes, had not harvested the crop. As a result, the stalks stood out in neat rows through the snow. Both Ullman and Gifford had been raised on farms and knew that a cornfield would be free of rocks and ditches. Word was sent back to the passengers that they were going to land. Ullman began the descent. Not only did he put the plane down in a perfect three-point landing, he inadvertently hooked the tail wheel on the top strand of a barbed-wire fence. "The barbed-wire helped bring us to a stop," said Gifford. "It was just like landing on an aircraft carrier."

As soon as the plane stopped, the passengers broke out in cheers. Residents of Carroll had gathered by the side of the road at the edge of the field. The townspeople helped the passengers through the snow to the road where they piled them into cars and transported them to the hotel in town. Pollard was the last of the Lakers to leave. He finally got into a long car and then discovered that his chauffeur was the local undertaker and that the vehicle was a hearse. "I had not been scared in the least while we were in the air or when we were landing," said Pollard. "But when I saw that stretcher in the back of the car, I realized how close we had come, and I got the shakes for a few minutes."[22]

Bob "Slick" Leonard was not bothered by the mode of transport. More than the hearse, he recalls a liquor cabinet in the hotel that was padlocked; however, Larry Foust (who ten years before had scored the winning basket in the 19–18 game and by this time was on the Lakers) twisted the padlock off, allowing the still-shaken players to have a belt and settle down.

The passengers from the plane took a bus back to the Twin Cities the next day, but the pilots stayed behind. Following a Federal Aviation Administration investigation, they also returned to Minneapolis, but a few days later, Ullman came back to pick up the plane. "They were going to have someone else fly it out," said Olofson, "but Vern wouldn't let them. He said, 'I put it in there. I'm going to take it out.'"[23]

The plane survived the ordeal, and it continued to serve the Lakers. Another thing the plane did was spur speculation that Short was looking to move the team to the West Coast. Short's purchase of his own plane made having a team that far away more feasible. In addition, the Lakers had been playing a number of their neutral-site games on the West Coast, including two in Los Angeles. In February 1960, Short dropped hints that the Lakers might leave Minneapolis, saying it was unlikely he would endure another financial loss. By the end of the month, the NBA gave him permission to move. Even though no specific destination was mentioned, it was clear Short favored Los Angeles.

The Lakers finished the regular season with a 25–50 record, still good enough to reach the playoffs, and the Lakers made another run, beating Detroit in the first round and then taking St. Louis to the limit before losing in seven games. The crowds at home were good during the playoffs, but it was too late. A month after the Lakers' season ended, Short announced the Lakers were moving to Los Angeles. "This time the city was ready for the decision," wrote Johnson in the *Minneapolis Star*. "Many hoped it wouldn't happen, but just as many got so tired of the threats that they lost interest."[24]

In Minneapolis the Lakers had won six league titles, although the first in the NBL is often ignored. The NBA traces its roots back to the BAA, and many record sources do not even acknowledge the existence of the NBL. The NBA credits the Minneapolis Lakers with five NBA championships, but the true record is one title in the NBL, one in the BAA, and four in the NBA. The Minneapolis Lakers also produced seven members of the Naismith Basketball Hall of Fame: Elgin Baylor, John Kundla, Clyde Lovellette, Slater Martin, George Mikan, Vern Mikkelsen, and Jim Pollard.

When the Lakers left, the local sports scene still had the Minnesota Gophers, which won a national football championship in 1960 and a trip to the Rose Bowl. In addition, two more teams were on the way that kept major league sports in the area: the baseball Minnesota Twins and the football Minnesota Vikings (with Winter part of the ownership group). A National Hockey League team, the North Stars, came along in 1967, along with another professional basketball team, the Muskies, in the new ABA.

For several years in the 1960s the Los Angeles Lakers returned to Minneapolis to play a regular-season game, but it was not until 1989, with the formation of the Minnesota Timberwolves, that the state got another NBA team. Short sold the Los Angeles Lakers in the mid-1960s and then picked up a baseball team, the Washington Senators. After the 1971 season, Short moved the Senators to Texas, creating another community that found him villainous for taking away a team.

The Twin Cities' major league sports teams now use Minnesota as the geographical designation rather than a city name, a recognition of both Minneapolis and St. Paul, as well as the entire region. The state has major league teams in every sport. The Minnesota Twins won the World Series in 1987 (and again in 1991), becoming the first major league team in the state to win an overall championship since the Lakers won it all in 1954. For some, it was the first title to be celebrated in their lifetime. Older fans, however, continue to remember the glory years of the Minneapolis Lakers.

As for the city, St. Anthony Falls continued to power the mills, although the milling industry was declining. The Washburn A Mill, part of General Mills, closed in 1965. On the other side of the river, across from downtown, the Pillsbury A Mill continued but finally closed in 2004. Nicollet Avenue became Nicollet Mall and no longer met up with Hennepin Avenue at the base of the bridge. The Gateway disappeared, having lost its earlier luster and became rundown.

To combat the deteriorating nature of the area, the city razed more than fifteen blocks and around two hundred buildings, unfortunately bulldozing with little discernment for what was worth keeping. More than fifty years later, the destruction of the 1899 Metropolitan Building still generates complaints and stands as the symbol of urban renewal run amok. Hubert Humphrey was by this time a US senator, soon to be vice president of the United States. Following in the footsteps of the Lakers' Jewish ownership, in 1961 his former aide, Arthur Naftalin, became the first Jewish mayor of Minneapolis, turning a page in the city's ugly history of anti-Semitism. The arrival of the Minnesota Twins and the Minnesota Vikings and a Rose Bowl-winning Gopher football team made up for losing the Minneapolis Lakers to a dirt-dry metropolis in California. If anyone were to ask about Los Angeles' oxymoronic nickname, they would get a rich history of the NBA's first dynasty.

## CHAPTER NINE

# Minnesota Ice

## The Eleventh Hockey Province

### DAVID C. SMITH AND SHELDON ANDERSON

## America's Biggest Hockey Tournament

The greatest hockey memory for many older American sports fans is the US Olympic team's defeat of the Soviets in the "Miracle on Ice" at Lake Placid leading to the gold medal in the 1980 Olympic Games. But that was not the highlight in the hockey life of Herb Brooks who coached that team to its miracle. Neither were the three NCAA championships he won as the coach of his alma mater, the University of Minnesota, in the 1970s. Playing in the 1964 and 1968 Olympics did not reach the pinnacle of memory for him, and neither did coaching four NHL teams. For Herb Brooks, what topped them all was holding the Minnesota high school hockey championship trophy while wearing the sweater of the St. Paul Johnson Governors in 1955.

> Of all of the thrills I've had in hockey, I can honestly say the biggest was winning the Minnesota State High School Hockey Tournament. No question about it. It's because you do that with kids you've come up through the ranks with. You lived for the day you had a chance to try out for the high school team, hoping you'd get the sweater number of some guy you admired. Then you lived for the day you made the tournament, so you could win it and share that with your mates. It sounds like bull, but that win in high school was bigger than the gold medal.[1]

DOI: https://doi.org/10.34053/scs2019.tcs.9

The boys' and the girls' tournaments draw more fans than any others in the country, and young hockey players throughout the state dream of playing in St. Paul in mid-March in what for most of them will be the biggest games of their lives. Mike Ramsey starred for Minneapolis Roosevelt before playing for the Minnesota Gophers and in the NHL. Ramsey was also on the 1980 Olympic team. After the US scored with twenty-seven seconds left in the game to tie Sweden 2–2 and help the US qualify for the medal round, an oft-forgotten step on the way to gold medal, Ramsey said, "That's the most nervous I've been before a game since the Minnesota High School Hockey Tournament."[2]

Even Canadian expats have been impressed with Minnesota's high school hockey spectacle. Moose Jaw native Glen Sonmor, who coached the Gophers, the Minnesota Fighting Saints, and the Minnesota North Stars, thought that the tournament was "the root of hockey in this state. I would tell people in Canada about it, and they were just dumbfounded. In other cities in the United States, hockey's an oddity. Here, it's so ingrained, so much a part of the fabric. I think this is the only place where that could happen."[3]

In the first half of the twentieth century, only a few high schools in northern Minnesota and the Twin Cities had hockey teams. St. Paul and Minneapolis held their first public school championships before World War I. St. Paul Mechanic Arts, St. Paul Central, and Minneapolis West were the most dominant teams in these early leagues; West had the advantage of skating on the nearby chain of city lakes where the Minneapolis park board had been conducting hockey leagues beginning in 1913. Beginning in 1924, West High hockey players also had artificial ice time a few blocks from school at the Minneapolis Arena on Twenty-Ninth Street and Dupont Avenue South, where the Minneapolis Millers played.

By 1930 about twenty-five high schools had teams, and a north-south rivalry developed between schools on the Iron Range and those near the Canadian border in the northwest and in the Twin Cities. In 1922 St. Paul Central beat Duluth Central 5–3, but a year later Eveleth crushed Mechanic Arts 9–2, winning what was billed as the "mythical" state championship. The competition heated up in 1929, when a team of Twin City high school all-stars narrowly beat Eveleth 2–1.[4]

St. Paul athletic director Gene Aldrich was the instigator of the first Minnesota State High School Hockey Tournament held at the St. Paul Auditorium in 1945. Twenty-six high school teams competed for the chance to go to St. Paul, where Eveleth beat Thief River Falls 4–3 for the first title. Eveleth's legendary

Minneapolis West High School was a powerhouse in hockey before World War II, in part because they could skate on nearby lakes. Minnesota Historical Society.

Finnegan-Grant-Celley line scored twenty-three of the team's thirty goals in the tournament. More than eight thousand fans attended the event. A decade later about sixty high schools were playing hockey, and the quality of play improved dramatically. St. Paul Johnson coach Rube Gustafson commented that "every team knew how to play good team hockey.... There was a time, you know, when we had teams that didn't know what the blue line was for."[5]

The state tournament slowly became one of Minnesota's marquee sporting events. By 1954 attendance had ballooned to 24,465 for the three-day, eight-team event, and by the end of the decade almost forty thousand people saw the tournament live, which strained the capacity of the 7,500-seat auditorium in downtown St. Paul.[6]

The first radio broadcasts of the tourney started in 1947, so residents of Roseau, more than 350 miles northwest of St. Paul, could follow their Rams in the tournament. The title game between Thief River Falls and International Falls was televised in 1956, and the whole tournament was televised from 1961 on.

The television play-by-play of the 2014 tournament was provided by announcing legend Gary Thorne, who for many Americans was the voice of hockey—NHL, NCAA, Olympics—on ESPN (as well as the voice of the New York Mets, then the Baltimore Orioles, in warmer seasons.) Why did he do a high school tournament? "I don't know of any other state that has anything remotely like this at the high school level, a tournament that takes on the size and importance that this one does," he said. "Hey, if you have a chance to be involved with it, why not?"[7] The year after Thorne's weekend in St. Paul, the Class AA semifinal games on a Friday night at the Xcel Center, home of the Minnesota Wild, set the all-time Minnesota record for attendance at a hockey game at any level of 21,609.

At first, some high school athletic directors were reluctant to fund hockey teams because of its reputation as a brutal, unsportsmanlike game. The North Americans were known for their physical style. When the US hockey team was awarded its silver medal at the 1952 Olympics in Oslo, "there was a stony silence from the usually cheering crowd of 27,000. Then a few 'boos' broke out." The Norwegians found the US team "too rough."[8] After the 1954 high school tournament, the *Star Tribune* wrote that "Gene Aldrich, who laid the ground-work for the first tourney, observed that this years' tourney should prove to the skeptical that prep hockey is not a dangerous stick-swinging, skull-cracking sport." Aldrich pooh-poohed this view of the game: "Look, in not one of the 11 tournament games was there anything so much as resembling a fight or any untoward incident."[9]

## Hockey Up North

For most of the tournament's history, hockey interest was focused in three regions of the state: the Iron Range in the northeast, near the Canadian border in the northwest, and the Twin Cities. The Range was a center of the lumber industry until iron ore was found at the end of the nineteenth century. The allure of mining jobs on the Range fueled immigration from Italy, Yugoslavia, and Finland, among many other countries. The Range was as close to diversity as Minnesota got. The state's liberal hue—even socialist in the 1930s—comes in part from the Range.

Rangers might remind you that Bob Zimmerman (aka Bob Dylan) and Frances Gumm (aka Judy Garland) hail from the region, but hockey—not music—has had the most indelible cultural stamp. Eveleth is in the heart of the

Mesabi Iron Range, about sixty miles north of Duluth. A town of four thousand now, down from seven thousand when mining jobs peaked, Eveleth built the state's first indoor hockey rink in 1922. It is home to the US Hockey Hall of Fame on Hat Trick Avenue and a number of famed Minnesota Gopher and US Olympic hockey players. The "World's Largest 'Free-standing' Hockey Stick," weighing more than three tons, is a downtown Eveleth tourist attraction.[10]

Eveleth not only won the first state high school hockey tournament in 1945 but it won four straight titles from 1948–1951 without losing a game—any game—for four years. Eveleth's early domination of high school hockey is not surprising given the town's already impressive history for hockey excellence. In the 1920s Eveleth had a team in the US Amateur Hockey Association (USAHA) that included St. Paul, Minneapolis, Pittsburgh, and Cleveland. Those early battles between Eveleth and Minneapolis and St. Paul sowed the seeds for the later north-south and intercity rivalries that naturally spilled over to high school hockey. The 1920s rivalries were stoked hotter when brothers Ching and Ade Johnson, Canadian players, left Eveleth to anchor the new Minneapolis team in the USAHA in 1923.[11]

Eveleth Junior College was considered one of the powerhouses of American college hockey in the late 1920s, ranked number one in the country in 1929. The coach of that team, Cliff Thompson, also coached the dominant Eveleth high school teams of the late 1940s and is revered as one of the great coaches in Minnesota hockey history at any level.

The game runs deep in the veins of the Iron Rangers and continues to create a sense of community. Grand Rapids, Hibbing, and Coleraine are the other Range towns that have won state high school championships. Hibbing's Joe Micheletti won a high school championship, an NCAA title with the Gophers, and played in the NHL. "In northern Minnesota, that is how it is," Micheletti recalls. "You're born, you go to school and you play hockey. You have to do it. Dad built a rink in the back yard, and we all went out there with our hand-me-down skates. Hockey was just part of our daily lives."[12]

Eveleth's claim to be the Capital of American Hockey could probably be disputed only by two towns twenty miles apart within a slap shot of the Canadian border to the northwest. Warroad and Roseau, with a combined population smaller than Eveleth's, have produced equally storied high school hockey teams and players even if they do not have Eveleth's history in amateur hockey.

Warroad has called itself "Hockeytown, U.S.A." for many decades, and put up the signs to prove it long before the Detroit Red Wings copyrighted the name in the 1990s. Warroad's hockey history is longer and deeper, and its claim to be *the* "Hockeytown" has nothing to do with selling a brand name.

Warroad sits on the west end of the Lake of the Woods, only two hours from Winnipeg, Canada. At the turn of the twentieth century Winnipeg's rail connections to the Twin Cities were as important as its east-west links to the other provinces, and Warroad picked up the game from its near neighbor to the north.

Even if Minnesotans could not locate Warroad on a map or know of its hockey history, they have probably heard of Warroad's Marvin Windows, a big name in high-end residential construction. Coach Cal Marvin was the man behind Warroad hockey, but his fame has been eclipsed for all but the most ardent fans by another family member—granddaughter Gigi Marvin, a stalwart of the US gold-medal-winning women's hockey team in the 2018 Olympics. One of six Marvin kids, Cal started a team at the University of North Dakota after World War II and then coached the amateur club Warroad Lakers in the Northwest Hockey League. Remarkably, five NHL players and seven US male Olympians hail from Warroad. The only other American towns in that ballpark per capita are Eveleth and Roseau.

The Red Lake Indian Reservation is nearby, and some of Warroad's great hockey players have Chippewa heritage, including NHLer's Henry Boucha and T. J. Oshie. Oshie gained fame by scoring on four of six shootout goals to beat Russia at the 2014 Sochi Olympics.[13]

Roseau has produced more NHL players than Warroad but fewer Olympians. Roseau also has the honor of being the hometown of Neal Broten, chosen by Minnesota Wild fans as the greatest hockey player in Minnesota history. Broten led the Rams to a state high school championship, and won an NCAA championship for the University of Minnesota, where he also won the inaugural Hobey Baker award as the top collegiate player in the nation. He was on the Miracle on Ice Olympic team, and won a Stanley Cup with the New Jersey Devils in 1995. He is the only hockey player ever to accomplish that. His NHL career included twelve seasons as a fan favorite with the Minnesota North Stars.

The Roseau Rams garnered five state titles before 1992, when the tournament went to two divisions. In the second Minnesota high school championship game in 1946, Roseau beat favored St. Paul Johnson 2–1. The Rams' thirty-four-state tourney appearances top all schools, and only Edina has won as many championships. When the tournament split, Roseau decided to play with the big boys in Class AA and has won two more state titles against high schools with enrollments larger than Roseau's total population. Roseau natives disdain Warroad's move in 1992 to play with the smaller schools in Class A. Before the split, the Warriors never won a championship, finishing second twice. Since then Warroad's boys have won four titles; the girls have won twice and been runner-up four times in a tournament otherwise dominated by Twin Cities private schools.

Warroad and Roseau are joined in state hockey lore by another border school, International Falls (one hundred miles east of Warroad on the Rainy River), which won six state titles from 1957 to 1972. The Broncos came closest to Eveleth's four-year winning streak when it won fifty-two straight in two undefeated state-title seasons in 1965–1966.

## St. Paul, the City of Hockey

The third hockey hotbed in Minnesota began in St. Paul and Minneapolis and gradually shifted and dispersed to the suburbs. While Minneapolis is now home to the Twins, Vikings, Lynx, and Timberwolves—"Oh yeah!?" St. Paulites would retort, "The only three Hall of Fame baseball players from the Twin Cities, Dave Winfield, Paul Molitor and Jack Morris, are all from St. Paul. And we have an NHL team!"

That St. Paul is the home of the Minnesota Wild is no accident.

Hockey, America's fifth most popular sport, fits into St. Paul's underdog mentality. The Saintly city cannot be bothered with the trappings of cosmopolitanism. St. Paulites pride themselves on their small-town feel with tight-knit neighborhoods, parochial schools, and small businesses—most importantly the local pubs and restaurants like Cosetta's and McGovern's near the Wild's Xcel Center adjacent to the original St. Paul Auditorium. St. Paul often seems to have more in common with the Range than it has with Minneapolis.

St. Paul hockey players began playing in organized leagues over a century ago, and the St. Paul Athletic Club was the first team to win the McNaughton Cup in 1916 and 1917, the mythical championship of hockey in the western United States. The star of the team was Francis Xavier "Moose" Goheen, a native of St. Paul suburb White Bear Lake. Most of the games in those days were played at the Hippodrome on the grounds of the Minnesota State Fair in St. Paul. The "Hipp" began serving as a skating palace in 1908. The Hipp rink was covered and enclosed but relied on outdoor temperatures for making ice. It was the largest "indoor" sheet of ice in the country.

The St. Paul team played seven to a side until 1920 when Goheen and the Athletic Club skated to a 2–2 tie with the hard-hitting Winnipeg Wanderers. The *Minneapolis Tribune* reported that "the game marked the formal introduction of six-man hockey and it might be said that the greater familiarity of the Canadians with the six-man game, more than any other factor, contributed to their successful battle."[14]

Minneapolis was playing hockey too, not only on the city's lakes but on a downtown rink and another at Lake Street and Girard Avenue. The vaunted Minneapolis Park and Recreation Board organized a recreation hockey league in 1913, and by 1920 the city had more than twenty hockey rinks, over half of them lighted for night play, some on natural lake ice, others on rinks flooded on park playing fields.[15] The 5,500-seat Minneapolis Arena, the first artificial ice in the Twin Cities, was built in 1924 for the Minneapolis Millers. But the Mill City never embraced the game the way the Capital City did.

The hubs of Minnesota hockey can usually be traced to a coach who organized and promoted kids' hockey, like Cliff Thompson in Eveleth and Cal Marvin in Warroad. Herb Brooks Sr. was one of the men behind the growth of hockey in the Phalen and St. Paul Johnson neighborhoods, along with coach Rube Gustafson. "Herb Sr. put in a lot of time, putting up the boards, maintaining the rink," remembered Lou Cotroneo, the backup goalie on the 1947 Johnson championship team and coach of four state-title teams in the twenty-one years he coached at his alma mater. "The kids would skate until 9:30, 10 at night, and then you would flood the rink before you went home. The only break was when someone brought some chili for everyone."[16]

It was fitting that the downtown St. Paul Auditorium hosted the first high school hockey tournament in 1945 and for the next quarter century. It was a blow to the capital city when the tournament outgrew the old auditorium and moved to Bloomington's Met Center in 1970. But the tourney returned to St. Paul to stay when the Civic Center opened next to the venerable auditorium in 1976, and stayed there except for a temporary dislocation to the Target Center in Minneapolis when the current Xcel Center was under construction in 1999 and 2000. When the state tournament was split into two classes in 1992, consolation bracket games were shifted to Mariucci Arena, the Gophers home ice on campus.

When girls started competing for state high school championships in 1995, the tournament was contested at smaller arenas: Aldrich Arena and the Hippodrome in St. Paul, then Ridder Arena, a 3,200-seat arena built at the University specifically for the Gopher women's team. Following an unsuccessful lawsuit in 2004 to force the girls' tournament to play at Xcel Center where the boys played, a gender equity argument, the tourney moved there anyway in 2006, giving the girls a chance to experience NHL ice at the cost of atmosphere with smaller crowds scattered in the huge arena.

The NHL awarded Minnesota an expansion franchise in 1966. The North Stars played at the suburban Met Center, a sort of compromise between the Twin Cities. The North Stars had a few good years, but never connected with St. Paulites as the Wild have. One NHL scout observed that "the Minnesota hockey fan does not sleep with his North Stars. The North Stars have to succeed to get a following. The Minnesota hockey fan sleeps with his high school hockey," which was linked to St. Paul.[17] Nonetheless, it was a blow to the Twin Cities when Canadian owner Norm Green moved the North Stars to Dallas in 1993, where the redubbed "Stars" added insult to injury by winning the Stanley Cup in 1999, something the North Stars never did.

St. Paul got a World Hockey Association (WHA) franchise in 1972, but the new league and the Minnesota Fighting Saints did not catch on in competition with the NHL. The St. Paul Civic Center hosted the second WHA All-Star game in 1973, and despite appearances by such hockey greats as Gordie Howe and Bobby Hull, the event drew only thirteen thousand fans, four thousand under capacity. Fighting Saints coach Glen Sonmor joked that he had a "folding room" at the team's practice facility: "It's where we would bring in the players and discuss whether or not the team was going to fold." One of the owners, Wayne Belisle, tried to keep hope alive by talking about "secret investors" poised to support the team. "They were so secret," Belisle later quipped, "I didn't even know who they were."[18] The team finally collapsed in 1976.

After the North Stars left, St. Paul was home to the Minnesota Moose of the International Hockey League. Minneapolis and St. Paul finally set their rivalry aside to support a new NHL team. In 1997 the NHL awarded St. Paul an expansion franchise, but in keeping with Minnesota professional sports tradition, they were called the Minnesota Wild. The team began play in 2000 and was an instant success. National Hockey League Commissioner Gary Bettman acknowledged that "it was obvious that we should never have left Minnesota."[19]

## The Decline of St. Paul and Minneapolis Hockey

Going to a Wild game is a pricey proposition these days, and playing organized hockey has become an expensive sport. That is true of many organized games, with the possible exception of basketball and soccer, which require a ball, a pair of shoes, and an open playground or field.

When hockey evolved as a sport at the end of the nineteenth century, it was a poor man's game. Norman Rockwell's "Boy Skating" that appeared on the January 1914 issue of *Boy's Life* depicts a boy with strap-on skates and a crooked tree branch for a stick. The puck was probably a piece of an old tire and goals a couple of stones. A used, folded up *Saturday Evening Post* provided cheap leg padding.

Early on in the tournament there was little disparity in the resources of the northern and southern schools. Old time hockey needed lots of water and lots of cold, but eventually neither was necessary. As more artificial ice rinks were built in the Twin Cities area, and sticks and skates became more expensive, the poorer, smaller northern schools could not keep up. Today most inner Minneapolis and St. Paul high schools do not even field a team.

With the loss of mining jobs on the Iron Range came a decline in school enrollments, stiffening the already daunting challenge of competing with larger, wealthier suburban Twin Cities schools, although the passion for hockey—and regional identity—has remained high. Rangers players and their fans have long been aware of the class differences. Rob Drobnik played goalie on Eveleth's 1945 championship team. He holds the record for fewest stops in a tournament game—one—in a 16–0 drubbing of Granite Falls. "Poor?" Drobnik recalled. "Why we only had one puck per block, and when that road apple dried up, a lot of times we didn't have any pucks. You skated all day because there was nothing else to do. No TV. You had to get out of the house."[20] Drobnik and his mates played in jerseys borrowed from Eveleth Junior College and had second-hand breezers and skates from the Chicago Black Hawks, who had their training camp in nearby Virginia.[21]

This bumper sticker was seen at the 1982 tournament: "IRON RANGERS: WE'RE NOT TOO SMART, BUT WE LIFT HEAVY THINGS." For most of them the trip to St. Paul was the first time they had stayed in a hotel. Tournament organizers had to institute the so called "Eveleth rule" to stop the Iron Range players from passing platefuls of food to friends and family from the all-you-can-eat training tables. As one Eveleth player put it, "We'd never seen so much food."[22] The kids from Hibbing could not afford to stay in a Twin City hotel, so they took a school bus four-and-a-half hours to St. Paul, and after the game, got back on the bus home. One journalist tried to commiserate with the students that this must be a long, boring day and night on the bus. One of the kids shot back, "Are you kidding? The bus rides are the best part!"[23]

St. Paul Johnson was the southern team to beat in the early years of the tournament, winning the title in 1947, 1953, 1955, and 1963. In 1955 Brooks' Governors beat an exhausted Minneapolis South High team 3–1 in the semifinal; the night before South had outlasted Thief River Falls 3–2 in eleven overtimes. South coach Rudy Kogl was seen taking a walk around the arena during two of the periods, just to get a breather and steady his nerves.[24]

Johnson beat Minneapolis Southwest 3–1 in the 1955 championship game, the first all-southern final. It was a portent of things to come. Southwest High School is in the wealthiest part of Minneapolis. The impact of money on the high school game—access to artificial ice year around, peewee hockey leagues, the sheer numbers of players, and intense competition in the Twin City area—slowly began to have an effect; discussions began about dividing the state tournament into two divisions.

Some officials pushed back. In 1982 Larry Larson, the MSHSL director of information and publications, observed that "the [hockey] tournament is the premier high school sporting event in the country. The Indiana basketball and Texas football people will debate that, I imagine, but I think I'm right. Part of the secret is having only one division—all 150 or so of the state's hockey-playing schools are in it—so you get the real David and Goliath games, the small schools that become Cinderella stories."[25]

When the northern teams lost the advantage of playing time outdoors, however, power shifted to the Twin Cities suburban schools. In 1975 parochial schools were allowed into the tournament, further tipping the balance south. From 1969 to 1991, only six of the twenty-three champions came from northern Minnesota. Of the forty-six teams that played those finals, thirty-three were southern teams, and among those only Rochester John Marshall came from outside the Twin City area.

Edina High School was the face of the suburban teams' increasing dominance. Edina is a wealthy inner-ring suburb on the west side of Minneapolis. In 2016 the per capita income was $65,245, and the median value of owner-occupied homes was $424,500.[26] A saying goes around in the Twin Cities that "nothing's finah than to come from Edina." To inner-city and out-state Minnesotans, Edinans were the quintessential "cake-eaters."

Until Edina won the championship in 1969, St. Paul Johnson had been the only Twin City team to take home the first-place trophy in the state tournament's twenty-four-year history. Edina was coached by Eveleth native and 1956 Olympic team goalie Willard Ikola, who guided the Hornets to eight championships. "We like Ike" became the Edina victory chant. Edina became the New York Yankees of the tournament—in the popular imagination an evil empire of privileged rich kids. Warroad was Edina's first victim in the 1969 final, a game the northerners remember for what happened to Warriors' star, future NHLer Henry Boucha. A hit from an Edina defenseman put Boucha out of the game. "About 15,000 people were ready to go over the boards," one fan recalled, "and lynch the entire Edina team." Warroad was down 4–2 at the time, but came back to tie the game, only to lose in overtime, 5–4. Coach Bob Johnson, a Warroader who won three NCAA championships at Wisconsin and a Stanley Cup with the Pittsburgh Penguins, quipped, "No one likes rich kids who are good."[27]

The dominance of the much larger schools in southern Minnesota and the rapid addition of schools playing hockey as smaller towns built indoor ice rinks eventually prompted a move to two divisions in the state tournament in 1992. Unlike the Minnesota boys high school basketball tournament, which was at one time the biggest in the country before going to four divisions, the dual hockey tournament continues to grow in popularity. In 2015 the tournament drew 135,618 fans, setting a new attendance record.[28]

St. Paul and Minneapolis high schools have not been able to keep up with the arms race in indoor ice time and expensive youth hockey programs. The once dominant Governors from the near East Side of St. Paul were as blue collar as their Iron Range or far-northern opponents. The last time Johnson made it to the AA state tournament was 1995, and Edison, in 1994, was the last Minneapolis school to make an appearance in the A division. Minneapolis now has only one co-op team, and St. Paul two; St. Paul Central plays together with Highland Park in the AA division, and Como and Johnson are combined on an A team.

One southern Minnesota high school hockey power does not even play in the girls' or boys' MSHSL tournament and exposes the infiltration of money into the game. Located in Faribault, about fifty miles south of Minneapolis, Shattuck was one of the oldest military schools in the state until it dropped the martial program in 1974. In 1972 Shattuck merged with St. Mary's, a neighboring girls' school.

In recent years Shattuck-St. Mary's has become one of the top hockey factories in the country, producing such NHL All-Stars as Zach Parise of the Minnesota Wild, Jonathan Toews of the Chicago Black Hawks, and Sidney

Crosby of the Pittsburgh Penguins. The boarding school is a costly affair; tuition tops $40,000 a year, with another $4,000 to play amateur hockey. *Sports Illustrated* wrote that "Shattuck-St. Mary's is to high school hockey what Harvard is to law school." ESPN called it the "Hogwarts of Hockey."[29]

Shattuck-St. Mary's has become a feeder for women's college and Olympic programs as well. Four women from Shattuck played on the 2014 US Women's Olympic Hockey team that finished second to Canada. With two more Shattuck grads on each of the Canadian and American men's Olympic teams at Sochi, the *Star Tribune* declared that Shattuck-St. Mary's is "one of the most prominent feeders of young hockey talent in the world, and its mix of male and female players is unprecedented."[30]

## Minnesota and US Olympic Hockey

The United States' Olympic teams, when successful, have relied heavily on Minnesota talent. The first Minnesota hockey Olympians were teammates on the St. Paul Athletic Club team: Moose Goheen, Tony Conroy, and Ed Fitzgerald, all from Mechanic Arts High School, and goaltender Cy Weidenborner. The inaugural Olympic hockey tournament in 1920 was not part of an official Winter Olympics but rather was played at the Summer Olympics in Antwerp, Belgium. The US team took silver, losing to Canada as expected. Goheen was offered a chance to play with the Toronto Maple Leafs and the Boston Bruins, but he decided to stay with his good-paying job with Northern States Power and play amateur hockey. In 1952 Goheen became the second American and first Minnesotan inducted into the Hockey Hall of Fame in Toronto.[31]

In those days the rules and regulations for eligibility were much looser, and the United States had two Canadians on the 1920 team. The system for choosing the US Olympic hockey team was haphazard at best. Easterners dominated the process, disadvantaging Minnesota players and teams when the official Winter Olympics began in 1924 in Chamonix, France. Clarence J. "Taffy" Abel was from Michigan but played for the Minneapolis Millers before joining the US Olympic team. Abel carried the American flag in the opening ceremonies in Chamonix. In an exhibition game in Boston, the Millers beat the US team 2–0. The *Minneapolis Tribune* wrote that behind 1–0 in the second period, the "Olympic players began to rough things a bit, but soon found they were up against a team of players who knew a bit about that style of play also. . . . The tactic profited the Olympics not a bit."[32]

The 1924 Olympic tournament was no challenge for the North Americans. The *Minneapolis Tribune* noted that at first the Canadians and Americans were somewhat discombobulated by the lack of boards surrounding the rink, writing that "the wing players were constantly passing out of bounds."[33] Nonetheless, in the early rounds Canada crushed Czechoslovakia 30–0, and the United States trounced Belgium 19–0. The semifinals were little closer, with Canada manhandling England 19–2, and the Americans blanking Sweden 20–0. Canada beat the United States 6–1 to take the gold.[34]

In 1928 the US Hockey Association selected the team from tiny Augsburg College to represent the United States at the Winter Olympics in St. Moritz, Switzerland. Augsburg is a liberal arts school that sits on the west bank of the Mississippi in the shadow of the University of Minnesota. Augsburg was founded as a Lutheran school, and until Minnesota Intercollegiate Athletic Conference (MIAC) rival St. Thomas University expanded its St. Paul campus across the river in the late twentieth century, Augsburg was the only private school in Minneapolis. Today Augsburg serves a diverse community in the heart of the city, including a large enrollment of students of Somali heritage.[35]

The 1928 Augsburg hockey team was a one-family show. The Hansen brothers—Oscar, Emil, Joe, Lewis, and Julius—dominated the ice time. Pat Larson, Merrill McInerney, and goalie Wallace "Moose" Swanson rounded out the team. With Si Melby as the Augsburg coach, McInerney was the only non-Scandinavian in the whole story. The original Hansen brothers were *not* the inspiration for the three Hanson goons in the 1977 movie *Slapshot*.[36]

Augsburg beat most comers in 1927 and was named the unofficial "state champion." The team went undefeated in 1928, blanking a St. Paul all-star team 4–0 and North Dakota State University 12–0. Pat Larson scored a goal in that game, but the Hansens tallied the rest.[37]

The invitation to play in St. Moritz came with the stipulation that the school had to raise $4,500 for the trip to Switzerland. That was no small sum in those days, especially for a small college of five hundred students. The University Club of Boston probably would have been the American Olympic Committee's (AOC) first choice, but it could not come up with the money. The Eveleth amateur hockey team was considered as well, but it did not have the means either. The University of Minnesota decided that the Olympics would interfere with its players' studies.[38]

The Augsburg community rallied around its team, with Professor S. O. Severson contributing $2,500. The South Side Commercial Club chipped in too, and the team played fund-raising exhibitions to raise additional funds. Augsburg met the goal.[39] The final step was to name Nick Kahler to coach the team. He had helped form the Minneapolis Millers, which won the 1925 US Amateur Hockey Association Championship. United States Hockey Association president William Haddock declared that "Augsburg College in Minneapolis has been selected, passports had been secured and the team was ready to sail from New York on January 25."[40]

The Eastern bias against teams and players from the Midwest was most evident in the rejection of Augsburg as the US Olympic representative. The AOC was headed up by none other than Major General Douglas MacArthur. MacArthur's secretary, Frederick Rubien, wrote Haddock, "MacArthur instructs to inform you that the hockey recommended is not regarded as a representative team and certification ... is disapproved." Haddock vehemently protested, but Rubien wrote back, saying, "This team Augsburg may be, as you say, as good as those which previously represented America in the Olympics, but has not demonstrated that ... in open competition." The University Club of Boston offered to play Augsburg to see if they were competitive, but it was too late.[41]

Minnesota hockey fans were bitterly disappointed. The *Minneapolis Tribune* wrote, "The attitude of the A.A.U. and the Olympic committee toward Augsburg is a slap at the Minneapolis school and is a reflection upon the sportsmanship of the United States. If an athletic team ... has to guarantee victory in order to be sent to the Olympic Games, it might be well for the United State to withdraw from competition in the international classic."[42] Some Minnesotans speculated that the AOC did not want to fork over its share of the money to send the team to St. Moritz.

MacArthur's reservations about the "representativeness" of Augsburg probably stemmed from the Hansen brothers' connection to Canada. The boys were born near Centerville, South Dakota, but their father John moved the family to Camrose, a small town about fifty miles southeast of Edmonton, where the Hansens played bantam and Junior B hockey. After moving to Minneapolis, the brothers enrolled at Augsburg, where they put together the school's first hockey team.

The AOC's rejection was a huge blow to Augsburg hockey. The college's 1928 yearbook promised that when "hopes of international competition failed of realization . . . the wearers of Maroon and Gray gave their undivided attention to intercollegiate hockey."[43] That was not to be. When the Hansons left after the spring semester of 1928, Augsburg did not field a team the next year.

Lake Placid, New York, was the site of the 1932 Winter Olympics. Minneapolis hosted the Olympic tryouts in the Midwest, including teams from Eveleth Junior College and the University of Minnesota.[44] In December 1931 Minnesota beat Eveleth 4–2, and a team from Detroit was scheduled to play in Minneapolis for the right to go East for more Olympic trials. Olympic organizers, once again showing their preference for teams from the East, changed their minds and invited both teams to travel East to play for the right to get into the semifinals. The *Minneapolis Tribune* again expressed its dissatisfaction with the process: "How silly! What bungling! It's all so typical of the way this Olympic hockey has been handled this year."[45]

On January 4, a team from St. Mary's of Winona, Minnesota, beat the would-be Olympic team from New York, throwing the Olympic trials into even greater turmoil. Three days later the Gophers beat Houghton, Michigan, 5–4, and then had to play an all-star team in Boston. The *Minneapolis Tribune* again criticized the bias against Minnesota: "The Gophers are short-enders in tonight's duel because they will be pitted against an all-star lineup, made up of the outstanding stick wielders in Chicago and New York." Minnesota lost 4–0, and a day later went down to Harvard, 7–6.[46]

No Minnesotans made the 1932 Lake Placid Olympic team, which won the silver medal again. Four years later, at Garmisch-Partenkirchen, Germany, the Gophers' Phil LaBatte played on the US team as a last-minute replacement for an Eastern player who could not attend. The Americans finished a disappointing third. Great Britain shocked the small hockey world by beating out favored Canada for the gold medal. In the 1948 Games, the US did not compete for a medal. A dispute between the AOC chairman Avery Brundage and the amateur hockey establishment over who should represent the US led to a showdown that nearly resulted in the cancellation of the entire American contingent in the Winter Games. In the end no American team was certified to participate in the Olympic hockey tourney that year.

The United States' Olympic hockey fortunes did not change until the power of Eastern hockey officials waned and more Minnesotans were selected for the national teams. The case can be made that the success of the US Olympic hockey team has always depended on how many Minnesotans were selected to play. Seven Minnesotans played on the team that won silver at the 1952 Oslo

Games, and another silver four years later at Cortina d'Ampezzo, this time with nine players from the Gopher state.

Minnesotans made up the core of both US gold medal-winning teams in 1960 and 1980. Nine played at Squaw Valley in 1960, including Roger and Billy Christian from Warroad, John Mayasich from Eveleth, and the hero of the Games, goalie Jack McCartan from St. Paul. An estimated twenty million television viewers watched the US beat the Soviet Union 3–2. The Americans then trounced Czechoslovakia 9–4 for the gold medal.[47] Mayasich later said, "At the time we were thinking it would be a great accomplishment if we could win a bronze, we had no idea we would win a gold. Beating the Russians was amazing and very similar to the 1980 team victory."[48]

Minnesota's pipeline to Olympic hockey is not limited to the men, although the opportunity for women to play in the Winter Games came much later. In the early twentieth century, when women doing sports was frowned upon anyway, girls found it nearly impossible to find places to play ice hockey, a game nearly as rough and tumble as football. In 1909 the *Minneapolis Tribune* reported, "Plans are under way to organize a [Minneapolis] team of fair young athletes to play the strenuous game." The Minneapolis Parks started a girls' recreation league in 1913, but it took another half century before hockey got off the ground.[49] In 1994 Minnesota became the first state to certify girls' hockey as a varsity sport, which led to the first girls' high school hockey tournament in 1995. Minnesota Gopher women's varsity hockey started in 1997 and was an instant success, winning the NCAA title six times from 2004 to 2016.

Gigi Marvin starred with the Minnesota Gophers, and then won silver with the US Olympic hockey team in 2010 and 2014. She was one of seven Minnesota women who played on the 2018 US team that won the gold medal in PyeongChang, beating archrival Canada in a shootout, 3–2. Pat Borzi of the *New York Times* declared that "Minnesota produces more girls and women hockey players than any other state by far."[50]

Warroad natives are keen to point out that only one time has an American hockey team won Olympic gold *without* a Warroad player on the team. That was the 1998 women's team, a team that featured only two Minnesota players. Although Warroad was not represented, the two Minnesotans, Anna Blahoski from St. Paul Johnson and Jenny Schmidgal from Edina, were from storied hockey communities just as familiar as Warroad to Minnesota's hockey fans.

## Maroosh and Minnesota Hockey

The Minnesota Gophers have been a perennial NCAA power for most of the last half-century. Much of the success of the hockey program can be traced back to Eveleth native John Mariucci. With future Hall of Fame Oklahoma football coach Bud Wilkinson in goal, Mariucci helped the Gophers win the 1940 National AAU Championship, and he was named an All-American. After a stint in the Coast Guard, Mariucci played for the Chicago Black Hawks from 1945 to 1948, becoming the first American to captain an NHL team.

Mariucci was one of the most famous pugilists in Minnesota hockey history and contributed to the game's earlier checkered reputation. Although he scored only eleven goals in his career, Mariucci was one of the toughest cookies ever to play in the NHL. One of his Hawk teammates said that "Maroosh" always had his back: "Anybody who tried to intimidate us had to have some pretty big balls because as soon as they went after us they would have to turn around and get ready for big John, who would come flying off the bench in a hurry."[51] One fight with "Black Jack" Stewart lasted a half hour. The toll it took on Mariucci was noted by one wit who said his face looked like a "blocked punt."[52] Lou Nanne played for Mariucci at Minnesota and later played and coached for the Minnesota North Stars. When Nanne told Mariucci that he wanted to become a dentist, Maroosh retorted, "You're supposed to knock their teeth out, not put 'em back in."[53]

Although Mariucci was known for his brawn, not brains, in 1952 he was hired to coach the Gophers, leading a .500 team from the previous season to second place in the NCAA tournament, losing to Michigan 7–3. The dapper Gopher coach, dressed in fedora, doubled-breasted suit, and bow tie, belied his earlier pugnacious ways. Mariucci credited a fellow Eveleth player for his early Gopher success: "John Mayasich brought college hockey to a new plateau. He was the Wayne Gretzky of his time." The Gophers made it to the NCAA final again in Mariucci's second year, falling to New York's Rensselaer Polytechnic Institute 5–4 in overtime. "It's a loss that sticks with me today," Mariucci said years later. "To lose in overtime was bitter."[54] Because of his success at Minnesota, Mariucci was named to coach the 1960 gold medal winning US Olympic hockey team.

The ice arena at Minnesota is named after Mariucci, although the University succumbed to the commercial way of collegiate sport, renaming it 3M Arena at Mariucci. Mariucci is in both the US Hockey Hall of Fame and the NHL Hall of Fame in Toronto. He is not only remembered for what he did for Gopher hockey but for championing the game throughout the country. After watching one NCAA final, he said, "It's asinine that the only two Americans on the ice for the college championship were the referees."[55]

Before Herb Brooks died in a tragic car accident in 2003, he gave Mariucci his due: "In all social causes to better an institution, there's always got to be a rolling force, a catalyst, a glue, and a magnet, and that's what John was for American hockey. The rest of us just filled in after him."[56] The Mooses, the Taffys, the Marooshes, and other pioneers of Minnesota hockey may be long gone, but no Zamboni can erase the indelible lines they left on blue and red lines throughout the state.

## CHAPTER TEN

# From DC Follies to Frostbite Falls

## Calvin Griffith and the Senators' Move to Minnesota

### JON KERR

*When I was trying to make a decision whether to come to Minnesota out of Washington I used to shut my eyes and say, 'Well, Unc', the time has come. Something has to give. We want to stay in baseball but we can't make it as it is right here.' I think he'd have agreed we were very, very fortunate to have Minnesota to come to.*

*—Calvin Griffith*[1]

Being baseball's "last dinosaur," as Chicago White Sox owner Bill Veeck termed him, was an almost constant fight for survival for the man who for a time found paradise in Minnesota.

Calvin Griffith began life as Calvin Robertson, orphaned son of an abusive, alcoholic father from Montreal. His fortunes seemingly changed after his adoption in 1922 by his uncle, Hall of Famer Clark Griffith. But the family-run baseball operation Calvin would eventually inherit in 1955 was itself a perennially underfinanced underdog operation kept barely afloat by business practices that would seem increasingly outdated in the second half of the twentieth century. On the field the Senators were known has hapless losers with the fitting slogan of "Washington: First in war, first in peace, last in the American League."

DOI: https://doi.org/10.34053/scs2019.tcs.10

With no Joe Hardy[2] in sight, the Griffith organization did not have the resources of the Yankees and others to withstand losses on the field and financially. After World War II, Washington DC was also changing with whites increasingly leaving the inner city for the suburbs. Baseball's traditional fan base in pre- (and for that matter post-) Jackie Robinson America was increasingly staying away from Griffith Stadium. The organization could not depend solely on ticket revenue. After inheriting the team from his uncle Clark, Calvin worried about the baseball side of the business: "When I took the club over in 1955 I think we had $25,000 in the treasury," he remembered. "What saved us was the Redskins playing in our ballpark seven or eight games a year. Rent and concessions, that's the only things that saved us. We didn't want to borrow money, cause if you borrow money in Washington, you're gonna owe so much you'll never make it."[3]

American League executives all noted the continually disappointing attendance of the Senators when their teams came to Washington. "We had complaints from all the other visiting teams," Griffith recalled. "They couldn't even pay their hotel bills, for chrissakes. We had some awful crowds, in the hundreds sometimes."[4]

A frustrated Griffith came to question whether baseball belonged in DC "What do our Washington fans want?" he asked in 1959, failing to understand why only 615,000 came out to see a Senators team finish last. Griffith was sensitive to the growing criticism of the sorry state of the franchise. Famed *Washington Post* journalist Shirley Povich remembered, "Calvin was thin-skinned and thick-skinned both. It was one thing his uncle hadn't been exposed to, he was so well liked. Calvin lacked the polish to deal with it often. So he was not a very popular figure in Washington, often."[5] Few fans recognized, as he did, that the team was showing signs of becoming a future powerhouse with sluggers such as Harmon Killebrew, Bob Allison, Roy Sievers, and Jim Lemon.

Media and public reaction were largely unsympathetic to Griffith's claims of financial hardship. Though he was being accused of cheapness even during those lean financial years, Griffith passed up opportunities to sell off his young stars. He would turn down Cincinnati's offers of a half million dollars apiece for Killebrew and his top pitcher Camilo Pascual.

But interest in the team from cities such as Los Angeles, San Francisco, Minneapolis, and Louisville began to attract Griffith. Clearly the family was arriving at a crossroads, though they tried to keep their discussions private.

"It was something you couldn't discuss," said Griffith of his uncharacteristic close-mouthed approach. "I was even afraid to bring it up to the board because they might object and then it would get out publicly. You couldn't afford to do what Chicago's doing because we were drawing so little and if they'd [fans] have boycotted us we'd have had to go to the bank and borrow, borrow, borrow and pay the interest. Then you're in bad shape."[6]

Calvin relied on his memory of conversations with Clark Griffith for guidance. "I talked to him about whether we were gonna move. He told me what to do and what not to do. He told me, 'You're not gonna make it here in Washington 'cause there's not enough money for radio and TV.'"[7]

Griffith initially denied interest in a northern city that was beginning to put out feelers for a major league franchise. He admitted to Washington reporters that he had received a telephone call from Minneapolis lobbyist Gerald L. Moore on August 21, 1957, but downplayed the contact. "He said his city was getting up a brochure pointing out what it had to offer a major league team. I told him it was a fine idea but we planned no future meeting," said Griffith. "What happens in the future I can't predict," he added, cagily. "But I'd definitely discount the Minneapolis story."[8]

Griffith's attention at that point was more directed toward another frontier, he later claimed. In what would have preceded the Dodgers and Giants historic moves to the West Coast, the Senators were seriously considering a move to Los Angeles in 1957. "Norman Chandler [publisher of the *Los Angeles Times*] guaranteed me that if we moved out there they would build a stadium for us equal to none. We were sure thinking about it."[9]

Griffith's California dreaming was even spurred on by an important legal counselor. None less than Supreme Court chief justice Earl Warren assured the Senators owner that there would be no trouble with moving his franchise, even against the opposition of other American League owners. Not only that, but Warren was also willing to help provide connections. "I used to go up there [Supreme Court] and talk to him in his chambers," remembered Griffith with obvious pride. "He was telling me I should go to California—either Los Angeles or the San Jose area. He said, 'Just let me know and I'll get those politicians together for you.'"[10]

Griffith was seriously considering the move for 1958. "But the first thing I know, California was taken up by the Dodgers and Giants."[11] Unwilling to take on those two established organizations, his interest in a franchise move was quieted most of the next year. In fact, in a bylined article in the *Washington Post* of January 15, 1957, he officially pledged not to leave the nation's capitol "Next year. The year after. Forever."[12]

It was a pledge that the Senators and future Twins president would often be reminded of—and years later blamed on a misunderstanding by the team's ghostwriter public relations man. "That caused a lot of concern. I got called a liar and every damn thing. But everybody's got a right to change their mind."[13]

Griffith's mixed feelings about leaving the city were apparent. "Being in Washington opened up so many opportunities for you," he remembered. "We used to have all kinds of [US] Senators come out to the ballpark. I remember Huey Long used to be out there all the time. They used to ring this bell when they had to be back for a vote or something. Senator [Lyndon] Johnson of Texas. He used to come out and eat hot dogs. I used to go out and sit with 'em and tell 'em about all these new ballplayers and who was coming in. . . . I used to go to Nixon's place when he was vice-president and talk baseball with him."[14]

Griffith Stadium's history and charm also had an obvious place in Calvin's heart. "It was a great old stadium," he said nostalgically. "The streetcars used to stop right at the ballpark and everybody'd empty out. You think back to the '24 Series and you're a batboy. You think of the Presidents behind you, all the diplomatic people, parties and every damn thing."[15]

Yet with only two hundred parking places adjacent to the aging ballpark, Griffith Stadium's future was falling victim to not only the Senators futility on the field, but also to the tides of suburban growth. Racial segregation and white flight led to the abandonment of inner-city ballparks along with other urban institutions not immediately accessible to the automobile.

"The problem that we had run into in Washington was that our ballpark was in a very black district," said Thelma Haynes, Clark Griffith's niece. "And people were afraid of getting their tires cut up all the time and things like that, not that whites don't do the same thing I don't mean that. But it was hard to control and we didn't have parking facilities like here [Minnesota]."[16] This was the organization's line, which Povich and other critics suggested only served as a convenient alibi.

When Congress considered a $6 million new stadium proposal for Washington, Griffith initially agreed. But he soon grew unhappy with the chosen site—across from the National Guard Armory in northeast Washington and in a largely black neighborhood. It was distant from the most rapidly growing southern and western suburbs.

As Congress failed to act on the measure and Washington continued its last-place ways both on the field and in attendance, public discussion of a possible Senators move heated up once again in 1958. "From the standpoint of baseball it is not good to be leaving the nation's capital," warned American League president Ford Frick. "But you have to think of the poor devil who is holding the franchise." Yet at the July 7 American League owners' meeting, the Washington owner reportedly took a verbal tongue-lashing for the timing of public statements suggesting an imminent move. Indeed just a few days later, Calvin was called before a senate subcommittee considering legislation that would affect baseball's exemption from antitrust action. It was not a friendly audience. Responding very respectfully to the sharp questioning, Griffith said that he "wanted to stay in Washington" and that he would seek no offers in the future to move elsewhere.

Griffith clearly could not count on support from his fellow American League owners. "A lot of these owners are in such big business that they didn't want Congress messing around with baseball 'cause it might affect their other businesses too," he complained. Griffith's leverage in American League meetings was somewhat limited, he admitted later. "They have cliques. Everybody has cliques in the League. I wasn't in any clique cause I was too damn independent. I didn't have any money to be in a clique. I couldn't agree to be in on this or that. I had to be with the regular group and wait and see what was what."[17]

Yet financial pressure continued to grow on the Griffith organization as new plans moved ahead for a publicly owned Washington stadium [later to be known as RFK Stadium] to include both the Senators and the football Redskins. "I am not worried about the seasons of 1959 and 1960," Griffith remarked. "What bothers me is what I might face after two years with expiration of our contract with the Redskins. The revenues we get from football and the concessions are important to us."[18]

That arrangement was part of the Griffith family's renewed attraction to a new frontier. Slowly but surely Minnesota had worked its way into Griffith's heart, even if only by working through his wallet. "They were promised so many times that they were gonna have a ballclub. They got slapped in the face so many times. [Minneapolis sportswriter] Charley Johnson used to come down and see Clark Griffith way back in the early 50s, maybe even the 40s," recalled Calvin. "I used to say, 'what the hell is he doing out here? Nobody's gonna move out there to Minnesota. It's too cold.'"[19]

Griffith laughed as he remembered a mid-1950s winter meeting in Minneapolis that confirmed his fears of Minnesota weather.

> Ossie Bluege and I were up at the Nicollet Hotel where the baseball meetings were. We stayed up there until two or three in the morning—nothing but smoke-filled rooms, geez it was terrible. We got outta there and decided we were gonna walk from the Nicollet to the Radisson [the hotel where they were staying]. And every street you went by, whew, it was cold. Then we get to the Radisson and they had this heater thing, around ten feet of space on the ground you walk over. And goddamn it almost blew my lungs out, my lungs were so cold and then to come up against that. And I turned to him and said, 'You know Ossie, you gotta be a goddamn fool to live up here.' And here we are![20]

But Minnesota is a summer beauty, complete with over ten thousand lakes. For an avid fisherman like Calvin, that was a big attraction. He began to chart Minneapolis weather and was pleasantly surprised that the weather would not have a negative impact on the baseball season in Minnesota. He even became convinced there might be a positive side to Minneapolis's cool spring and fall weather. "We always felt that playing in Washington took a lot of life out of our ballplayers," he remembered, making a comparison to the often-noted, late-season fatigue of Texas Rangers players. "We wanted to go to a place where the ballplayer could get rejuvenated. That's one reason why we liked Los Angeles and Minnesota. They were cool in the evenings."[21]

But more importantly, the persistence of the Minneapolis delegation paid off. Gerald Moore, the head of the Minneapolis Chamber of Commerce, made numerous visits, some unexpected and under an assumed name, to Washington's Griffith Stadium. "He'd come walking in and I'd say, 'Now if I introduce you to anybody it's as Gerry White or Gerry Brown, but no Gerry Moore,'" admitted Griffith. "I didn't want it getting out and everybody getting all excited."[22]

Griffith was now even facing opposition from his immediate family. "I went out to his house and met the family," remembered Moore. "His wife at the time wanted to stay in Washington. She was into society and all that. So it was pretty touchy. . . . And the press in Washington was really against it. So he had a lot of pressure."[23]

Yet the Senators' owner was clearly growing excited at the financial incentives being thrown in his direction. The clinching offer may have come from a beer company: "Hamm's Brewing Company offered us a three-year contract for $750,000 a year. Back in Washington we were [only] taking in $150,000 or $200,000, or $250,000 for our radio and TV. I never dreamt of anything like that."[24] Press reports in 1959 indicated further Minneapolis guarantees were made to Senators' attorney Leo D'Orsay of a minimum attendance of 750,000 and minimum net profits for the Griffith franchise of $430,000 a year for five years, although that offer was apparently later dropped.

Povich described Griffith as starry eyed in reaction to the offers being thrown his direction from Minneapolis. "They seduced him. He saw it as almost a new sex life out there," remembered Povich with a touch of sarcasm. "The rosy picture they painted—and they made good on almost everything.... Nobody was more persuasive than Minneapolis."[25]

Griffith was already impressed by the profits reaped from a quickly arranged exhibition game in Minneapolis on July 21, 1958. The Senators made the trip for a sold-out contest with the Philadelphia Phillies at the then shiny, new, state-of-the-art Metropolitan Stadium in suburban Bloomington, which had been awaiting a major league tenant since its opening in 1956.[26] "[Met Stadium Manager] Chet Roan practically bribed me with $10,000 for that game," Griffith recalled with a smile. "That's when we were getting maybe in the hundreds for playing exhibitions most places, even in Chicago and New York. They really wanted to get us up here to show us around."[27]

But Minneapolis's wine-and-dine strategy almost backfired at a luncheon in a restaurant overlooking a busy highway in Bloomington. "Every car that went by had a boat on the back," Griffith remembered. It looked like every Twin Citian was heading to the lake on the weekend. "That wasn't too good a information [sic]. But still we only played twelve Sundays over a year so I decided not to worry about it."[28]

Calvin was determined to be more cautious after his embarrassment at the 1958 owner's meeting. There was good reason, because Senator Estes Kefauver was heading up a major study of baseball's antitrust status, and House Judiciary Committee chairman Emanuel Celler was also warning of more hearings should the Senators move from Washington.[29]

"Young Griffith wants to go to Minneapolis because he thinks he can make more money there," the Brooklyn congressman said, likely remembering how his Dodgers had so recently left for Los Angeles. "If baseball is a sport, then what Griffith is thinking of doing is not likely to happen. But if it's really a business, as it seems to me, then it is only natural for Griffith to move where he can get

Before moving to Minnesota, Twins owner Calvin Griffith was worried about Minnesotan fans leaving the Twin Cities to head north with their boats. Here he presents Twins slugger Harmon Killebrew with a runabout. Minnesota Historical Society.

the most shekels for his team." Griffith agreed: "Some people [owners] were always saying remember about the politicians in Washington. I said, 'I can't worry about Washington. I've gotta make a living. Politicians don't pay for X number of seats in the ballpark.'"[30]

Baseball's winds of change finally started to sweep in Griffith's direction. In particular, Branch Rickey's widely publicized promotion in 1958 of a third baseball league, the Continental League established to serve growing cities like Minneapolis, drew the attention of the existing major leagues—though the plans never came to fruition.[31]

The Washington Senators owner accidentally got an early earful of information on the Continental League one night in a Miami hotel room.

"I was lying in bed and I hear all this noise and I said, 'That sounds like Rickey.' He was in the next room talking about the Charge of the Light Brigade or some battle like that. 'We gotta be like them and lead the charge,' Rickey said. "Boy, he could use those words! But we were never really worried."[32]

Minneapolis businessman, and later Twins board member, Wheelock Whitney maintained that major league baseball owners were very worried by Continental League's efforts to force major league expansion:

We decided we would go after the major leagues in the place where they were weakest, which was in the reserve clause. You could get legislation through Congress that would abolish that reserve clause if you could get enough support from Congress by convincing them it was that reserve clause that was keeping baseball tied up so there was no mobility of players, making it impossible to have expansion.[33]

The gravelly-voiced Whitney recalled that "this is what we did, and it resulted in the long run in expansion, which is what we wanted." He cited an oral agreement worked out with major league expansion committee heads Walter O'Malley and Del Webb in August, 1960: "We never wanted a third major league."[34]

By their October 26, 1960, meeting, American League owners were ready to take action. In fact, the speed of the process struck even some insiders as surprising. "I told Minneapolis [supporters] before the meeting there's no way there's gonna be any expansion," Griffith remembered. "It wasn't on the agenda. Then I sat there [at the meeting] like a damn fool wondering what the hell was going on." Griffith and the Minneapolis delegation were not totally unprepared, however, having met the evening before to hammer out their own final agreement. "At 5:15 on Tuesday evening the Minneapolis people brought to my hotel a proposal I felt I could not turn down," he told reporters after the next day's League meeting. "It guaranteed me nearly a million admissions for three years. It gave us full concession rights and a low stadium rental. It changed my thinking and I decided to ask permission to move."[35]

Charley Johnson would later write in the *Minneapolis Tribune* of an even more dramatic midnight meeting at the Savoy Hilton in which Griffith gave a list of demands to be met by 8:45 the next morning. Included was $250,000 worth of indemnity payments to the Boston Red Sox and the Dodgers for the removal of their minor league teams from the Twin Cities, in addition to other admissions and concession demands that the Minneapolis delegation quickly accepted.

But there still remained several twists and turns in an American League owners meeting that was one of the most tumultuous in history.

"There was something going on," recalled Griffith, chagrined. "They voted and I got voted down. So I said to myself, 'Calvin old boy, you have attended your last meeting in baseball. When you get back to Washington they're [fans and media] gonna ride the hell out of us 'til we have to sell.'"[36]

It was a low moment that Griffith remembered soon turned in yet another unexpected direction. "Then we recessed for lunch and [Yankee President] Dan Topping came over and he said, 'Calvin, are you really serious about moving to Minnesota?'" For whatever reason, Griffith's cause was now taken up by the powerful New York organization. "They brought it up again after lunch and voted on it again and I was allowed to move to Minnesota," said Griffith matter-of-factly.[37]

At long last the Senators were leaving Washington, as the sports world would soon learn to its general surprise. Even the Robertson boys, Calvin's brothers who had spent the afternoon at a Silver Spring, Maryland, country club playing the game they had learned from Clark Griffith, were taken off guard by the news. "We came off the golf course that day with Willie Wolk, a doctor, a good friend of ours," remembered Jimmy Robertson. "And we come in off the golf course and a guy comes up and says, 'Nice going, you son-of-a-bitch.' Another guy comes up and he's cussing out me and Billy and Sher. And these was good friends! So we said, 'Willie, go in the clubhouse and find out what's going on.' When he came back he was white," recalled

Robertson. "He said, 'You son-of-a-bitches moved to Minnesota.' That was our first inkling of it."[38]

As co-owner of the team, Calvin's sister Thelma Haynes was kept better informed of her brother's lobbying efforts at the New York owners' meeting. "I told Calvin it [Minnesota] sounds like Antarctica to me," she remembered with a chuckle. "But if that's what you've got to do to survive it's all right with me."[39] Less convinced, at least initially, was Calvin's wife. Whitney said, "I was there [in New York] trying to comfort Natalie that Minnesota wasn't as cold or as bad a place as everybody said. Having lived in Washington all their lives they were pretty scared about it. She was particularly concerned about moving. Natalie wasn't all that excited about leaving Washington."[40]

Minnesotans were, of course, elated at the news of the decision. Banner headlines and reactions from public officials and local fans dominated newspapers, nudging out the Kennedy-Nixon presidential race for one day. Calvin's own brief greeting to the Twin Cities was to assure them that he had never forgotten Minnesota since his first visit there three years before. "I never got Minneapolis and St. Paul out of my mind," he said, expressing his regret at delays in the move.[41]

Popular reaction was of course very negative in Washington, although a minority of fans welcomed the chance for a new franchise that would be more appreciative of the city. Nearly 750,000 fans had come out in 1960 to see the Senators finish in fifth place. "It isn't quite true that they weren't drawing," argued Povich years later, while nevertheless also expressing continued personal fondness for Calvin. "Relative to the teams they had, they were drawing very well. And he took the team out just at the time it was maturing and blossoming."[42]

But Calvin's conscience was apparently clear. "It was difficult to uproot our fan tradition in Washington," he told reporters. "But I would like to emphasize that it was my own stipulation that Washington fans would not be without a major league team."[43] Years later, Calvin would simply shrug off the criticism. "We had all kinds of people fussing at us. I don't remember what I said, to tell you the truth. But we did it to stay in baseball."[44]

Washington fans were disappointed that after years of suffering with a bad team, Calvin was turning his back on the nation's capital just as the Senators were getting better. Older fans doubted that Clark Griffith would have approved a move, but Calvin claimed, "When I was trying to make a decision whether to come to Minnesota out of Washington I used to shut my eyes and say, 'Well,

Unc', the time has come. Something has to give. We want to stay in baseball but we can't make it as it is right here.' I think he'd have agreed we were very, very fortunate to have Minnesota to come to."[45]

The Washington Senators were now the Minnesota Twins. "A lot of the people in Washington thought we'd named the club after me and Jimmy," remembered Billy Robertson with a laugh that caused him to take off his glasses to wipe his eyes.[46] The team name, of course, really referred to the Twin Cities—with nearly everyone—including Calvin—claiming credit for the idea.

After fifty years in the nation's capital, the Griffith family finally had taken their business northwest to baseball's newest frontier. "It was hard," said Thelma Haynes, who still retained some of her Southern accent even in the late 1980s. "When you've been brought up in Washington and made friends there for twenty or twenty-five years, it's hard to take up roots and go somewhere else."[47] If Griffith shared that feeling, he hid it well. "We said to ourselves, 'We're in baseball and it don't matter where we go. We're gonna make more friends, especially going to an area where" they really want you."[48] For a singularly possessed baseball man like Griffith, roots existed anywhere that four bases were thrown down in a diamond shape.

The thrill of going to the White House to give out presidential season passes was his biggest personal loss in leaving Washington. "That was the biggest thing. Just the idea of going in and sitting down with the president and talking," he remembered, sounding partisan in describing the Republicans who inhabited the White House when he left—before catching himself. "Eisenhower and Nixon were really good fans. Richard Nixon was a real good baseball fan. I used to go up to his house for parties. But Uncle always told me to stay out of politics."[49] Griffith kept his display of presidential photos and other Washington memorabilia on prominent display at his new Metropolitan Stadium office. Also included were numerous pictures of Clark Griffith, a small statue of Babe Ruth, scores of autographed baseballs, and a giant marlin fish mounting, which hung for years over his desk.

Physically moving the franchise in time for a season less than six months away was itself no easy task. "We brought practically the whole organization with us," Griffith said, with only slight exaggeration. "We had to put them up in a hotel and pay their meals for a month 'til they got established. We had to have people we knew were honest. You can get a lot of kickbacks and bribery in concessions and buying stuff."[50]

Again, it was primarily family members on whom Calvin would most count. But there would be others, including Howard Fox, George Brophy, Ossie Bluege, Charlie Daniels, Tom Mee, Don Cassidy, Dave Moore, Jack Alexander, Gil Lansdale, and Angelo Giuliani who would either come with the team or soon join the organization in Minnesota as long-term, trusted employees.

Past friendships in the baseball world also helped the cash-short Griffiths make the transition. Owners Tom Yawkey of the Red Sox, with brother-in-law Joe Cronin again helping to pave the way and Walter O'Malley of the Dodgers, gave lenient terms on the $450,000 owed for their minor league territorial rights in the Twin Cities. "They were nice to me," remembered Calvin. "They didn't make me pay them the money I owed 'til July. They were good to me or else I would've had to borrow $200,000 more to pay them off."[51]

Calvin would later complain that the promises of Minneapolis's businessmen to reimburse him for his expenses were often forgotten. "I spent nearly $790,000 coming from Washington out here," he complained. "I was told I was gonna get $500,000 back and I got $250,000 in receipts on stock in the ballclub. So a lot of things didn't come around the way it should have been."[52]

Nevertheless, the love affair that fall and winter of 1960–61 continued as Minnesota welcomed its first major league baseball team and its owners. Calvin's first visit on November 4, after the decision to move the team, rated a front-page photo on both Minneapolis and St. Paul daily newspapers as well as an airport greeting from both the mayor of Minneapolis and the Minnesota governor.

"I think it was the happiest time of Calvin's life," said Billy Robertson. "Hell, everybody was happy. We knew everybody from bartenders up to vice-presidents."[53] Griffith was even named state chairman of the Christmas Seal campaign and given honorary keys to the Twin Cities. Newspapers profiled Griffith and Natalie when they bought a house on Lake Minnetonka. "Calvin was a hero. People loved him and overlooked his shortcomings," remembered Twins media relations director Tom Mee. "The guys in the early years around the [baseball] beat respected him. They were all knowledgeable about the game, and they recognized that he was. Even though he didn't speak well, they respected him."[54]

There was plenty of reasons to be optimistic about the Twins, both on and off the field. Advance ticket sales were topping many complete season attendance figures in Washington, improvements in Metropolitan Stadium were on schedule—enlarging the seating capacity of the former minor league ballpark to thirty thousand seats—and lone holdout Harmon Killebrew was signed early in spring training for the then-princely sum of $22,500. Griffith was feted at luncheons and favorably portrayed in nearly every media description. "It has made a new man of my husband," Natalie Griffith said of the move. "He looks ten years younger and acts twenty years younger." Mrs. Griffith went on to add that she also was, by necessity, an ardent baseball fan. "I think it's good that I am, or I might not see much of my husband. We talk baseball at home but only when it's going well."[55]

Things were certainly going well early that first spring. On April 12, 1961, the same day the Russians launched the first cosmonaut into space, Minnesota newspaper headlines screamed of the Twins season-opening 6–0 win over the New York Yankees behind Pedro Ramos's three-hitter. "It's important to get a good start when you move into a new community," Griffith told reporters. "And it couldn't have been better."[56]

Griffith was convinced that he had made the right decision to move to Minneapolis: "Those first few years at the Met were like paradise. We got big crowds all the time. Everybody was so goldarn happy. . . . I got a license plate that said 'TWINS' on my car, and people would drive by me, honking their horns and smiling and waving. Not like later on, when they'd give me the finger."

Nothing was probably more damaging to his reputation than Griffith's 1978 description, quoted by *Minneapolis Tribune* columnist Nick Coleman, of his decision to move the franchise to Minnesota when he realized that there were only fifteen thousand African Americans in the state. According to the *Tribune* article on a meeting of the Waseca Lions Club, Griffith said that "black people don't go to ballgames, but they'll fill up a 'rassling ring and put up such a chant it'll scare you to death. It's unbelievable. We came here because you've got good, hardworking, white people here."[57]

"The words were misunderstood, taken out of context," Griffith claimed in newspaper accounts afterward. "I had had a couple of drinks and was trying to be funny."[58] The president of the Waseca Lions Club and others at the dinner corroborated that account and suggested that Griffith's words were only said in jest and without malice. "It didn't come out that way in the program," local businessman Ken Lenz said. "I wasn't offended and don't know anyone who was. . . . I think Calvin is getting a bad rap out of it. Our community is just reeling. But I'm sticking to my guns—that the story in the *Tribune* was one hundred percent distorted all the way. He [Coleman] didn't write it all."[59]

Coleman later argued that Waseca residents were just embarrassed and angry that the privacy of the Lions Club had been violated. "I felt bad for the community because Waseca was acutely embarrassed for some time," Coleman said, recalling a different reaction amongst most of the crowd. "People were sucking breath in the room. He may have thought he was joking, but the people in that room that night did not react like it was humorous."[60]

Lions Club members who came to a Twins game at the Met nearly a year later sounded anything but embarrassed. "Everybody knows how to spell Waseca thanks to the *Tribune*," said the vice president of the Chamber of Commerce. "Calvin Griffith is one of the ten greatest Americans of our time," added another Waseca resident. "He is for us." For whatever reason, Lions Club members were publicly standing behind Calvin's version of the Waseca incident. "It was a real good laughing affair," said another. "Ninety-five percent of us weren't bothered at all."[61]

Elsewhere in Minnesota there was an immediate and negative public reaction to the newspaper account. A Bloomington state representative called for a full investigation of Griffith by Major League Baseball and suggested the Twins might no longer be welcome in Minnesota. The local chapter of the Urban League suggested that the Griffith family and the Twins might be more at home under apartheid in Johannesburg, South Africa.

Griffith's explanations and protestations did not satisfy many Twins players and fans either. Baseball commissioner Bowie Kuhn, who had worked for Griffith in Washington, publicly rebuked his former boss. Twin City newspapers called for Griffith to sell the team. Star player Rod Carew would soon demand a trade, saying, "The days of Kunta Kinte are over," and "I refuse to be a slave on his plantation and play for a bigot."[62]

Carew's anger would be lessened by the time of his 1991 induction into Baseball's Hall of Fame when he quickly called Calvin to thank him for his 1967 role in jump-starting his career decades before. In 2010 a statue honoring Griffith would be placed outside Target Field at the same gate (number twenty-nine) where Carew's jersey is honored. Carew voiced no objections.

Griffith would always describe their clash as temporary and based more on tensions over Carew's expiring contract and pending free agency interests. As in describing the move from Washington DC, the former Twins owner denied any connection to racial tensions resulting from his actions or attitudes.

Griffith's immediate explanations did not lend great credence to his case. Caught by a reporter while on a fishing trip immediately after the story was published, he stumbled. "I thought everything was off the record. I don't even know who the hell Nick Coleman is. I thought he was a state representative or something," Griffith said, mistakenly referring to Coleman's father, then Minnesota Senate majority leader.[63]

"Look, I'm no bigot," Griffith would later tell another reporter. "When we sign a prospect, I don't ask what color he is. I only ask 'Can he run? Hit? Throw?' After this season. I'm going to ask one more question. 'Can he field?' We made so many errors this season . . . ah, never mind."[64]

Griffith's candor, combined with an often-comical inability to correctly articulate his thoughts, often made him likeable in the public eye. But in this case it might have been a bad and very unfunny combination. "I guess I'm too honest," he said shortly after Waseca. "I was brought up to tell the truth and told that it wouldn't get you into trouble. But it's caused me a lot of headaches. From now on, I'd better start thinking up some lies."[65]

Twins media relations director Tom Mee noted that all attempts to write Calvin's speeches for him had only worsened matters. "He couldn't pronounce a lot of the words. Not that Calvin was dumb, but he just wasn't good with words. Malaprops, I think you'd call it," said Mee of Calvin. "When you got to know him, you knew that he wasn't dumb—that he really knew this game of baseball. But he didn't have that knack for public speaking."[66]

That night in Waseca, argued Mee, Calvin's speaking foibles were unfortunately mixed with an unfamiliar reporter. "Had anybody been there who'd been around Calvin a little, they would have thought nothing of it 'cause they would have realized Calvin does not use the language like you or I do. Regular reporters would have known it didn't mean anything. Calvin talked that way about a lot of things."[67]

Remarkably, a Chicago reporter had written a similar account some twenty years before when he had accidentally, he maintained, found that he was able to overhear a private major league owners' meeting through listening at a hotel floor vent. Bill Furlong's account in the *Chicago Daily News* had quoted Griffith as feeling out the possibility of moving his franchise to the Twin Cities because, "The trend in Washington is getting to be all colored."

Minnesota Twins attitudes about race would also be called into question, briefly, in 1964 when it was revealed that blacks and whites were being housed separately during spring training in Florida. Griffith refused to apologize for the segregation, arguing, "There are six so-called integrated hotels in Orlando. But they are nothing we would stop at. We are not going to a third- or fourth-rate hotel just to accommodate the civil rights people. If we are going to integrate, let's go first class."[68]

It was an approach that Tony Oliva insisted was shared by the team's blacks, who preferred the food and atmosphere of the tiny Statler Hotel to that of the whites' Cherry Plaza. "He put us in the best place available. In Orlando, we stayed in this nice little motel. Then after the World Series [1965] they [the Sheraton] want everyone. We weren't too happy to go over there."[69]

Others blacks in the Twins organization also defended Griffith. Longtime Griffith family employee and handyman Charlie Daniels remembered it was a personal loan from Calvin Griffith that got him his first house in Minneapolis in 1962 when local banks refused to lend to a black man. "Calvin is just a guy who says a lot of things before he thinks," said Daniels.[70]

Thelma Haynes suggested yet another interpretation of the Waseca speech. "He [Calvin] was trying to be sarcastic. When the people did come to Washington to try and prevail on us to come to Minnesota, they did use the fact that there were not many colored people in Minnesota as one of their selling points. They thought that was a good selling point. They just said there's mostly white people out there, only ten percent colored people," she recalled.[71]

Griffith did not rely on that explanation, though he agreed that the low number of blacks in Minnesota was mentioned to him. "But the only thing I said about blacks [at Waseca] was that they didn't go to ballgames. I read it in the paper. And they're still saying it. You read articles all the time. Is that radical, er . . . racist?" Griffith described his reported Waseca description of blacks turning out in great numbers for non-baseball events at Washington's Griffith Stadium as factual, not racist. "All I did was talk about the noise at wrestling matches," he protested.[72]

> I said it was like if you go to an Indian pow-wow they're all over there humming like mmmmm [making sound]. . . . I said that's the way black people were at wrestling matches. They'd be making that noise. Now is that racist? They used to have black and white matches and they'd root like hell for the blacks. But I didn't say nothing like that. I didn't say nothing like that.[73]

That Calvin was not conscious of any racism in his attitudes appeared to be true when he later described the Waseca incident. "I'm not a racist. If I were a racist I'd say so. I know what it is. . . . A lot of these Northern blue-bloods maybe went to college with them [blacks]," said Calvin. "But a lot of people don't go to college or experience them in real life."[74]

Griffith pointed out with pride the family's long association with blacks in Washington, which included Clark Griffith Sr.'s creation of a special bleacher section called "the pavilion" priced and designed for low-income fans. "We even had a black rooter down there—'Greaseball'. He'd get those people stirred up," remembered Calvin. "The ministers asked him [Clark Griffith] to do it. They didn't have much money, those people."[75]

Special rentals of Griffith Stadium to black groups continued even after Clark Griffith Sr.'s death. "How could I talk about blacks when our ballpark had 350,000 of 'em every year and I practically knew half of them," Calvin said. "They've been good to us. They were our bread-and-butter in Washington. The Homestead Grays [Negro League] brought in money all summer—fourteen games or so. You're not gonna knock anybody that kept you alive."[76]

The entire Griffith family was defensive about their racial attitudes for years after Waseca. "I had more colored friends in Washington than anybody," said Jimmy Robertson in 1986. "We used to have a lot of fun together. If they were good guys, they were good guys. I used to have all colored vendors in Washington," he continued. "[But] I fired three or four of 'em because some guy was booing 'cause a colored guy [player] had popped up and they were all excited. I told 'em if they paid their money they could boo anybody, me, you. I don't care whether they're black, white, yellow, purple, long as they come in the ballpark."[77]

Attitudes about race are often learned in youth. But Griffith insisted that before moving south he had already learned to live with blacks as equals:

Hell, I went to school with black people in Montreal, Canada and I didn't even know what they were, who they were outside of they were human. They talked just like we did. I used to talk with 'em, play with 'em just like anybody else. In Washington I played ball with them in the backyard. I went into their stores and bought sandwiches, milkshakes from them and every other damn thing.[78]

In contrast with most descriptions of Washington, DC, as still largely Southern and segregationist at the time of his youth, Griffith recalled childhood games with mixed-race, neighborhood kids in the Griffith Stadium parking lot. "We used to pick up a game with the blacks and the whites and we just had fun. The funny thing about it was nobody knew, nobody even talked about it, somebody being of the opposite color."[79]

Povich was mixed in his assessment of the Griffith family's racial attitudes. "They had a Southern strain," he said. "I don't think that he was sincerely prejudiced though, nor was Mr. [Clark] Griffith who was [nevertheless] a holdout against blacks in the Major Leagues."[80]

Early in the century, the Griffith organization was arguably one of baseball's early pioneers in interracial relations. In 1911 Clark Griffith was among the first to scout Cuban players, signing Rafael Almeida and Armando Marsans for Cincinnati. While not an overt attempt to break the color barrier, Griffith's multiracial Cubans still represented a risk. American blacks had been known to pose as Cubans in an attempt to slip into the major leagues.

But Calvin Griffith clearly did not come from a risk-taking background on many subjects. His focus was always on keeping the struggling family business going, something he was able to continue until he sold the Twins in 1984. His main concern, even then, was on providing baseball jobs or other returns for those close to the Griffith family.

Yet Calvin also felt a certain loyalty to his adopted state. He passed up multiple opportunities to sell at higher prices to a number of out-of-towners, including a New York developer named Donald Trump. Instead, the Griffith family enterprise handed over its baseball tradition to a local banker named Carl Pohlad. Griffith later regretted that choice but not that the Twins remained in the Twin Cities:

> Minnesota has been so good to me, I never did really want to move out of Minnesota. The only way I woulda was if I couldn't have done something here in this state. 'Cause they accepted us in 1961 with open arms and we had a lot of wonderful years here. So we weren't gonna come in here and be turngoats, I mean turncoats. We came in here and appreciated what they did for us and we did our utmost to give them the best baseball humanly possible—the way we had to operate.[81]

## CHAPTER ELEVEN

# The Minnesota Twins, Tony Oliva, and the Cuban Baseball Players

## BLAIR WILLIAMS

Describing the appearance and disappearance of Cuban talent, not only from the Minnesota Twins' roster but from Organized Baseball, requires examining how Clark Griffith and his son Calvin Griffith intervened in Cuban baseball.[1] From the 1920s until the mid-1980s, the Griffith family owned the Washington Senators, a team that moved to Bloomington, Minnesota, and was renamed the Minnesota Twins in 1961. Clark Griffith and his adopted son Calvin Griffith operated their baseball business on a frugal budget and signed players to short-term contracts at lower than market value. Though this would be a common business strategy for any team owner, the Griffith family differentiated themselves by a disproportionate recruitment of cheap Cuban baseball talent from the 1940s until the mid-1960s. This chapter uses Tony Oliva, the most well-known product of the Griffiths' Cuban initiatives, to illuminate the emergence of two different eras of baseball. The first period spanned roughly from 1890 until 1959, when players from across the Americas cycled through regional professional baseball leagues to increase their wages, and the second era dates from 1960 onward when American Organized Baseball controlled the labor market for players in the Western hemisphere, regardless of ethnicity. Therefore, the focus of this chapter is less about the playing career of Tony Oliva than about how Oliva reflected the history of Cuban baseball players who migrated

DOI: https://doi.org/10.34053/scs2019.tcs.11

throughout baseball leagues in the United States, Mexico, and the Caribbean, and how the Griffith family took measures to control this annual migration such that it flowed almost entirely into their baseball franchise.

The Griffith family's actions transformed Cuba into the second-highest producer of Major League Baseball (MLB) players throughout the 1950s and 1960s and established the Minnesota Twins as the most common destination in the United States for ethnic Cuban baseball talent.[2] Although controlling this pipeline of Cuban talent turned the Twins into a winning franchise in the 1960s, it also damaged relations with Cuban baseball to the point that Fidel Castro dismantled baseball in Cuba to prevent further meddling by the Americans. Castro's actions were predicated on a durable historical relationship between American and Cuban baseball, of which the Griffith family was a major actor nearly from the start. However, the Griffith family's pipeline of Cuban talent did not survive the souring of Cuban-American relations during the Cold War. That political shift ultimately led to the disappearance of Cuban players, not only from the Minnesota Twins roster after 1976 but almost entirely from Organized Baseball from the 1980s until the early 2000s.

## The Origins of Baseball in Cuba

Nineteenth-century Havana was a cosmopolis of the Caribbean, acting as a colonial host port to traders from Spain, Peru, and the Philippines while simultaneously interacting with the popular culture of its neighbor, the United States. Although at the time a Spanish colony, the Spaniards' preferred sport of *fútbol* (soccer) was rejected by many Cubans who defied their colonial masters. The introduction of baseball to Cuban culture is credited to Nemesio Guilló in 1867, though there is evidence that ball games similar to baseball were played in Cuba prior to that time. Guilló became interested in baseball while studying in America and returned with baseball equipment to Havana around 1867.[3] By 1886 there were regular exhibition games between American Organized Baseball teams and Cuban teams. Bolstered by increasing anti-Spanish sentiment and the cosmopolitan images of American culture, by 1890—less than thirty years after the establishment of major league baseball in the United States—there were two hundred baseball clubs in Cuba (*clubes de verano*, "summer clubs").[4] In 1890 the New York Giants major league baseball club began the tradition of spending the winter in Havana in order to train in the off-season.[5]

The Cuban-American baseball relationship was thrust into the spotlight after the *USS Maine* was sunk in Havana Bay in 1898 and the United States military responded under the pretext of liberating the people of Cuba from Spanish imperialism. American newspaper mogul William Randolph Hearst bolstered domestic support of the Spanish-American War by reporting that the men of the *USS Maine* were lovers of baseball and that like-minded Cubans were prevented from playing baseball by their Spanish colonial masters.[6] Cubans fleeing the violence in their homeland helped to further disseminate the sport of baseball as they relocated to the Dominican Republic, Venezuela, Mexico, and Panama, ultimately helping to establish a number of independent baseball leagues throughout the Caribbean.[7]

Arguably the most significant development in Cuban baseball was the emergence of the mobile Cuban baseball player, who traveled throughout different professional baseball leagues in the Gulf of Mexico in an effort to earn a living wage. Perhaps the best representative of these mobile players was black ethnic Cuban Martín Dihigo. In a career that spanned from 1922–1950, Dihigo was a superstar in Cuba comparable to America's Babe Ruth. Dihigo also traveled regularly to play in the American Negro League and the Mexican League, ultimately entering each league's Hall of Fame.[8] Although Dihigo is an exceptional case, from the 1920s until the 1940s, several dozen Cubans traveled to America and/or Mexico every year to play baseball and earn additional wages, which made them both the most common and the most mobile ethnic group among the baseball leagues throughout the Gulf of Mexico.

From the Cuban point of view, mobile baseball players were both a blessing and a curse. Cuban-born players were being hired to play against the best international competition, but this success also pulled ethnic Cubans from Cuba's own leagues. From the point of view of Organized Baseball, however, Cuban players like Dihigo represented cheap and talented foreign competition to the more expensive homegrown American players. The Griffith family and the Washington Senators were the first team in Organized Baseball to take full advantage of the cheap Cuban baseball player market.

## Thinking Locally, Signing Globally: Griffith, Cambria, and the Mobile Cuban Players

Clark Griffith spent nearly two decades as a pitcher in Organized Baseball before taking over as manager of the Cincinnati Reds in 1911 and eventually becoming full owner and president of the Washington Senators in 1920. A self-made man, Griffith managed all of his business decisions by balancing a sense of thrift against the league-wide inflation of baseball players' salaries.[9] A cornerstone of Griffith's fiscal strategy was the acquisition of Cuban talent by becoming the point of first contact for Cuban players, which was accomplished through the work of Joe Cambria.

Joe Cambria was born in 1890 as Carlo Cambria in Messina, Italy; in 1893 Cambria boarded a ship with his family and immigrated to the United States, where he moved with his family to Massachusetts and changed his name to Joe.[10] Cambria's minor league baseball career began in 1910, and he spent some time playing in Cuban winter ball in 1911. Following Cambria's military service in World War I, he purchased several minor league baseball teams; Calvin Griffith, Clark's nephew and adopted son, played on one of these teams. In 1934 during the Great Depression, Calvin introduced Cambria to his uncle Clark, and thereafter Cambria transitioned from minor league team owner to a player scout for the big-league Washington Senators. Cambria was relocated to Havana and within twenty years signed an estimated four hundred players from Cuba, most of them destined for the Senators' and Twins' minor league affiliates.[11] Cambria's specialty was signing players for well-below market price, even admitting he signed a prospect in exchange for an ice cream cone.[12] Although other major league teams were signing Cuban players, Cambria's activity presaged the later Organized Baseball investment in Caribbean leagues, in which teams developed their exclusive baseball camps in the Dominican Republic.

Although Organized Baseball prohibited black Americans from being employed on their teams, light-skinned Latinos were regularly seen on MLB teams, and Native American and Japanese American players appeared on minor league teams.[13] Most interestingly, Griffith used six black Latino players in the period from 1911–1947; these men were actually Caribbean-born men of African ancestry who were considered racially distinct from black Americans.[14] The appearance of these dark-skinned Latinos in Organized Baseball undermines the historical narrative familiar to most Americans that Jackie Robinson broke the racial barrier in 1947.[15] Griffith's use of black Latino players in Organized Baseball also reveals that the Negro leagues—the black-owned, black-operated, and black-community supported baseball businesses—were in reality an economic competitor with Organized Baseball.

The mobile black and Latino players working for the Negro leagues, Mexican leagues, and Cuban leagues often had wages comparable to their white counterparts in Organized Baseball.[16] Salaries from this era were not commonly reported, and verifiable data is scarce, which makes this lack of data a challenge for direct comparison. Historian Peter Bjarkman uses the example of the black American player Wilmer Fields, who reported an annual income of $12,000 by playing in the Negro leagues, barnstorming, and playing in Mexico throughout the 1940s and 1950s. For context, the average salary for a major league baseball player in 1967—nearly twenty years after Fields' career ended—was $19,000.[17]

Although Fields was a celebrated player and his earnings were not the norm, his situation illustrates a significant point: nonwhite baseball players migrating throughout the Caribbean could make wages comparable to the majority white players in Organized Baseball. The high wages for these mobile players presented a problem for those white owners of Organized Baseball who wanted to recruit cheap talent for their teams among the pool of nonwhite Caribbean players. Therefore, after World War II Organized Baseball sought to eliminate its economic competitors by monopolizing the pathway through which men— white or black, American or Latino—could become baseball players.[18] The first steps to this control began with the integration of Organized Baseball.

Jackie Robinson's integration was indeed a triumphant moment for wider racial integration throughout America, but the inclusion of black Americans in Organized Baseball dealt a fatal blow to Negro League baseball. Within one decade of integration—by the late 1950s—the last Negro League teams disbanded; the teams were not permitted to join Organized Baseball, and the teams received no compensation for their lost players. Historian Japheth Knopp uses a case study of Kansas City, Missouri, to show that although the integration of Organized Baseball was a precursor of the greater desegregation of America, it also came at the cost of dismantling the black businesses and social circles affiliated with the local Negro League Baseball team, the Kansas City Monarchs.[19] Knopp argues that the price of black communities being integrated into Organized Baseball was the crumbling of the financial foundations that had once built and sustained these communities. Thus the cost of integration was not necessarily felt by the player himself but by the community that once supported him.

Clark Griffith owned the Washington Senators as well as a "lucrative" stake in the Pittsburgh-based Negro League team the Homestead Grays, which played many "home" games in Washington, DC, in the same stadium as the Senators.[20] Fearing the depreciation of his diverse baseball investments, Griffith opposed the entrance of black Americans like Jackie Robinson into Organized Baseball despite having used black Latinos on his teams for over thirty years. In an effort to strengthen his Caribbean investments, Griffith had Joe Cambria form the Havana Cubans team in 1946, attaching them to the minor league AAA Florida International League, which made them the first Organized Baseball team to be located within Cuban territory. This effectively formalized Griffith's interest in using Cuba as a farm system for Organized Baseball.[21]

In 1947 the Cuban leagues correctly foresaw the combination of the integration of Organized Baseball alongside Cambria's harvesting of young Cuban talent as a move to control the fates of young black and Latino baseball players. Cuba feared that with greater integration in the Organized Baseball leagues, there would be an even larger migration of their talented youth to the United States. In an effort to regain some control over the situation, the Cuban leagues agreed to a pact with Organized Baseball regarding the management of young Cuban baseball players.[22] This pact had two main effects: first, it forced Organized Baseball to respect any previously existing contract on a Cuban player; second, it gave Organized Baseball the right to insert American players arbitrarily into Cuban teams for the purposes of training and development.[23] In other words, the wider-scope effect of the Robinson-era racial integration of Organized Baseball dismantled more than just the black communities in America; by allowing Americans to intervene in the composition of Cuban League teams, it put cracks in the foundations of Cuban baseball as well.

The mid-1950s were a watershed moment when the stories of the Griffith family and Cuban baseball were inexorably enmeshed. For a period of thirty years, Clark Griffith dominated the Cuba-to-America flow of baseball talent, profiting from a pipeline that directed whites, blacks, and Latinos into Organized Baseball at large and, more specifically, to the Washington Senators. Despite the intricate system of investments that Griffith had developed over the first half of the twentieth century, his empire faltered due to the Senators' lack of success on the playing field. The team reached its nadir when word of the Senators' failures spread to even non-baseball fans by means of the 1955 Broadway production of *Damn Yankees*, in which a Senators fan makes a deal with the devil in return for his team's success.[24] That same year Clark Griffith passed away and left his baseball holdings to his adopted nephew, Calvin Griffith. With the younger Griffith tasked to turn around the team's record, he relied on the services of Joe Cambria.

## The "Age of Gold" and the Departure of Organized Baseball from Cuba

In 1952 Fulgencio Batista took power in Cuba via a military coup and instituted an authoritarian state until he was ousted in 1959. The economy during this seven-year period benefitted the country's wealthy elite and ushered the game of baseball in Cuba into an "age of gold."[25] Player salaries in the Cuban leagues skyrocketed due to an increase of white American players from Organized Baseball—including later Hall of Famers Brooks Robinson, Jim Bunning, and Tommy Lasorda—flocking to Havana to increase their income by playing in the Cuban winter leagues.[26] This period of wealth was a long-term effect of the aforementioned 1947 pact: American baseball team owners were increasingly in favor of using the Cuban leagues as a competitive development league, while the Cuban owners enjoyed that fans packed the stadium to watch teams composed of the best young international baseball talent in the western hemisphere. The end of this "age of gold" came when rebel groups, led in part by Fidel Castro, began their assault on Batista's regime in late 1958. In response to the violence, Organized Baseball commissioner Ford Frick and Calvin Griffith requested that all American winter-ball baseball players withdraw from Cuba.[27]

During Castro's first year in power in 1959, he maintained a tenuous political relationship with the United States while welcoming competition with American baseball. Although it is a myth that Fidel Castro was a talented baseball player, it is true that Castro had an intense interest in the sport and regularly appeared at games. Perhaps most notably Castro's presence was strongly felt in the fall of 1959 during the "Junior World Series" of Organized Baseball's AAA minor league when the Havana Sugar Kings played the Minneapolis Millers.[28] The first few games in Minneapolis were nearly snowed out by early winter weather, attracting a maximum of two thousand people, but the deciding games were played in Havana, where Millers players reported that Castro walked menacingly past their dugout while brandishing a gun. The Sugar Kings—a team consisting of mostly Cuban nationals—won the championship, and Millers' player Ted Bowsfield recalled, "We were just happy to get it over and to get out of town with our hides."[29] The immediate effect of this threat resulted in the commissioner of the International League forcibly moving the Havana Sugar Kings to New Jersey, a move which caused the ethnic Cuban managers and coaches to resign in protest.[30]

That tense championship series signaled a rapid deterioration of the relationship between Organized Baseball and the Cuban League. Castro believed that the 1947 baseball pact gave America too much presence in Cuban baseball and made the Cuban leagues too reliant on non-Cuban talent. As a countermeasure, Castro ordered the 1960 Cuban League championships to be played by teams consisting solely of ethnic Cubans. He intended to promote domestic baseball and undermine America's grasp on the Cuban national game, but ultimately he undermined the Cuban leagues by stripping the cosmopolitan Havana teams of their top international talent and leaving them skeletons formed from leftover Cuban players. Many local fans were uninterested, afraid, or simply unable to afford to attend an all-Cuban baseball game entrenched in revolutionary politics. Historian Roberto González Echevarría reports that at one game in Havana only twenty-nine people bought admission tickets; league officials ultimately recruited school children, prison inmates, and the elderly to fill the stadium seats.[31] These events heralded the eventual dismantling of the Cuban leagues, which ended quietly in the winter of 1961 when the league president, Narciso Camejo, fled the country. Cuban players were faced with a choice: they could stay in Cuba and wait for baseball to return in some incarnation created by Castro, or like so many of their fellow countrymen had done before, they could try playing in America, Mexico, or one of the other Caribbean leagues.

At the same time as the Cuban leagues were collapsing, Calvin Griffith moved the Senators to Minnesota.[32] Owing to the Griffith family's longstanding relationship with Joe Cambria in Cuba, combined with the disappearance of the better-paying Negro leagues, the Minnesota Twins were uniquely situated to benefit from the end of the Cuban Leagues by signing young ethnic Cuban players to cheap contracts. In 1961 Griffith already had six Cubans on the major-league team and no less than fourteen Cuban players in the minor-league system.[33] In terms of major-league talent in 1961, the Twins rostered one-quarter of all Cubans in MLB (twenty-three Cuban MLB players on eighteen teams).[34]

## The Name of the Game:
## Oliva as Pivotal Moment in Organized Baseball

The most notable of the Twins' minor league talent was the quiet, black Cuban Tony Oliva. Oliva's arrival straddled the end of the era when mobile Cuban baseball players traveled throughout the Caribbean and America to play in different leagues throughout the year and the beginning of the era when Organized Baseball dominated the baseball labor market throughout the western hemisphere.

Oliva is unarguably a luminary icon within the history and community of the Minnesota Twins. Among the thousands of players who have played for the Minnesota Twins since 1961, Oliva is one of seven players honored by the Twins with the retirement of his jersey number. Oliva has served the team for over fifty years in multiple capacities, from player to hitting coach to public spokesperson.[35] The narrative of Oliva's rise from humble beginnings in the western Cuban province of Pinar del Río to baseball stardom in America is well documented by baseball historians and sports journalists.[36] Because Oliva became an icon with the Minnesota Twins, however, historians have regularly overlooked his unique status as a black Latino and an accidental immigrant to the United States. Moreover, in 1961 Oliva held a closely guarded secret about his true identity: he was not actually eighteen-year-old Tony but twenty-three-year-old Pedro. Therefore Oliva's story is rich with drama and intrigue that illuminate the interplay between the Twins baseball club and the life of a black Latino player in the United States in the 1960s.

Pedro Oliva was born in 1938 into a poor farming family in the western province of Pinar del Río, Cuba, about a two-hour bus ride from Havana.[37] At the age of nineteen, Oliva earned a roster spot on a winter league club, and at the age of twenty-three a teammate introduced Oliva to Joe Cambria. In February 1961 Oliva signed a minor league contract with the Minnesota Twins with instructions to attend spring training in Florida.[38] Oliva had never obtained the necessary birth certificate to get a passport to enter America, so he took his younger brother Antonio's birth certificate as his own. Thus Pedro Oliva assumed Antonio Oliva's identity and eighteen-year-old age.[39] Calling himself Tony, he boarded a plane and left Cuba on April 9, 1961, with every intention of returning home to Pinar del Río at the end of the American minor league season, following the migratory practice that his fellow countrymen had been doing for decades. At the end of Twins spring training, Oliva was handed a dismissal slip and almost returned to Cuba, but instead he convinced team coaches to let him play for the Wytheville Twins, the organization's lowest-ranked developmental team located a short drive north of their A-level Charlotte affiliate.[40]

But what was once an annual circuit of traveling Cuban baseball players quickly became unidirectional from Cuba to America after the dissolution of the Cuban leagues in the spring of 1961. The collapse of these leagues was just a precursor to far more severe international crises that resulted in Oliva's extended sojourn in America.[41] At the same time as Oliva began his first spring training in Florida, a group of American-trained Cuban soldiers launched a surprise attack on the Castro regime, more commonly known as the Bay of Pigs Invasion. After the Castro-led defeat of the insurgents, Cuban-American relations deteriorated rapidly with the nadir reached in 1962 when the Soviet Union supplied Cuba with nuclear missiles, subsequently bringing Cuba to the frontlines of the Cold War and cementing the United States' decision to embargo the importation of goods from and travel to Cuba. Three years later, the US Congress passed the 1965 Immigration Act, which greatly increased the number of Cuban immigrants allowed into America every year, most of whom were fleeing the Castro regime in order to seek protection and a new life in the United States.[42] Although Oliva did not intend to be one of the first of this wave of Cuban immigrants to the United States, it is productive to think of Oliva both as the tail-end of the era of mobile Cuban players and as the forefront of a new wave of Cubans who were seeking political refuge. Oliva could not return to Cuba because to do so meant his forfeiture of any future career in baseball.

Like all players in the 1960s, Oliva did not control his own financial security. Oliva played almost his entire American career (1961–1976) under the "reserve clause," an enduring legal definition which allowed MLB owners to retain the rights of a player even after the expiration of his contract. The reserve clause was dismantled in 1975, after several legal battles, perhaps most notably when the black American baseball player Curtis Flood charged that the reserve clause likened baseball contracts to slavery. Flood's case went to the US Supreme Court, which ultimately decided in favor of Organized Baseball, even though the court argued that the reserve clause was tenuous at best.[43] In 1975 Andy Messersmith helped dismantle the reserve clause after playing a full year without a contract, and free agency was introduced into Organized Baseball thereafter.

In 1961 baseball journalists quickly nicknamed Oliva the "Cinderella Kid" because he had performed poorly in spring training and then became the premier hitter in the Twins' minor league system, earning the Silver Slugger Award for his league-leading .410 batting average with the Wytheville Twins of the Appalachian League.[44] But Oliva's success belied the quiet pain he endured on a daily basis because, as a black man, he did not receive the same civil liberties as his white teammates. Playing in the segregated American south, he was not allowed to reside in the same hotel as his white teammates, instead regularly staying with prearranged host families for black players, where he

TONY OLIVA     Outfielder     MINNESOTA TWINS
68-52

Cuban Tony Oliva was a feared left-handed hitter, winning three American League batting titles. He was the most iconic of Cubans who played for Calvin Griffith's Minnesota Twins. Minnesota Historical Society.

often had trouble expressing his needs due to his poor command of the English language. On the occasion that the team stopped at a restaurant that would serve blacks alongside whites, he carried two notes with him, one that read "Fried Chicken" and the other "Ham and Eggs," so that he could hand them to a server and receive food. More often, Oliva waited on the team bus while his white teammates ate, hoping that his colleagues would bring him some food that he could eat as they traveled.[45] Although Cuba had its own racial hierarchies, Oliva's previous experiences in the Pinar del Río winter leagues were on integrated teams where players were never asked to wait on the bus while teammates ate in a restaurant.

At the end of 1961, Oliva had two paths to follow to continue his baseball career. The first path was to follow his original plan and return to Cuba, although professional baseball had all but disappeared there and was being replaced by a predominantly Cuban, state-run nationalist league. The other path he had not planned for but ultimately chose: that was to live life as Tony Oliva within the confines of Cold War America's structural racism. Other Cubans playing in the major leagues were faced with the same dilemma, and the winter of 1961 proved to be the last chance for most Cuban players to return to their homeland.

The Twins' management did their best to keep their players in America, partly out of concern for the tense political situation in Cuba and partly out of the developing realization that the Cuban winter ball circuit was exhausting their talent. For example, in the fifteen-month span between the 1960–1961 MLB season and the final Cuban winter league in 1960, pitcher Pedro Ramos threw 491 innings.[46] Twins' rookie shortstop Zoilo Versalles was so exhausted from playing Cuban winter ball—and worried about his family's safety in Cuba—that he disappeared to Cuba for one month in the middle of the 1961 MLB regular season; Twins management firmly told him to stay in the United States and rest in the winter of 1961.[47] In lieu of pitcher Camilo Pascual playing winter ball, he was given a coaching position in the Florida International League where he would assist minor league players like Ramos to have a less intense off-season workload. With the majority of successful Cuban players on the Twins' major league roster agreeing to remain in America in order to earn more money and have a safer future, Oliva decided to play winter ball in Florida instead of returning to Cuba.[48] This decision ended any possibility of his return to Cuba for over a decade.

Fortunately for Oliva, he endeared himself to the Twins organization and his teammates by demonstrating beyond a doubt that he was one of the best young talents in baseball. After his 1962 minor league season in Charlotte, he missed his second consecutive batting title by a fraction of a point. It was this success that saved him from deportation at the end of the 1962 season when Organized Baseball discovered that Oliva had illegally entered

America using his brother's birth certificate. A Twins public relations writer, Herb Heft, had approached Oliva hoping to write a biographical sketch of the "Cinderella Kid." Heft was baffled why Oliva could not recall his own birthday. Heft ultimately wrote that Oliva was somewhere between "19 and 24 years old."[49] Their suspicions raised, Twins officials began investigating the discrepancies in Oliva's story. When confronted, Oliva confessed through an interpreter that he was actually Pedro, and admitted he could not remember his brother Antonio's birthday. Commissioner Ford Frick forgave the incident and allowed the Twins to retain Oliva's contract because the Twins had signed Oliva in good faith. Inadvertently, Oliva did not know his actual birthdate and continued to report himself as twenty years old instead of his actual age of twenty-three.[50]

Oliva continued to call himself Tony, and though he never officially faced punishment for his actions, he was held back in the Twins' AAA minor league affiliate in Dallas for an additional two years where he was regularly embarrassed or terrified. While prepping for these minor league games, the Dallas players were forced to wear cowboy outfits, a practice which Oliva disliked but took in stride. When the Dallas team traveled, they had a faulty DC3 plane nicknamed the "knuckleball" that players prayed remained airborne; Oliva regularly spent the flight with a towel covering his face.[51] Although Oliva continued to play well in the minor leagues, he did not become a regular player on the Twins' roster until 1964. Oliva was disappointed that he was held in the minor leagues for such an extended period, but given the new status of Organized Baseball as the arbiter of baseball careers in the western hemisphere, he had no other choice but to wait until Twins management finally promoted him to the majors.

After coming up to the majors, Oliva became a key figure in the success of the Twins franchise in the 1960s. Yet that success came with a cost that was often overlooked by historians. Like other black players, Oliva was regularly subjected to racism and segregation; like other Latinos, his English ability was ridiculed; like all baseball players, his body deteriorated, and he endured seven separate knee surgeries and chronic pain throughout his career.[52] Meanwhile, the frugal Calvin Griffith refused to sign Oliva to a multiyear contract until 1971, by which time Oliva's career encompassed seven consecutive all-star appearances (1964–1971), a two-time batting champion (1964–1965), a World Series appearance (1965), and two American League Championship appearances (1969–1970).[53]

## Calvin Griffith: Race, Ethnicity, and Business

Oliva's situation raises the delicate question of whether Calvin's personal beliefs about race and ethnicity undermined his business practices. Although Calvin was well known for speaking his mind without a filter, the damning evidence came in late 1978, when he was invited to speak at the Lions Club of Waseca, Minnesota. Griffith was himself a Lions Club member and familiar with the decorum of these meetings, so he believed the speech would be off the record. However, unbeknownst to Griffith, *Minneapolis Tribune* reporter Nick Coleman was in attendance and reported the speech the next day in his newspaper column. Griffith spoke sternly on topics ranging from his player's personal lives to perceived on-the-field laziness, but two inflammatory comments in particular had enormous repercussions.

First, Coleman reported that Griffith said he moved the Senators to Minnesota because "you had only 15,000 blacks here. Black people don't go to ball games, but they'll fill up a rassling [sic] ring and put up such a chant it'll scare you to death. It's unbelievable. We came here because you've got good, hardworking, white people here."[54] Second, Griffith lambasted black Panamanian player Rod Carew, who in the 1970s had taken up the mantle of Oliva as the icon of the Minnesota Twins, saying, "Carew was a damn fool to sign [his] contract. He only gets $170,000 and we all know damn well that he's worth a lot more than that, but that's what his agent asked for, so that's what he gets."[55] *Minneapolis Tribune* writer Howard Sinker conducted a follow-up interview in which Griffith explained that his remarks were supposed to be off the record and were made only to get laughs from the audience, although Coleman reported that the audience seemed uneasy at Griffith's possibly alcohol-slicked rhetoric. Nonetheless, Griffith confirmed to Sinker that he did move the Twins to Minnesota because of the state's small population of black people. Griffith denied any racist intention to his remarks, saying to Sinker, "What the hell, racism is a thing of the past. Why do we have colored ballplayers on our club? They are the best ones. If you don't have them, you're not going to win."[56]

Regardless of his intent, Griffith's comments both demoralized and incensed his team. When Rod Carew heard the comments for the first time before a regular season game, he responded by going to the locker room and removing his uniform in preparation to leave the stadium. Carew ultimately decided to return to the game without comment. He later said to *Minneapolis Tribune* reporter Gary Libman, "I will not ever sign another contract with this organization. I don't care how much money or how many options Calvin Griffith offers me. I definitely will not be back next year."[57] Carew made good on his promise, and the Twins traded him to the California Angels in 1979.

Griffith seemed to have no change of heart in how he handled his players and continued to treat black players in a harsh manner. In 1982 Griffith sold Greg "Boomer" Wells, a black American, to the Hankyū Braves of the Nippon Professional Baseball Organization in Japan. Wells described the process by which he went to Japan to Robert Fitts in an interview in the early 2000s:

> Why did I go to Japan? Because I was sold like a slave! I was with the Twins, playing ball in Puerto Rico when my agent called and said, 'You've just been sold to Japan.' I was like, 'Wait a minute—they can do that without my permission?' . . . I said, 'No Way! I'm not going over there' . . . Finally, Calvin Griffith, the Twins' owner, called me directly and said, 'Look, we've already sold your contract, and you're going . . . If you don't go to Japan, there's no telling where I'll send you next year!'[58]

As Wells negotiated with the Hankyū Braves over his pay, Griffith continued to harass his former player to ensure that a contract was signed quickly. Ultimately Wells settled for less money than he desired in return for a smooth contract signing process.[59] Although the Twins owed a significant portion of their success during the 1960s to their pipeline of Cuban talent that they had inherited from Clark Griffith's Washington Senators, Calvin Griffith's frustration with the end product of cheap access to minority players became increasingly evident throughout the late 1970s and 1980s. Calvin Griffith sold his control of the team to Carl Pohlad in 1984, making Wells one of the last targets of the long-term plan of frugality.

When viewing the long history of the Griffith family's baseball business, there are repeated examples of prioritizing financial frugality at the cost of a player's financial security and morale, and the unintended result was the near elimination of Cubans from the entirety of Organized Baseball. Griffith's pipeline of Cuban talent began to dry up after the Castro revolution, and later incarnations of the Twins' teams became entirely devoid of Cuban players. By 1970 there were only four Cuban players on the Twins' major league roster (Tony Oliva, Luis Cardenas, Minnie Mendoza, and Luis Tiant) and after Oliva retired in 1976, there were no further Cubans on the Twins' roster under the Griffith regime. More broadly, in the five-year period after Carew's departure in 1979 until Calvin Griffith sold the team in 1984, there were only three Latino players who made the Twins' roster in any capacity, despite ethnic Latinos comprising nearly twelve percent of major league roster spots annually.[60] In summary, the result of Griffith's stinginess throughout the 1950s and 1960s led to the disappearance of not only Cubans but almost all Latinos from the Twins roster in the early 1980s.

The repercussions of the Griffith family's intervention in the Cuban leagues was felt long after the end of the Cold War in 1991, as Cuban baseball continued to distance itself from its American counterpart. From 1970 until the early 2000s, there were only a handful of ethnic Cubans who played in major league baseball, a number that reached its nadir in the mid-1980s, with only three players of Cuban origin.[61] More broadly, with Cuba closed to investment from Organized Baseball, owners turned to other Caribbean states to acquire cheap talent, namely the Dominican Republic, Puerto Rico, and Venezuela. Beginning with the notable defection of Liván Hernández and his brother in 1997, Cuban baseball players became increasingly common in the major leagues in the 2000s. Cuban-American relations improved after Raúl Castro assumed power in Cuba in 2008 and US President Barack Obama loosened decades of embargo policies in 2015. As of 2016 there were as many Cuban players in the major leagues as there were in the 1960s. However, due to free agency in MLB, these current Cuban players possess a far greater control over their financial security than their predecessors. In the past few years, players like Yoenis Céspedes and Yasiel Puig signed multiyear contracts for tens of millions of dollars before having played a single game in the United States. In 2015 an MLB-affiliated minor league baseball team sought to locate itself in Cuba, and representatives from each country wanted to ensure mutual profit and respect during the negotiation process.[62]

Despite the United States' renewed relations with Cuba and its talented ballplayers, the Twins' current ownership group has not benefitted from this comparatively cordial environment. The poorly performing and low-budget Twins were nearly removed from MLB in the early 2000s before having a sudden turnaround and becoming a perennial winning team throughout the mid-2000s. It was a situation that harkened back to the poor-performing Senators in the 1950s and their sudden turnaround after a change of ownership and location. But the role of Cuban players in the major leagues has flipped from its 1960s status: now Cubans are well paid and generally employed by high-budget teams. Although the current Twins' roster ranks in the middle of MLB salary expenditures, if highest paid player Joe Mauer's annual contract of $23 million were removed, then the 2018 Twins would have the third lowest salary in major league baseball.[63] It is ironic that in the longer history of the Griffith family's intervention in Cuban baseball, the Twins benefitted from a short burst of Cuban talent in the mid-1960s punctuated by the career of Tony Oliva, but in the long-term the team has not received any great benefit from the recent return of Cubans to Organized Baseball.

Tony Oliva remains a lifelong advocate for the Twins organization and a staunch supporter of the Minnesota community. Now nearing eighty years old, Oliva continues to reside in Bloomington, Minnesota, and attends Minnesota Twins off-season promotional events and serves in an unofficial capacity as a hitting coach during spring training. He is perhaps best known among recent baseball aficionados for the debate as to whether he should be admitted to the Baseball Hall of Fame. In 2014 the "Golden Era Committee" came up one vote short of inducting Oliva into the Hall of Fame. Oliva responded, "The Hall of Fame is not fair. For some people, it's beautiful. For a lot of people, it's not fair."[64] Oliva knows all too well the capricious nature of fairness; because baseball is a game of statistics, it is too easy to forget the social environment that affects how players perform. In order to play baseball in the United States, Oliva endured the loss of his homeland, decades of unequal treatment, a drastic shift in his personal identity, and multiple surgeries on his body. Despite these challenges, he was perhaps the most productive member of the Minnesota Twins from 1964–1971, putting up numbers comparable to many existing Hall of Fame players while at the same time leading the Minnesota Twins from national laughing stock to perennial contender for the championship. As of 2019 the Hall of Fame's Golden Era Committee has not voted Oliva into the Hall.

## Conclusion

As the Griffith family claimed cheap Cuban talent for their baseball team, it set into motion a series of events that played into greater Cold War tensions over American influence in Cuba. At the middle of these events—both topically and chronologically—the man born as Pedro Oliva began his storied career as one of the first black Cuban migrants to America in the post-Batista era. Tony Oliva's familiar narrative of endurance and success exemplifies a shift in both world politics and locus of control for baseball in the Western Hemisphere where Organized Baseball monopolized the paths by which a man—regardless of his race—could play baseball. The Cuban government's counterresponse to Organized Baseball's regular intervention in the Cuban leagues prevented ethnic Cubans from following a similar career path in America. It is in this way that a Minnesota-based sports business managed to affect global migration and shape the Cold War policy with long-term ramifications for how athletes operated.

## CHAPTER TWELVE

# Of King Tuts and Kewpies

## Professional Boxing in the Twin Cities

SCOTT WRIGHT

## Early Years

Boxing first achieved popularity in the Twin Cities in the 1880s and early 1890s. Well-known boxers like John L. Sullivan and Bob Fitzsimmons were featured on local fight cards, and several area boxers gained national reputations.[1]

The appearance of John L. Sullivan in 1883 in St. Paul gives a good sense of the popularity of the sport at the time, especially in a city that, unlike its neighbor to the west, was an Irish town. Sullivan was at the peak of his fame, having won the heavyweight championship five years earlier, and his appearance in St. Paul was as much that of a celebrity as it was of a professional boxer. The *St. Paul Daily Globe* described his appearance the morning following the event in a column and a half of small, tightly packed print (newspaper layouts in those days contained almost no white space, photo reproduction was not yet possible, and the front page had no banner headlines). The account, which was the lead article on page two, was titled "The Maulers," and reported that people began entering Market Hall at about seven o'clock in the evening, and within an hour a capacity crowd of 1,500 had arrived. The article makes particular note of the fact that "there was not visible a single lady" in the crowd, indicating that boxing was primarily a male form of entertainment at that time. Following a preliminary bout, it was announced that Sullivan would now "appear in a set-to with Morris Hafey, of St. Paul, who was anxious to stand up with the champion and test his nerve and wind." In return for this exhibition, Hafey would receive $500 "if he

DOI: https://doi.org/10.34053/scs2019.tcs.12

was not knocked out by the end of the fourth round." The two men then came forward, and the champion "looked superb, having massive and symmetrical proportions, the easy grace and supple carriage of a gladiator." He was "stripped to the waist, his limbs clad in pink tights, white stockings and gaiters." As the bout began, Hafey was sent to the floor by Sullivan's first punch, got up, and was then sent down a second time. At this point the champion himself stopped the bout, which lasted no more than "fifteen or twenty seconds." Later Sullivan engaged in two exhibitions with somewhat more competent opponents and the evening ended—or in the colorful newspaper language of the day, "the jig was up"—at 9:30 p.m.[2]

Despite the infancy of the sport in the Twin Cities, several local fighters managed to gain national prominence during this period. Two of the best were Danny Needham of St. Paul and Harris Martin of Minneapolis. Needham, who campaigned as both a lightweight and welterweight, fought in one of the longest fights on record—a one-hundred-round, seven-hour draw against Patsy Kerrigan in San Francisco in 1890—and held both the Lightweight Championship of the Northwest and the Welterweight Championship of America during his thirteen-year boxing career. [3] Martin, an African American boxer who fought under the nickname "The Black Pearl," was born in Pennsylvania but fought out of Minneapolis during his boxing years. Although he was considered one of the best middleweights of the period, he was never given a chance to fight for the world championship due to the racial attitudes of the time.[4] He did, however, win the Colored Middleweight Championship of the World, defeating Frank Taylor, known as "Black Frank," in a bout in Minneapolis in 1887.[5]

Boxing was under fire in those days for its brutality and lethality. In 1892 a significant change occurred on the local boxing scene when, following a controversy the previous year between then governor William R. Merriam and a group attempting to promote a match in St. Paul featuring world middleweight champion Bob Fitzsimmons, the Minnesota Legislature passed an anti-boxing law.[6] Under this legislation anyone participating in a boxing match in any manner—fighter, promoter, or referee—could be fined $10,000, sentenced to up to five years in prison, or both.[7] As a result, boxing became technically illegal in Minnesota for the next twenty-three years until the law was repealed in 1915.

Despite the prohibition, boxing continued to flourish in the Twin Cities and in numerous other places around the state on an underground basis. George A. Barton, who served for many years as executive sports editor of the *Minneapolis Tribune* and from 1942 to 1969 as chairman of the State Athletic Commission, which oversaw boxing, offers a colorful portrait of boxing during this illegal period in his autobiography, *My Lifetime in Sports* (1957). In his early years, Barton was an active participant in the sport, both as a fighter himself and as a manager and referee, and he relates how "illegal or 'sneak' fights were . . . held in small halls, gymnasiums and even barns [and] during the summer months . . . in wooded areas along the Mississippi and St. Croix rivers." Information on upcoming fights was spread largely "by word of mouth," but the fight results were covered in considerable detail in the daily papers. [8] Thus Barton's career as a budding journalist during this period found no conflict of interest with his participation in the matches themselves. The role of newspapers during this era is also shown by the fact that boxing records often indicate the winners and losers of bouts by what were called "newspaper decisions," since official judging of bouts did not exist on a regular basis as it does today.

During the early period of the sport—both legal and illegal—there were few clear-cut rules governing it. The length of fights was negotiable, lasting twenty or thirty rounds, compared to a maximum of twelve rounds today. Some fights were also "fights to the finish," or to the point where one of the fighters was unable to continue. The sport overall was extremely brutal, even by modern standards. Boxers generally wore two- or four-ounce gloves (as opposed to the ten- or twelve-ounce gloves used today) resulting in more physical damage to the opponent as well as a higher frequency of hand injuries. Referees seldom stopped fights, and there was no standing eight count as there is today after a fighter has been knocked down. Only the corner "throwing in the towel" would normally end a bout before a fighter had been rendered unconscious or the agreed-on number of rounds had been reached. It was not uncommon for one or even both participants to be taken to the hospital after a fight.[9]

By the second decade of the twentieth century, however, changes were taking place in the local boxing scene that would propel the Twin Cities to the forefront of the sport. The most important of these occurred in 1915 when the state legislature repealed the anti-boxing law.

## A Golden Age

At the time that the sport again gained legal status, there was a new generation of local boxers emerging, mostly from St. Paul, who were ready to take local interest in the sport to a whole new level. Given the early ethnic makeup of the two cities—St. Paul with a high percentage of Irish and German Catholics,

Minneapolis comprised more of Scandinavians of Lutheran background—these St. Paul boxers, not too surprisingly, had names like Gibbons, O'Dowd, Malone, and Miske. They not only stimulated local interest in the sport but also helped to gain for their home city a reputation as an important boxing center. Boxing remained highly popular in Minneapolis during this period but did not produce boxers of the caliber that St. Paul did.

Several of these St. Paul fighters fought in the middleweight (160-pound) weight class. The first star to appear was Mike Gibbons. Born in St. Paul on July 1, 1887, Gibbons began his boxing career in 1907 when the sport was still illegal. From 1910 to 1921, Gibbons faced the best in his weight class, remaining undefeated in 106 fights. His tremendous boxing skills gained him the name "The St. Paul Phantom." Unfortunately these skills also resulted in an unwillingness of any of the middleweight champions of the era to fight him, and for many years he was known as the "uncrowned champion."[10]

Gibbons finally got his chance to fight for the championship in 1919 against fellow St. Paul Irishman, Mike O'Dowd. Seven years younger than Gibbons, O'Dowd had won the world middleweight title two years earlier and had already defended it six times. The Gibbons-O'Dowd fight took place in the St. Paul Auditorium on November 21, 1919, and set both attendance and gate records.[11] As was frequently the practice at the time, the fight was scheduled as a "no-decision" bout, meaning that the title would only change hands if Gibbons could knock out the champion. The fight went the distance. O'Dowd's youth and aggressive style led most at ringside to view him as the winner. Although he never won the championship, Gibbons is usually ranked among the all-time greats of the middleweight division and as perhaps Minnesota's greatest fighter.

O'Dowd kept the middleweight title until 1920 but remained competitive until being challenged by another St. Paul great, Jock Malone, who KO'd him in one round in 1923. These three St. Paul middleweights—Gibbons, O'Dowd, and Malone—were clearly among the elite fighters of their generation.

Two other St. Paul boxers who made their mark on the sport during this period were Tommy Gibbons and Billy Miske. Gibbons, the younger brother (by four years) of Mike Gibbons was, like his brother, a very skilled boxer. Larger in size, he campaigned chiefly as a light heavyweight (175 pounds) and heavyweight. He is remembered for his epic battles with archrival Miske and with future middleweight champion Harry Greb,[12] as well as bouts with many of the top heavyweights of the period, including Jack Dempsey, Georges Carpentier, and Gene Tunney.

The bout with Dempsey remains one of the best-remembered sporting events of the period. Taking place in Shelby, Montana, on July 4, 1923, the bout drew national attention. Dempsey was in his prime as heavyweight champion and a greatly feared puncher, but Gibbons was able to use his boxing skills to go the full fifteen rounds without receiving serious damage. Dempsey kept his title, but adding to the notoriety of the event, his manager, Jack Kearns, absconded with the gate receipts immediately following the fight, bankrupting the town and leaving Gibbons with a mere $5,000 for training expenses. (He had been promised between $75,000 and $100,000 as his share of the gate.) Gibbons, however, was able to cash in on his marketability following the fight, landing a $50,000 vaudeville tour, which took away some of the sting of the Shelby debacle.[13] Following the end of his career, Gibbons went on to become Sheriff of Ramsey County,[14] a position he held for twenty-four years until his retirement in 1959.

Tommy Gibbon's chief rival on the local boxing scene was Billy Miske. Of German immigrant background, Miske was born in St. Paul on April 12, 1894, and began his boxing career in 1913. Fighting primarily as a light heavyweight and heavyweight, he took on the best of the era in the middleweight, light heavyweight, and heavyweight divisions. He split in four bouts with light heavyweight champion Battling Levinsky, defeating him twice by decisions before Levinsky won the title. Like Gibbons, Miske fought middleweight great Harry Greb several times. He was best known nationally, however, for his three bouts with Jack Dempsey, fighting to a draw in their first fight in 1918 and then losing twice, the third fight for the heavyweight title in 1920.

On the local scene, it was Miske's five-bout series with Gibbons that is best remembered. The two fought for the first time in Hudson, Wisconsin, in 1914 when boxing was still illegal in Minnesota; then in St. Paul in 1915; in Minneapolis in 1919; in New York's Madison Square Garden in 1922; and for the last time, in December of 1922, in St. Paul. Gibbons won three of the bouts by decision, Miske won once by disqualification, and they fought to one draw. Gibbons may have been the superior ring technician, but Miske's fighter's heart and indomitable will made all of the fights competitive.

Tragedy surrounded Miske's final fight. Shortly after his fourth bout with Battling Levinsky, in the summer of 1919, the boxer was diagnosed with Bright's disease, a serious kidney ailment that at the time was largely untreatable. Although strongly advised to retire from the ring, Miske continued to fight since it was the only way he knew to support his family. He continued

Jack Dempsey and St. Paul's Billy Miske prior to their first fight at the St. Paul Auditorium on May 3, 1918. This was fourteen months before Dempsey won the heavyweight title. The fight ended in what was known as a "newspaper draw." Also pictured is Twin Cities sportswriter and boxing referee, George A. Barton. Minnesota Historical Society.

to win the majority of his bouts, despite the toll the sport took on his body. After a fight in January of 1923, his condition worsened and he did not fight again until the end of the year. On November 7, 1924, he entered the ring for the last time. In desperate financial straits, he was determined to fight one last time to give his family a decent Christmas. He managed to knock out his opponent in the fourth round. With the money that he made from the fight (reported in the neighborhood of $2,400)[15] he gave his family the Christmas he had promised but died just a few days later, on New Year's Day, 1924, at the age of twenty-nine.[16] The story of his last fight gained Miske national attention and is still recalled today as a testament to the fighter's tremendous guts and heart.

Several other fighters from this period in Twin Cities' boxing were prominent on the national scene, among them St. Paul bantamweight Johnny Ertle.

Known as Kewpie because of his small stature (he stood just four foot eleven) and youthful appearance, he was the only other Minnesota boxer besides Mike O'Dowd to claim a world title during the 1910s. Beginning his career in 1913, when boxing was still illegal in Minnesota, he won the World Bantamweight (118-pound) championship from Kid Williams in 1915 in St. Paul and defended it numerous times before losing it to "Memphis" Pal Moore in 1918.

Finally, no discussion of the Twin Cities' Golden Age would be complete without the inclusion of the famous rivalry between two upper Midwest lightweights of the period—Billy Petrolle and Henry Tuttle. Of Italian immigrant background, Petrolle was born in Pennsylvania but later moved with his family to the northwestern Minnesota town of Dilworth. Since many of his early fights took place across the border in Fargo, he acquired the nickname *the Fargo Express*, although he never resided there and later considered Duluth, Minnesota, his home. Fighting as a lightweight, junior welterweight and welterweight, and managed by the great boxing impresario Jack Hurley, Petrolle soon became well established on the national boxing scene where he was considered one the best lightweights of the period.

In Twin Cities' boxing circles, however, Petrolle is best remembered for his six-bout series with another regional favorite, Henry Tuttle, better known as *King Tut* (a name Tuttle's manager gave him early in his boxing career, inspired no doubt by the discovery of King Tut's tomb in 1922). Although born in Wisconsin, Tuttle was headquartered for most of his career in Minneapolis where he enjoyed strong support. Tuttle and Petrolle met in the ring for the first time in St. Paul on August 2, 1927, with Tuttle losing by disqualification due to low blows. They fought again thirteen days later, also in St. Paul, this time with Petrolle winning by decision. In the years that followed, they fought four more times. Tuttle scored decision victories in Minneapolis in 1928 and in Detroit the following year, and the series ended in 1931 with Tuttle scoring a one-round knockout of Petrolle in a fight in St. Paul on February 2. Petrolle avenged that defeat with a fourth-round knockout of Tuttle in New York's Madison Square Garden three and a half weeks later. The bouts between Petrolle and Tuttle clearly constitute one of the great local rivalries. They also serve to highlight the fact that fighters fought far more frequently in those days than they do today and were not required to remain out of action for set periods following knockout losses.

As a final note on this period, it was during this time that the first "mixed race" boxing match took place in Minnesota. Although other states (New York and Michigan, for example) had lifted bans on such bouts, there was still a rule in Minnesota prohibiting them. Following a campaign led by a group that included a writer from a local African American newspaper, a district judge officially lifted the ban in April of 1923. The first mixed-race match occurred in Minneapolis in October. It featured Clem Johnson and "Tiny" Jim Herman. Johnson, who was born in Guyana but fought out of New Orleans (and ended his career with a less-than-spectacular fourteen wins, thirty losses, and three draws), lost by TKO in the eighth round. Herman, boxing out of Omaha, Nebraska, had a somewhat more impressive career record of forty-seven wins, thirty-one losses, and twelve draws. Both Johnson and Herman were heavy-weights, but the fact that they were allowed to fight each other had little over-all effect on the heavyweight division at the time. No black heavyweight was permitted to fight for the heavyweight championship in the years between Jack Johnson's loss of the title in 1915 and the arrival of Joe Louis on the scene in the mid-1930s.[17]

## The 1930s

By the 1930s boxing in the Twin Cities was declining, but there were still big fights as well as local and regional boxers who made their marks on the national boxing scene. Among these were heavyweights Charley Retzlaff, Art Lasky, and Lee Savold, and Jack Gibbons, who competed chiefly in the middleweight and light heavyweight divisions.

Born in North Dakota but living in Duluth during his boxing career, Retzlaff fought two future heavyweight champions, James Braddock and Joe Louis. Retzlaff entered the ring with Braddock in 1932, three years before Braddock became champion. Retzlaff won a split decision. The fight with Louis took place in 1936, just a year and a half before Louis won the title and one fight before Louis's devastating defeat at the hands of Max Schmeling in June 1936. The loss to Schmeling stood as the only loss on Louis's record at the time, and he would not lose again until 1950.[18] Thus, despite the forthcoming loss, he was just entering his prime at the time he fought Retzlaff.

The Retzlaff-Louis fight in Chicago provides a good example of the con-tinuing popularity of boxing in the Twin Cities at this time. Both the St. Paul and Minneapolis papers contained daily coverage of the final preparations the fighters were making for the bout. On the morning of January 16, the day before the fight, the *St. Paul Pioneer Press* ran an article with the headline: "Louis

Out to Win in a Hurry; 'No Use Fooling,' He Remarks." Below this, a smaller headline read: "Retzlaff Says Down in His Heart He Knows He Has What It Takes to Win."[19] The banner headline on the sports page the morning after the fight tells the rather predictable outcome: "LOUIS KAYOS RETSLAFF IN 1:25 OF FIRST."[20] Despite the loss, Retzlaff was a good enough boxer to get the fight. He ended his career four years later with a remarkable record of sixty-one victories, fifty-four coming by knockout, against only eight defeats and three draws.

Fighting at roughly the same time as Retzlaff, Art Lasky, who used Minneapolis as his home base for most of his boxing years, also fought two future heavyweight champions, losing decisions to Primo Carnera—"the Ambling Alp"—in St. Paul in 1932 and to James Braddock in Madison Square Garden in 1935.

The third member of the trio, St. Paul-based Lee Savold, arrived on the scene slightly later and competed, albeit in losing efforts, against such heavyweight greats as Billy Conn, Joe Louis, and Rocky Marciano.[21] He ended his amazing nineteen-year pro career in 1952 having scored one hundred victories, seventy-two by knockout, against thirty-eight losses and three draws.

Jack Gibbons, like his father (Mike) and uncle (Tommy), was an extremely gifted boxer. In his five-year boxing career (1932–1937), he won sixty-nine of his seventy-five fights and at his peak, in 1936–37, was ranked fourth among the world's middleweights and sixth among the light heavyweights. After his ring career, Gibbons was appointed to the Minnesota Boxing Commission, where he served from 1956 until 1975, and as executive secretary from 1965 to 1975.

With fighters of the caliber of Retzlaff, Lasky, Savold, and Gibbons active on the local scene, boxing in the Twin Cities continued at a high level during the years immediately preceding World War II. The Minneapolis Armory was the site of bouts featuring such famous fighters as Henry Armstrong and Sugar Ray Robinson.[22] Rocky Marciano refereed a Golden Gloves tournament there, and in 1959 World Heavyweight Champion Ingemar Johansson made an appearance at a National Basketball Association doubleheader featuring the Boston Celtics against the Philadelphia Warriors, a matchup of Hall of Fame centers Bill Russell and Wilt Chamberlain. Although Johansson did not fight, it was a big deal for the local Swedish population to see their champ. *Minneapolis Tribune* society columnist Barbara Flanagan gushed that "Ingemar Johansson is a double-helping of Swedish smorgasbord with shy blue eyes and dimple on his chin."[23]

## Post-World II Resurgence

Following the war a new group of fighters would emerge to recapture at least some of the glory of the Golden Age. On October 18, 1946, a nineteen-year old Irishman from St. Paul named Glen Flanagan made his boxing debut on a fight card in Minneapolis. In the bout, Flanagan, who had only recently been discharged from the navy, defeated Emmett Yanez of St. Paul in a four-round decision.[24] Reporting on the fight the following day, the *Minneapolis Tribune* noted that Flanagan "had his foe on the deck in every round" and the *St. Paul Pioneer Press* called it "one of the better preliminaries."[25] Flanagan eventually gained national prominence and was among the first group inducted into the Minnesota Boxing Hall of Fame in 2010. Glen and his younger brother, Del, also became key figures in the resurgence of boxing in the Twin Cities in the post-World War II era.

When Glen Flanagan fought professionally for the first time, boxing was much like it had been in the prewar era. The sport was popular in the Twin Cities, and both Minneapolis and St. Paul had frequent, often monthly, boxing cards. But very few of the great boxers of the earlier period were still active, and the war had kept many of the next generation from entering into and developing in the sport. Payment for preliminary level fighters was not high, ranging from $50 to $200 per fight (with one third going to the fighter's managers). By moving up to main event status, fighters could get as much as 25 percent of the gate, but the big money fights were less frequent than they had been earlier.

Following the Yanez fight, Glen Flanagan, fighting primarily on local fight cards, ran up a record of twenty-one wins against five losses. His first main event occurred on January 15, 1948, in St. Paul, against Minneapolis boxer, Norman Mastrian (later known for his role in the Carol Thompson murder case[26]). Flanagan easily defeated his less-skilled opponent and moved on to higher-level opposition. Fighting as a featherweight (126 pounds), he split two bouts in 1949 with another Minnesota Boxing Hall of Fame fighter, Jackie Graves from Austin, Minnesota, losing by decision in October of 1949 but knocking Graves out in a rematch a month later. During the years that followed, Glen fought many of the top fighters in both the featherweight and lightweight (135 pound) divisions. His only fight for a world title, however, ended in a loss by decision to Tommy Collins for the National Boxing Association World Featherweight title in 1952. Glen retired in 1960 with a record of 84–32–13 during his fourteen-year professional career.

While Glen's career in many ways resembled the pattern of the prewar era, that of his brother Del, two years younger, typifies more clearly the changes occurring in the sport in the postwar years. For one, Del benefited from top-level amateur experience that served to prepare him for his professional career. Fighting as a lightweight, Del won city and regional Golden Gloves titles in 1945 and 1946 and went to the national tournament as an alternate in 1946.[27] In April of the following year he fought for the first time as a pro, scoring a technical knockout in a four-round bout in St. Paul. A year later he won his first main event against Herman Mills, who the *St. Paul Pioneer Press* called "a worthy Chicago trial horse."[28] At this point Del was riding the crest of a twenty-two-fight winning streak, fourteen by knockout, and had gained a sizeable local following.

Another difference between the brothers also emerged at this time. Following his victory over Mastrian in January of 1948, Glen travelled to California for a series of fights. When he returned home later in the year, he jettisoned his manager and decided to take a shot at self-management, which proved only marginally successful. Del, on the other hand, in December of the same year, signed on with well-known East Coast fight manager Lou Viscusi, who appeared to have the connections and experience needed to move him along more smoothly in his career.

Into this mix too came the arrival of television and its impact on the sport. Boxing provided a good fit with the new medium. Its confined area of action made it easy to cover, especially with the early technology of TV, and its pacing—three-minute rounds broken up by one-minute rest periods—provided excellent opportunities for the placement of commercials. By the early 1950s, boxing cards were a mainstay of network TV, with CBS, NBC and the old DuMont networks all offering weekly boxing programs. Television offered a good way for fighters to gain national exposure, but it cut into attendance for local bouts.

While both Flanagans appeared on television, the medium generally worked better for Del. His superior managerial and promotional connections, and simply the fact that he was two years younger and had come on the scene a little later than his brother, put him in a better position to take advantage of the opportunities TV offered. It also led to Del's role in a series of big money fights that took place in the second half of the decade, which clearly marked a high point of the sport locally in the postwar era.

In 1957, under new manager Bernie Glickman of Chicago and fighting now as welterweight (147 pounds), Del embarked on a series of fights aimed at getting a shot at the world welterweight title.[29] In a series of fights promoted by Jack Raleigh, a Somerset, Wisconsin, restaurant owner, Flanagan first took on two local rivals—Jim Hegerle of St. Paul and Joe Schmolze of Minneapolis. Defeating Hegerle by decision in January and knocking out Schmolze in one round in February, he then fought nationally known West Coast welterweight Ramon Fuentes in March, winning a "one-sided decision."[30] These fights, all of which took place in St. Paul, were well advertised and promoted. Along with numerous newspaper articles in the period leading up to the fights, public workouts were held in the Ryan Hotel on Sixth and Robert Streets in St. Paul. The Fuentes fight drew a crowd of 6,953 and gate receipts of $27,478 and set up a match against former champion Kid Gavilan in April. Although Gavilan was somewhat past his prime (he had lost the welterweight title in 1954), the fight was another highly successful promotion, with Flanagan winning a unanimous decision and the fight setting a Twin City gate record of $43,653.[31]

Unfortunately, personal issues interrupted the road to a title shot when both Del and Glen were arrested on a disorderly conduct charge following an incident in Minneapolis in May 1957. The charge resulted in a workhouse sentence for Del and the loss of his number six rating by the National Boxing Association. When he returned to the ring in July against Gil Turner, he was overweight and lost by a unanimous decision. Although he continued to fight and defeat top-level fighters—scoring a nontitle victory over then welterweight champion Virgil Akins in September of 1958 and avenging his loss to Gil Turner two months later—he was never again in line for a title shot.[32] A disastrous one-round knockout loss to future middleweight champion Joey Giardello in June of 1959 effectively ended his status as a contender. He fought his last fight in June of 1964, retiring with an overall record of 105 wins (thirty-eight by knockout), twenty-two losses, and two draws.

At the same time that St. Paul promoter Jack Raleigh was building highly successful fight cards around Flanagan, his Mill City counterpart, Tony Stecher, was doing likewise with featherweight Jackie Graves. Graves, whom Glen Flanagan fought twice in 1949, also gained considerable prominence in the postwar era. Born in Austin, Minnesota, in 1922, Graves had a remarkable amateur record of 284 wins against only six losses and had won a national amateur championship in his weight class before turning pro in 1944. Stecher promoted his career from the beginning, with the vast majority of Graves's fights during his twelve-year pro career occurring in Minneapolis. Among his biggest fights were three fights with Glen Flanagan (the third in 1956 at the end of Graves's career), one with Del Flanagan (a knockout loss in 1950), and one against featherweight champion Willie Pep. The Pep fight, which took place in Minneapolis in July of 1946, drew a crowd of over nine thousand and a gate of $39,866 and was a seesaw battle with both Graves and Pep hitting the canvas before Pep finally prevailed by an eighth-round TKO.

Glen Flanagan, Del Flanagan, and Jackie Graves, all in their own ways, were key figures in Twin Cities' boxing after World War II. It was a time when boxing enjoyed tremendous popularity in both cities. In addition to the quality of the fighters themselves, boxing also flourished because of the work of colorful and dedicated local sportswriters, like Dick Cullen of the *Minneapolis Tribune* and Don Riley of the *St. Paul Pioneer Press*, who provided day-by-day coverage of the sport. Boxing was a mainstay of Riley's popular column, "The Eye Opener," and he also appeared on local TV promoting interest in the sport. In the late 1950's, local Twin Cities TV station WTCN (Channel 11), ran a weekly show called the "Ringside Roundtable," hosted by Hal Newell and featuring a panel that included Riley, former boxer Jack Gibbons, and boxing historian Bernie Slater. The show, which was sponsored by El Producto cigars, discussed boxing on both the local and national scenes.[33] Thus the local media kept public interest in the sport at a high level.

## The Twin Cities Fight Scene in the 1960s and '70s

With the arrival of major league baseball, football, and hockey to the Twin Cities in the 1960s, interest in boxing in the area began to decline.[34] During this period a number of fighters gained national prominence, but they fought less frequently on smaller fight cards, appearing instead in larger-scale shows at the Met Center in Bloomington, which had been built in 1967 primarily as a home for the Minnesota North Stars. Among the local fighters who gained prominence during this period were heavyweights Jim Beattie, Duane Bobick, and Scott LeDoux.

Born in 1942 in St. Paul, six-foot-six Jim Beattie won the St. Paul Golden Gloves Heavyweight title four times between 1959 and 1962 and the Northwest Golden Gloves Heavyweight title three of those years. After turning pro in 1962 and scoring knockout victories in his first two bouts, he signed on with Kid Galahad, Inc., a New York management group hoping to discover and groom a future heavyweight champion. Under the group's sponsorship, he moved to New York, received an apartment and a salary, and was given the opportunity to train at the famous Gleason's Gym. The years in New York saw Beattie win fifteen bouts, fourteen by knockout, and lose only three times. Two of the losses, however, were to another young fighter with title aspirations, James J. Woody. When the second fight to Woody ended in a TKO loss in 1965, the Galahad group lost interest in their protégé, and Beattie returned to Minnesota.

Under the management of former boxer Glen Flanagan and now appearing primarily in the Twin Cities, Beattie again established a winning record with many of his fights ending by knockout. In 1968, however, in a bout held at the Met Center, he lost by knockout to former title contender Buster Mathis. After another knockout loss in Las Vegas the same year, Beattie retired from the sport. Eight years later, at the age of thirty-four, he launched a comeback. Fighting chiefly in the Twin City area, he once again put together a string of victories before facing another local boxer on the rise, Scott LeDoux, in a bout also held at the Met Center in 1979. Shortly after losing by TKO to LeDoux (who was seven years younger), Beattie retired for good with a professional record of forty wins (thirty-two by knockout) in fifty fights. As a footnote to his boxing career, Beattie also made a brief appearance in the highly regarded 1970 movie *The Great White Hope* as the fictional character the Kid (based on heavyweight champion Jess Willard), who won the title from Jack Jefferson (based on Jack Johnson) at the film's end.

The second Minnesota heavyweight to gain national prominence during these years was Duane Bobick. Born in Bowlus, Minnesota, in 1950, Bobick also had an impressive amateur career, including a National Golden Gloves title and a gold medal in the 1971 Pan-American Games (where he scored a decision over the great Cuban amateur, Teofilio Stevenson). In 1972 he defeated future heavyweight champion Larry Holmes to make the US Olympic team, but lost early in the Olympic tournament in a rematch with Stevenson.

Bobick began his pro career in 1973. He won his first thirty-eight fights, thirty-two by knockout, before suffering a devastating first-round knockout to future WBC heavyweight champion Ken Norton in May of 1977.[35] He got back on track in the two years that followed, winning eleven times, all by knockout, with only one loss, before losing in February of 1979 (another first round knockout) to John Tate, who would briefly hold the WBA heavyweight title two years later. After losing again in July 1979, Bobick retired with an overall record of forty-eight wins in fifty-two fights, forty-two by knockout. During his six-year pro career he fought several times in high profile fights at the Met Center, including two wins over popular local fighter

Scott LeDoux, the third Minnesota heavyweight to gain national attention during this period.[36]

Born in Crosby-Ironton, Minnesota, in 1949, LeDoux, like Jim Beattie and Duane Bobbick, had considerable amateur success, winning Upper Midwest Heavyweight titles twice, in 1968 and 1973. He turned pro in 1974 under the direction of legendary Minneapolis trainer and manager "Papa" Joe Daszkiewicz. During the nine years that followed, LeDoux faced the best of the heavyweight division, including George Foreman, Leon Spinks, Ron Lyle, Ken Norton, Mike Weaver, Larry Holmes, and Greg Page—and in a five-round exhibition in 1977, Muhammad Ali. Losing in most of these bouts, LeDoux nonetheless always remained competitive.[37] Several of LeDoux's big fights took place at the Met Center, including his losing effort against Larry Holmes for the WBC Heavyweight title in 1980. The first of his two fights with Duane Bobick, both of which also took place at the Met Center, set a state attendance record of 13,789 that stands to this day. Among the other interesting moments in his career was the time, captured on national television, when an angry LeDoux accidentally knocked off fight announcer Howard Cosell's toupee in the aftermath of a highly disputed loss to fringe contender Johnny Boudreau.[38] LeDoux, who retired in 1983 with a record of thirty-three victories in fifty fights, will certainly be remembered as one of the state's most colorful boxers. He died prematurely of ALS in 2008 at the age of sixty-two.[39]

Along with heavyweights Beattie, Bobick, and LeDoux, several other Minnesota fighters in lighter-weight classes also attained national prominence during the 1970s. African American middleweight Doug Demmings of Minneapolis, whose pro career lasted from 1973 to 1983, fought many of the top middleweights of his era, including former Olympic champion Sugar Ray Seales, John Mugabi, and world title-holders Marvin Hagler and Alan Minter. Most of his biggest fights, however, took place out of the area.

Following a somewhat similar pattern was the career of junior middleweight Rafael Rodriguez, also of Minneapolis. Fighting between 1970 and 1983, Rodriguez amassed a record of twenty-eight wins and twenty-one losses, with most of the losses coming by close decisions outside of his home region. Among Rodriguez's best-remembered local fights were back-to-back victories in 1978 over aging local light heavyweight Pat O'Connor.

The careers of Demmings and Rodriguez serve to highlight the fact that the Twin Cities did not produce large numbers of top-level African American and Latino fighters over the years. Many of the great black and Latino boxers of their respective time periods fought there, but home-grown fighters of either group who attained success on the national scene were relatively few in number—due, one suspects, to the small population of both groups in the Twin Cities prior to the 1970s.[40]

Local light heavyweight Pat O'Connor was one of the most gifted of all the local boxers of the period, but he never achieved his full potential. After a promising amateur career that saw the Rochester, Minnesota, native winning a national Golden Gloves title at the age of sixteen, O'Connor fought his first professional fight the day after his eighteenth birthday, in 1968. He went on to win thirty-one fights without a loss before facing title contender Andy Kendall at the Met Center in September of 1972. A lethargic and unprepared O'Connor gave a weak performance, ending in a TKO loss in the seventh round. His career after that never regained its former glory. After losing twice to former North American Boxing Federation middleweight champion Denny Moyer in 1973 and the two losses to Rodriguez in 1978, O'Connor retired at the age of twenty-eight, remembered more for his great potential than for his actual achievements in the ring.

## Twin City Boxing in Recent Years

Although the Twin Cities in recent decades has continued to produce high-quality fighters, few have reached the level of earlier times. Among those who achieved national attention in recent years was African American light flyweight Will Grigsby. Standing only five foot four and fighting in one of boxing's lightest weight divisions (108 pounds), Grisby won Upper Midwest Golden titles in 1985, 1987, and 1988. After turning pro in November of 1988, he won his first professional title—the USBA flyweight title—in 1996. Two years later, in 1998, he won the vacant IBF World light flyweight title. After losing the title the following year, he regained it in 2005. Due to frequent layoffs and difficulties in finding opponents, Grigsby fought only twenty-two times in his nine-year boxing career. Still, he is considered to be one of Minnesota's best ring technicians and was inducted into the Minnesota Boxing Hall of Fame just three years after his retirement.

Unfortunately, given the declining local interest in the sport, Grigsby fought only three of his bouts in the Twin Cities, twice in Minneapolis and once in his hometown of St. Paul. Super lightweight Mike Evgen, whose fighting years extended from 1989 to 1997, fought locally more frequently. Hailing from the

Rice Street area of St. Paul, Evgen appeared several times early in his career at the Roy Wilkins Auditorium in St. Paul, and in the latter part of his career, at Treasure Island Casino in nearby Red Wing, Minnesota. He briefly held the IBO world super lightweight title and made two unsuccessful challenges for other world titles during the course of his eight-year pro career.

Since 2000 most Twin Cities boxers have either competed outside of the area or in small-scale local promotions, many of the latter at gambling casinos. Among those who achieved some degree of success were super welterweight Matt Vanda and super lightweight Jason Litzau, both of St. Paul, and super middleweight Anthony Bonsante of Minneapolis.

The rise of major league sports teams in baseball, football, hockey, and basketball has undoubtedly been a major cause for the declining interest in boxing in the Twin Cities in recent decades. It has led to the virtual disappearance of high-profile local fight cards. While boxing continues to takes place at area casinos, the promotions seldom involve boxers likely to be headed for top-level national competition. In addition, coverage of the sport—at either the local or national levels—has almost totally disappeared from area newspapers. Despite its glorious past, boxing in the Twin Cities does not seem to be headed for a revival in the foreseeable future.

## CHAPTER THIRTEEN

# "How 'Bout Dat, You Turkey Necks!"

## The Heyday of Twin Cities Pro Wrestling

### SHELDON ANDERSON AND BRAD LUNDELL

*First of all, I was a wrestling fan when I was young. Even when I figured out what wrestling was, I was still a fan.*

—*Film director John Carpenter*

It was no accident that the Twin Cities became one of the top pro wrestling franchises in the country after World War II. In the heyday of Twin City wrestling in the 1970s, one of the patsies—so-called jobbers—was "Sodbuster" Kenny Jay, a fitting nod to wrestling's deep Midwestern roots. The country's midsection is college wrestling's heartland. Oklahoma State has won thirty-four NCAA Division-I Wrestling Championships, Oklahoma seven, Iowa twenty-three, and Minnesota three. The Gophers' Minneapolis neighbor Augsburg College has captured eleven NCAA Division-III titles. College football is king in Oklahoma, but wrestling is a hallowed sport there too. And without any pro sports teams to contend with, Iowa wrestling has maintained its popularity. There are two college wrestling halls of fame, one in Stillwater, Oklahoma, and one in Waterloo, Iowa.

The melodramatic mayhem that is professional wrestling came of age during the Great Depression. Desperate Americans hungered for some fun, and they found it in Hollywood and sports. The advent of talkies in the late 1920s took the movies to the top of the entertainment business. Until the passage of the

DOI: https://doi.org/10.34053/scs2019.tcs.13

Hayes Film Code in 1934, movie stars could also titillate their audiences with suggestive dialogue and skimpy clothes.

Horse racing, baseball, and boxing were at the height of their popularity as well. Crowds flocked to see Seabiscuit and War Admiral, Babe Ruth and Lou Gehrig, and Joe Louis and Barney Ross. They followed their exploits on radio and in newspapers and newsreels.

Pro wrestling gained in popularity as a bridge between legitimate sport and the fantasy world of the cinema. In Europe and the Middle East, wrestling was viewed as one of the pure, classical Olympic sports of the ancients depicted on Grecian urns. The sport had a rural, lower-class character in frontier America, epitomized by the tales of Abraham Lincoln's grappling prowess. In contrast to the upper-crust lawn games of golf and tennis, wrestling was the lowest of the lowbrow sports—a macho, sweaty, bloody, down-and-dirty backyard brawl.

In the late nineteenth century, carnivals and circuses brought big burly "champions" to small towns to take on local challengers. Some wrestlers had learned the sport in Civil War camps. The informal barnstorming nature of wrestling was both chaotic and dangerous. Most of these so called "rough and tumble" matches were not rigged, and without standard rules, combatants were often injured and even killed.[1]

Around the turn of the twentieth century the catch-as-catch-can style began to dominate the pro wrestling scene. More consistent rules were developed and matches moved from open ground or wooden floors to padded, roped rings.[2] The rules of boxing had been standardized by then as well, and fight audiences increasingly turned to that sport. Boxing was appealing because of the knock-down and the knockout, with one fighter ending up flat on his back. Boxers such as Jack Johnson, Jim Jeffries, and Jack Dempsey became household names.

As boxing grew in popularity after World War I, the spectacle of two wrestlers grabbing, holding, and hugging lost its lure. Promoters transformed wrestling into a bawdy theater of colorful characters and phony plotlines. Promoters and wrestlers were not geniuses of casting or scriptwriting, but they knew how to tap into ethnic loyalties and hatreds, break gender norms, and feed on working class prejudices.

Frank Gotch from Humboldt, Iowa, was the last so-called legitimate heavyweight wrestling champion.[3] By the 1930s the enterprise became entirely "worked," the term for the phony theater that pitted the good guys against the bad guys, the "cleanies" versus the "meanies."[4] It was a familiar plotline from Greek tragedies to Western folklore. The wrestlers and promoters had a code word for keeping up the farce—*kayfabe*—a sort of oath of fealty to a secret society.[5] Noted sports journalist Frank Deford once cracked, "I believe that professional wrestling is clean and everything else in the world is fixed."[6] Old-time wrestlers got testy when asked about the fakery, protesting that they often got hurt. Today wrestlers and fans alike share the fiction, no holds barred. "Shooters" were technically proficient wrestlers who would actually use wrestling moves to pin their opponents or get them in a submission hold. Going off script was a sure way to run afoul of promoters and fellow grapplers.

The kingpin of Twin Cities' wrestling was Vern Gagne from Robbinsdale, a near northern suburb of Minneapolis. In the late 1940s, Gagne was a good football player and a better wrestler at the University of Minnesota, winning two national individual titles in 1948 and 1949. After an aborted attempt at pro football, Gagne went back to the wrestling ring. In those days, a top pro wrestler made more than an NFL player anyway.

Gagne was a proud man who was never completely comfortable with the bogus side of pro wrestling. Gagne fashioned himself after the great heavyweight champion Lou Thesz, the epitome of the good guy "scientific" wrestler who never resorted to dirty tactics unless the dastardly deeds of the opponent forced him to. Thesz declared, "I am a wrestler. Not a wrassler, not a clown. A wrestler."[7] Gagne's character confirmed in Minnesotans what they thought of themselves; nice, levelheaded, and fair. The "heels" were evil outsiders.

Gagne was determined to become a "world champion," but promoters with the National Wrestling Alliance (NWA) denied him the title. In the mid-1950s the US Justice Department investigated the organization for violating anti-trust laws. The NWA admitted no guilt but eventually did not stand in the way of other promoters starting regional franchises and agreed not to blackball free agent wrestlers.[8] In 1960 Gagne and promoter Wally Karbo established the American Wrestling Association (AWA). At first they gave the championship to Pat O'Connor, probably with an eye on the large Irish population in St. Paul. As the local favorite, however, Gagne soon took over the belt, and he was the face of the franchise for a quarter century. Just to keep up the charade that wrestling was competitive, Gagne periodically relinquished his title to the Crusher, Dick the Bruiser, or Maurice "Mad Dog" Vachon.

Television catapulted the fortunes of pro wrestling after World War II. The new medium needed cheap programming, and wrestling and boxing were ideal. One static camera could film the action, and the frequent breaks provided ample time for commercials. Wrestling became regular TV fare. Quebec native

VERNE GAGNE

Minneapolis Robbinsdale native Verne Gagne—a "scientific good guy"—was the ringleader of the glory days of Twin Cities professional wrestling. Minnesota Historical Society.

Paul "The Butcher" Vachon (Maurice's brother) recalled that when Canadians wanted to buy a TV in those days, "they said they were gonna get themselves a 'wrestling set.'"[9]

Every week at the high-brow Calhoun Beach Club in south Minneapolis, Gagne's AWA troupe filmed the "All-Star Wrestling" show on WTCN Channel

11. The Georgian Revival building first served as a hotel and athletic club for the upper crust, and from 1963 to 1972 it was a home for the elderly. One can only imagine the looks on the old folks' faces when they ran into the likes of "Hard-Boiled" Haggerty and Stan "Krusher" Kowalski.

The syndicated TV shows acted as a teaser for the big arena cards on the weekend; in the "squash" matches, the star pinned a patsy within minutes and used post-match interviews to stir up hatred for the arena foe. Wrestlers who could give an outrageous interview and build a phony rivalry were more valuable than those who could actually wrestle.

Wrestling fan Rich Renikoff remembers taking a bus with his Northeast Minneapolis buddies from Tony Jaros's joint to a TV match at Calhoun Beach, all wearing "Roger Kent for President" T-shirts in honor of the WTCN wrestling announcer. It was a memorable night because they witnessed one jobber beat another jobber (a rare matchup) when Kenny Jay beat George "Scrapiron" Gadaski with a "victory roll." That same night "Rock 'n Roll" Buck Zumoff smashed a boom box and the Crusher crushed one of his stogies. The fan took pieces of the boom box and the cigar on the bus back to Jaro's, along with a flattered Roger Kent and a keg of beer.[10]

Between the weekend arena shows, AWA wrestlers barnstormed the small towns like their predecessors had a century before. Taking place in school gymnasiums or civic auditoriums around the Upper Midwest, these road shows helped cement the popularity of the sport for fans who had only seen their favorite wrestlers on TV.

As independent contractors, wrestlers had to mold and remold their personas to draw fans. The heel might go to the rescue of the good guy and even become one himself. When some wrestlers lost their appeal on either side of the evil meter, they donned a mask to create a new, unknown, "mysterious" character. The AWA's Mr. M was the most famous of that lot. Dr. Bill Miller was a veterinarian who had earned nine athletic letters at Ohio State University, hardly an intimidating resume to bring into the ring. If none of these acts made money, the wrestler had to make like the end of a Western movie and get out of town, hopefully to make his fortune with a different wrestling franchise.

Ethnic stereotyping, bending gender roles, and class warfare were standard themes in creating rivalries and fodder for the dreaded death matches, cage bouts, and battle royals, in which ten or more wrestlers tried to throw each other out of the ring. It was like watching the extras in a Cecil B. DeMille film milling around at the back of a big battle scene, faking blows.

Wrestling borrowed from boxing in building audiences through ethnic identities. Ethnic groups often embraced these caricatures and rooted for their heroes to do them proud. African Americans were devastated when Max Schmeling knocked out Joe Louis in 1936 and overjoyed when he knocked out the German two years later. Irish fighters displayed their toughness and iron jaws, while Jewish fighters were supposedly scientific and sneaky, "jabbing, feinting, blocking, and sidestepping punches." Some in the fight game denigrated this as a "cowardly enterprise," so several Jewish fighters took Irish names to confirm their rugged, pugnacious bona fides. When Jewish fighters such as Battling Levinsky, Benny Leonard, and Ross beat all comers, some Irish fighters adopted Jewish names.[11]

Gagne and local wrestling promoters could not leverage his French heritage to build a fan base. The French were a small minority in the Twin Cities, although three main downtown Minneapolis avenues pay homage to French explorers Father Antoine Hennepin, Robert de La Salle, and Joseph Nicollet. Gagne did work up a routine as a hot-tempered Latin whose fuse was short and his revenge *brutale*.

For many years Gagne's foil was the French-Canadian Mad Dog Vachon, whom Gagne had met at amateur wrestling competitions. Mad Dog was the antithesis of what Gagne brought to the ring; Vachon was ill-tempered, inarticulate, and "unscientific." At the bell Mad Dog would rush across the ring to rain down blows on an opponent's head. His matches bore no resemblance to a real wrestling match, a sham that Gagne pitched to his fans. In interviews, Mad Dog would get rabid, foaming at the mouth and spitting at the poor guy holding the mike. Mad Dog liked to bite his opponents, which for gullible young fans begged the question: did the bitee have to go to the hospital for a painful round of anti-rabies shots? Mad Dog and his brother Paul the Butcher were among the AWA's top tag-team attractions.

Pro wrestling in those days was a gory spectacle. Some wrestlers concealed a small shard of a razor blade to cut their foreheads, producing a gush of blood into the eyes and face. It did no permanent damage, but it lent credence to the notion that wrestling was "really real!" The Crusher and Mad Dog had no qualms about "getting color," as the wrestlers put it. One photo of the bloody twosome could have come out of a Sam Peckinpah movie.

The AWA played to two big ethnic communities in Minneapolis, Native Americans in the Phillips neighborhood and Poles in Northeast. At the height of the AWA's popularity in the 1960s and 1970s Minneapolis had one of the largest urban Native American populations in the country. The American Indian Movement (AIM), the most militant advocate of Red Power, was based in Minneapolis. As the civil rights movement grew in the 1960s, wrestling promoters were reluctant to adopt Hollywood's portrayal of cowboys in white hats fighting wild Indians. Native Americans such as Billy Red Cloud (Bill Wright) and Gene "Wahoo" McDaniel were almost always good guys, fighting tough hombres like "Black Jack" Lanza and "Black Jack" Mulligan, big bad outlaws in black hats.

Pro wrestling was most popular in Northeast Minneapolis, an enclave of Polish-Americans on the east side of the Mississippi River. The devout Catholic Poles there have more in common with the "ethnic" Irish and Italians in St. Paul than with the Protestant Nordics on the west side of the river. Several wrestlers were beloved in "Nordeast." Bronco Nagurski starred for the Gophers in the 1920s, helping Minnesota win the 1927 Big Ten football championship. In 1933 Nagurski debuted on a pro wrestling card in Minneapolis, and local promoter Tony Stecher gave him the National Wrestling Association title in 1937.[12] Stan Mayslack also came on the wrestling scene in the 1930s, but he become more famous after the war for his restaurant; for over sixty years Twin Citians have happily clogged their arteries with Mayslack's signature four-inch-high roast beef sandwiches.

The favorite wrestler in Nordeast was Reggie Lisowski from Milwaukee, known in the ring as "The Crusher." As a dim-witted, beer-guzzling, inarticulate tough guy, he played up every Polish stereotype. Weight training, he said, was lugging around beer kegs. He punched up his interviews with a gravelly "How 'bout dat!" Chomping on a big cigar, the Crusher bragged that after he finished off some "turkey neck," he was going up to Nordeast for some beers and "dollies." The Crusher could barely keep a straight face. He was so funny in interviews that he went from being one of Gagne's most hated rivals to a good guy, even inspiring the Novas' 1964 novelty song "The Crusher."

The cold war made for good wrestling storylines, especially for Polish Americans. In 1939 Adolph Hitler, in cahoots with Joseph Stalin, attacked and partitioned Poland. Germany's brutal five-year occupation of the country resulted in 6.5 million deaths, three million of which were Polish Jews. After defeating Germany at the end of the war, the Soviets installed Polish communists to head the new government in Warsaw. Instead of a free state, Poland got a Peoples' Republic. Polish Americans hated the Germans, but they loathed the Russians.

Promoters all over the country hired commie bad guys. Gagne had several "Russians" in his stable, including the brutal Bolshevik Nikita Koloff, whose real name was Nelson Scott Simpson, another Robbinsdale native. The Crusher and Dick the Bruiser fought for America against the "Soviet" Kalmikoff brothers, Ivan and Karol, who were really Edward Bogucki from Detroit, and Karol Piwoworczyk from Holyoke, Massachusetts. Both names are Polish. The Crusher called them the "Carmel Corn Brothers."

The Red Scare in the ring ended when Soviet Premier Mikhail Gorbachev decided to end the cold war. On a visit to the Twin Cities in June 1990, Gorbachev was met by cheering crowds holding up signs such as "We're with you, Gorby," and "Go Glasnost." The hated Russian was no more, so Koloff cleverly morphed into a good guy, tag teaming with Dusty Rhodes, also known as the "American Dream."[13]

The former Axis powers provided some villainous characters too. Wrestling fans probably did not know much about German history, but they could relate to hating guys with names like Otto von Krupp (after the steel company in Essen) and Fritz von Goering (after Hitler's rotund right hand man). It made no difference that West Germany and Japan were allies of the United States after World War II; the caricature of the German brute and the Japanese double-crosser was too juicy for wrestling promoters.

In the AWA the image of the rampaging Prussian-German Nazi was invoked by the goose-stepping, sadistic "Baron" von Raschke, who was really James Raschke from Omaha. Raschke was teaching middle school when he decided to join Gagne's troupe. The Baron got his signature move in the middle of a match with O'Connor in St. Louis. Caught in a headlock, O'Connor told the Baron to put "The Claw" on him, but the befuddled Baron had no idea what that was. O'Connor told him to put his hand on O'Connor's head like a faith healer and squash his brain into submission. Fritz von Erich of Texas wrestling fame was the first to use the hold. It was a perfect move for the German, who could threaten opponents by stomping around the ring holding up "The Claw" like a Nazi salute.[14]

Mitsu Arakawa was one of the many AWA wrestlers who personified the role of the supposedly sneaky, diabolical Japanese. After tossing some ceremonial salt over his shoulder—paying some kind of homage to sumo wrestling—Arakawa threw the rest of it in the eyes of innocent, unsuspecting opponent. Obviously the dirty double-cross was meant to invoke the surprise attack on Pearl Harbor. Ironically, Arakawa made his home in Hawaii. One of his tag-team partners, fellow Japanese bad guy Robert "Kinji" Shibuya, was born in Utah and raised in Los Angeles. Shibuya and other Japanese characters such as Mr. Fuji and Tor Kamata used the same "salt in the eyes" trick, portraying the pious and polite East Asian on the one hand, and a backstabbing, bloodthirsty inquisitor on the other. Mr. Fuji was really Harry Fujiwara, a Japanese American from Honolulu. Kamata's given name was MacRonald Kamaka. He was Hawaiian too, and even served in the air force.[15]

The Iranian hostage crisis in 1979 ushered in yet another ethnic bad guy— the Middle Eastern Muslim. Gagne enlisted Khosrow Vaziri to play the role of the Iron Sheik, and the former Billy White Wolf changed to Colonel Adnan El-Kaissie, who was actually Iraqi born. El-Kaissie claims to have gone to school with Iraqi dictator Saddam Hussein. Jerry Blackwell made a miraculous conversion to the Sheik Ayatollah Jerry Blackwell. Vaziri had been a talented amateur wrestler in Iran, competing in the 1968 Mexico City Olympics. When the United States went to war with Hussein in 1991, the Iron Sheik dropped that persona in favor of Iraqi Colonel Mustafa. Of course, the differences between Iran and Iraq, Persians and Arabs, and Shiites and Sunnis were lost on American wrestling fans. The Iron Sheik was the mortal ring enemy of American patriot Sergeant Slaughter (Eden Prairie, Minnesota High School graduate Robert Remus), who proclaimed that "we're going to clean up America. We don't want Iranians around, Russians invading us. We're going to clean up America of all this trash."[16] But in the early 1990s, the US sergeant teamed up with Colonel Adnan to form a particularly traitorous tag team.

Wrestlers also pandered to fans' gender prejudices. Gender roles were clearly prescribed in the 1950s. Television shows such as *The Adventures of Ozzie and Harriet* and *Father Knows Best* reinforced images of the dominant, allknowing father figure and the demure, domesticated housewife. Most wrestlers were the epitome of the macho working man—manual laborers with big muscles and small brains. One of their favorite jabs at another wrestler was "your mama pays me to go easy on you." Women wrestling fans loved these "real men." Their husbands probably had a hard time matching up.

In the 1940s George Wagner and his wife Betty developed a wrestling character that defied all gender norms; their "Gorgeous George" was an effeminate, pompous, arrogant sissy. Gorgeous dyed his hair platinum blonde, curled and pinned up his pretty locks, and pranced into the ring in a gaudy, baubly cape while his valet, Jeffries, sprayed disinfectant at the opponent. Hibbing, Minnesota, native Bob Zimmerman—soon to be Bob Dylan—met him in the

1950s: "[He was] a mighty spirit. Crossing paths with Gorgeous George was all the recognition I would need for years to come." A lot of acts were blowing in the wind of Gorgeous George. James Brown, the "Godfather of Soul," admitted that the wrestler had inspired his cape act, in which the exhausted singer would be draped by an assistant and miraculously come back to life.[17]

What an entertainer Gorgeous George was. Women loved his zany act, and playing to the rabidly homophobic temper of the time, men loathed him. His spiel was the height of narcissism and utter disdain for the average man—which was, of course, his main audience. Gorgeous George was the highest of high heels. He once told another wrestler, "Tell them how pretty you are, tell them how great you are. And a lot of people will pay to see somebody shut your big mouth." Muhammad Ali, the "Louisville Lip," learned his lessons from the great wrestler: "I saw fifteen thousand people comin' to see this man get beat. And his talking did it. I said this a gooood [sic] idea." Indeed, it was. In the 1950s Gorgeous George and New York Yankee star Joe DiMaggio were each making $100,000 a year.[18]

Georgeous George, also known as the "Human Orchid," spawned a long line of platinum-blonde, pretty-boy heels, including "Nature Boy" Buddy Rogers, "Luscious" Lars Anderson, and Gagne-trained Ric Flair from Edina, Minnesota. Flair billed himself as a "Nature Boy" too, perhaps a reference to an innocent, scantily clad Tarzan running around in the jungle. "Rowdy" Roddy Piper once said of Flair, "Oh, here he comes now, the Mae West of pro wrestling." In his role as the precocious, gender-bending Scot, Piper bragged that "real men wear kilts." When Luscious Lars's vanity act went sour, he changed his name back to Larry Heineimi so as not to be confused "with all of the stupid Swedes and Norwegians [in Minneapolis] named Anderson."[19]

The tag team of Larry "Pretty Boy" Hennig and "Handsome" Harley Race was a big AWA draw in the 1970s. The Crusher dubbed them the "Dolly Sisters." In one promotion Hennig and Race would have to wear dresses if they lost the match. These pitches in no way furthered gay rights, but they sold tickets.

The ethnic and pretty boy characters in pro wrestling banked on fans' fears of outsiders and norm breakers. America was in turmoil in the 1960s at the same time that wrestling was gaining popularity. Gagne and his fellow good guys were counted on to bring order back to an America racked by civil unrest. The times had changed, however, and stirring up ethnic animosities and anti-gay prejudices was no longer seen as a benign wrestling hustle. By the 1980s the ethnic angle was wearing off anyway. West Germans and Japanese had proven their democratic credentials and reliability as US allies, and Gorbachev changed the image of the dangerous Russian. Middle Easterners were the only ones left to play those roles, but second-tier powers like Iran and Iraq were not existential threats to the United States.

Playing up class differences seemed to be a less dangerous way to sell fights. Anti-intellectual, working class populism was a tried and true way to build ring rivalries. Boxing promoters had used this plot line for decades. In his fights against the rugged pug Jack Dempsey, the media billed Gene Tunney as the well-spoken East Coast intellectual who hung out with the likes of George Bernard Shaw. "Cinderella Man" Jim Braddock was the people's choice to beat Hollywood playboy Max Baer. Even Muhammad Ali played on subtle class differences in portraying hulking rivals Sonny Liston and Joe Frazier as "field hands," and then switching it up to cast Floyd Patterson as the Negro hope of the black (and white) middle class.

The average wrestling fan was not going to the Minnesota Orchestra on Friday and then to All-Star Wrestling on Saturday. The fans at the Minneapolis Auditorium were unlikely to rub shoulders with the refined Guthrie Theater set down the street, or dine with them at Nye's Polonaise Room in near northeast. Gagne tapped into the wrestling fans' odium for the arrogant, articulate sophisticate by elevating handsome, blonde-haired Nick Bockwinkel to the top of the organization. A former Oklahoma University football player, Bockwinkel billed himself as the "smartest wrestler alive." Bockwinkel was a pedantic, arrogant heel.

In 1981 Gagne announced that a title match against Bockwinkel at the St. Paul Civic Center would be his last. Still longing for legitimacy, Gagne invited some of his old Gopher football teammates, including the great Minnesota Vikings coach Bud Grant. Gagne orchestrated a farewell victory, and then handed the title to Bockwinkel.[20] Gagne embarrassed Grant when he came out of retirement, wrestling for several more years.

Giving Bockwinkel the title was a good business move for the AWA, because the glib pretty boy was a gifted raconteur. While the Crusher growled and grunted his way through an interview, Bockwinkel's erudite lectures demeaned his thick-headed opponents and delineated the cerebral methods he would use to defeat them. Bockwinkel ratcheted up the Mensa routine by bringing on manager Bobby "the Brain" Heenan, who like all ringside assistants shamelessly interfered in matches to assure a Bockwinkel win.

Heenan patterned himself after the two-timing manager and wrestler Lord Alfred Hayes. A blue-blooded heel was the perfect way to stir up class conflict. The highlight of Lord Hayes's AWA career was a "tuxedo match" with the Crusher, the champion of the common man. Whoever could de-pants the other would win the match. The image of the doofus Crusher in a dinner jacket evokes Louisiana Governor Earl Long's old joke that "a four hundred-dollar suit on him would look like socks on a rooster." The Crusher won the match, and in the end the Lord had no clothes.[21]

The wrestling audiences were supposed to despise the haughty know-it-all, but they came to appreciate Bockwinkel's showmanship. He turned good guy to fight for America against the cowardly sheiks and ayatollahs from the Middle East, the new US enemy in the post-cold war world. His bouts with Colonel Adnan El-Kaissie were bloody affairs. Gagne wrested another bad guy from promoter Vince McMahon's World Wrestling Federation (WWF)—the great Hulk Hogan—arguably the biggest box office draw in pro wrestling history.

McMahon was as ruthless in the business world as the wrestlers were supposed to be in the ring, and he exacted his revenge. After the anti-trust suits of the mid-1950s undercut the power of the National Wrestling Alliance, the AWA and other regional wrestling franchises had thrived on local and regional connections. Now McMahon sought to crush the competition by creating a new national enterprise. He lured Hogan back by giving him the WWF title. Another AWA draw, Jesse Ventura, bolted to the WWF as well. McMahon began scheduling shows in AWA territory, with Hogan and Ventura on the cards. Bockwinkel was aging, and new talent such as Gagne's son Greg and his "Highflyer" partner Jim Brunzell could not keep the organization afloat. Some wrestlers accused Vern Gagne of nepotism. The glory days were over.

The AWA folded in 1991, but the biggest story of Twin City wrestling was yet to come. Jim Janos grew up in south Minneapolis, and played football and swam at Minneapolis Roosevelt High School. After graduating he enlisted in the US Navy, where he served with an elite underwater demolition unit. Janos lifted weights fanatically and came out of the service a six-foot-four, 280-pound behemoth. Like Gagne, Janos wanted to be a football player, but he was too slow and plodding. After a disappointing gridiron stint at Normandale Junior College, Janos went into Gagne's stable.

Unlike Gagne a generation before, Jim Janos had no local crowd appeal, so he copied "Superstar" Billy Graham's colorful act and became the bleach blonde Jesse "The Body" Ventura from San Diego. While Bockwinkel and Lord

Alfred Hayes drew Midwesterners' ire as the slick intellectual and the privileged English don, Ventura featured himself as the super cool, muscle-bound southern California beach bum. He was good at it. His bad-boy schtick was to spew vitriol about the crappy Minnesota weather and the dumb Midwest hicks. Minnesota was flyover country. His belligerent anything goes "Hollywood" attitude flew in the face of Minnesota "nice" and the conservative family values of its humble, hardworking, persevering people. Few knew that he was a hometown boy himself.

Ventura retired from wrestling in 1986 and moved to Brooklyn Park, a northern suburb of Minneapolis. After several run-ins with the municipal government, in 1990 he ran for mayor and won. Eight years later Ventura launched an independent campaign for governor of Minnesota. Promising less government and lower taxes, the straight-talking Ventura made a populist appeal targeted at men, the less educated, and rural Minnesotans. His blustering, boastful campaign style differed little from his wrestling persona: "I'm big, I'm loud, and I'm not afraid to say what I think."[22]

Ventura's simple message to "get government off your back" worked. Winning only thirty-seven percent of the vote, he beat the weak Republican and Democratic candidates. Many voters chose Ventura never imagining that he would win. St. Cloud State University political science professor Stephen Frank quipped that young voters "for the most part regarded the election as a giant kegger."[23] As it became apparent on election night that victory was his, Ventura shouted to his followers, "We shocked the world!"[24]

Ventura muddled through four years of divided state government. His uncompromising bullying did not translate into effective governing. Ventura's major achievement was a light-rail line from downtown Minneapolis to the airport, which ran right through his old neighborhood. Frustrated that he could not beat the establishment and change Minnesota politics, Ventura stepped down after one term. His Reform Party became irrelevant.

By the end of Ventura's stint as governor, McMahon's WWF (now the WWE) had a choke hold on the pro wrestling business. The WWE has become a sordid soap opera with a relentless barrage of violence and crude sexual innuendo. McMahon even deigned to step over the line in ethnic stereotyping. One of his wrestlers made this comment about African American wrestler Sylvester Ritter, also known as the Junk Yard Dog: "Watch your wallet, don't turn your back on him, he grew up in the projects."[25] Many old-time wrestlers were disgusted with the X-rated show. "It's all about shock value," Baron von Raschke complained. "It's low class. . . . We had ethnic heels and heroes back then, but we never slurred anyone's nationality, and to be honest, I never remembered hearing a curse word."[26] Mad Dog Vachon, who regularly "colored up" to sell the real deal in the ring, called McMahon's product "a complete disgrace."[27]

McMahon and his family are regulars on the show. Theirs is not a *Leave it to Beaver* America. In one episode in the ring McMahon turned to his wife and WWE CEO Linda and announced that he was divorcing her.[28] The crowds yelled "bitch" at her. One study of fifty WWE "Raw" broadcasts found over 1,600 instances of crotch grabbing, over 150 times of giving the finger, and 128 simulated sex acts. "Suck it" is a favorite crowd chant. Some might wonder whether the puerile wrestling audience can distinguish between the real and the fantasy of sex and violence.[29]

In 2000 real estate mogul and reality TV star Donald Trump came to Minnesota to raise money for Ventura's Reform Party. Trump liked McMahon's phony wrestling show and began staging WWE matches at his hotels. With his outrageous dishwater blond coif and unrelenting braggadocio, Trump fashioned himself as the pretty boy wrestler, worthy of scorn. He took no offense at the WWE's misogyny and saw himself in McMahon's conceited histrionics. The wrestling promoter once told a jeering crowd, "I'm Vince McMahon. Hell, I'm a billionaire. . . . I could buy and sell every one of you in this arena tonight. . . . Shut up when I'm talkin'!"[30] In 2007 Trump began to appear on WWE shows. In one challenge Trump and McMahon agreed to shave their heads if their respective surrogate wrestler lost. McMahon lost his locks. President Trump showed his loyalty to the McMahons by naming Linda McMahon to head the Small Business Administration.

In 2009 nursing home patients Vern Gagne and ninety-seven-year old Helmut Gutmann came to blows. Both men suffered from dementia, but Gagne remembered some of his old wrestling moves and broke Gutmann's hip. The old man died from complications three weeks later. Police ruled it a homicide but prosecutors declined to charge Gagne, who could not recall anything about the incident.[31]

Some reports had Gagne killing Gutmann with a body slam. Like good pro wrestling theater, in the end the truth did not matter. The tragedy was pure black humor, and an ironic footnote to the colorful history of Twin City pro wrestling that Gagne and his buddies the Crusher, the Dolly Sisters, and Mad Dog Vachon helped write.

# Notes

## Introduction

1. Most of the movie takes place in the Twin Cities and the Brainerd area.

2. The Lakers and the Utah Jazz have the most oxymoronic nicknames in sports.

3. In 2018 the nonprofit Trust for Public Land named Minneapolis the best park system in the country for the sixth year in a row. St. Paul came in second.

4. *Star Tribune*, May 18, 2017.

5. Today the site is home to the Mall of America, the world's largest indoor shopping mall. The exact location of Metropolitan Stadium's home plate can be found on a marker inside the mall.

6. US Census, 1950, US Census Bureau, www.census.gov.

7. The Gopher women's hockey team has done much better recently, winning six national championships from 2004 to 2016.

## Chapter 1

1. When selecting the name for the new settlement, "Lowell" was a frontrunner because it honored another city with a great milling heritage: Lowell, Massachusetts. Ultimately, civic leaders believed that it was important to develop a new name for this new (to them) place. The Dakota word for water and the Greek word for city were combined to make Minneapolis. See Jocelyn Wills, *Boosters, Hustlers, and Speculators: Entrepreneurial Culture and the Rise of Minneapolis and St. Paul, 1849–1883* (St. Paul: Minnesota Historical Society Press, 2005), 129. Wills wrote that one early industrialist and booster in particular envisioned Minneapolis as a Lowell of the West, but with flour replacing textiles as the main product; and Warren Upham, *Minnesota Geographic Names: Their Origin and Historic Significance* (St. Paul: Minnesota Historical Society Press, 1969), 223.

2. Galen Cranz, *The Politics of Park Design: A History of Urban Parks in America* (Cambridge, MA: MIT Press, 1982), 5–8.

3. Daphne Spain, *How Women Saved the City* (Minneapolis: University of Minnesota Press, 2001), 24. Italics in the original.

4. For more Progressive Era reformers' connections of physical fitness and good character, see Dominick Cavallo, *Muscles and Morals: Organized Playgrounds and Urban Reform, 1880–1920* (Philadelphia: University of Pennsylvania Press, 1981).

5. Minneapolis Civic and Commercial Association, "Minneapolis, Where You are Always Welcome," Minnesota Historical Society Archives F613.M15 M58 1912z, cover, 21.

6. The 2013, 2014, 2015, and 2016 Parkscores from the Trust for Public Land has placed Minneapolis as number one in the United States. Their ranking system assesses the amount of land in public parks and the quality of that land. In 2016 Minneapolis received a score of 86.5 out of 100; St. Paul came in at number two with a score of 82.5. "Parkscore," The Trust

for Public Land, accessed January 20, 2017, http://parkscore.tpl.org/rankings.php; Kevin Duchschere, "Minneapolis, St. Paul Tie for Title of Best City Parks," *Star Tribune*, May 20, 2015; Alan Tate, *Great City Parks, Second Edition* (London: Routledge, 2015): 293–304; Alexander Garvin, *What Makes a Great City* (Washington, DC: Island Press, 2016), 230–36; and Aaron Rupar, "Mpls Unveils $400 Million Plan to Convert Star Tribune Land into Downtown's Biggest Park," *City Pages*, May 14, 2013.

7. Horace William Shaler Cleveland, *Landscape Architecture, as Applied to the Wants of the West: With an Essay on Forest Planting on the Great Plains* (Chicago: Jansen, McClurg, 1873), particularly chapter 4, "Advantages to be secured by timely forethought," 46–50. In fact, it was this 1873 text that coined the term "landscape architecture." Historian Norman T. Newton claims that Cleveland's *Landscape Architecture as Applied to the Wants of the West* was the first book to use the phrase, though Olmsted had included it in earlier pamphlets; and Norman T. Newton, *Design on the Land: The Development of Landscape Architecture* (Cambridge, MA: The Presidents and Fellows of Harvard College, 1971), 312.

8. Lance M. Neckar, "Fast-Tracking Culture and Landscape: Horace William Shaler Cleveland and the Garden in the Midwest," in *Regional Garden Design in the United States*, ed. Therese O'Malley and Marc Treib (Washington, DC: Dumbarton Oaks Research Library and Collection, 1995) 82–83.

9. In 1883 the state legislature created the Minneapolis park board and, despite lingering local opposition, the board immediately took an activist role. Composed of appointed men, it had the power to make special assessments and condemn or acquire land as it saw fit. After 1884 people were elected to hold seats on the park board and, for the most part, they have remained independent from the mayor's office or city council. *First Annual Report of the Board of Park Commissioners of the City of Minneapolis* (Minneapolis: Harrison & Smith, Printers, 1883), 3; and David C. Smith, *City of Parks: The Story of Minneapolis Parks* (Minneapolis: Foundation for Minneapolis Parks, 2008), 23.

10. Horace W. S. Cleveland, *Suggestions for a System of Parks and Parkways, for the City of Minneapolis* (Minneapolis: Johnson, Smith, & Harrison, 1883).

11. Shen Hou, *The City Natural: Garden and Forest Magazine and the Rise of American Environmentalism* (Pittsburgh: University of Pittsburgh Press, 2013), 188.

12. Cleveland focused on the Mississippi riverfront, and during his time engaged with Minneapolis, he consistently pushed civic leaders to preserve riverfront property so that it could eventually become park space. Cleveland, *Parks and Parkways*, 4, 6.

13. Newton, *Design on the Land*, 316. For a more detailed discussion of Cleveland's work on Como Park in St. Paul, see: Andrew J. Schmidt, "Pleasure and Recreation for the People: Planning St. Paul's Como Park," *Minnesota History* 58, no. 1 (Spring 2002): 40–58.

14. The sentiment is clear in many of Cleveland's writings, including: Horace William Shaler Cleveland, *Landscape Architecture, as Applied to the Wants of the West*; it can also be found in park board writings, such as the 1894 annual report of the Minneapolis park board in the President's Introduction, penned by Charles Loring: *Twelfth Annual Report of the Board of Park Commissioners of the City of Minneapolis* (Minneapolis: Harrison & Smith, Printers, 1893), 13.

15. Cranz, *Politics of Park Design*, 5–7, 63.

16. Cleveland, *Parks and Parkways*, 43–44.

17. *Twelfth Annual Report of the Board of Park Commissioners of the City of Minneapolis* (Minneapolis: Harrison & Smith, Printers, 1894), 1; *Fifteenth Annual Report of the Board of Park Commissioners of the City of Minneapolis* (Minneapolis: Harrison & Smith, Printers, 1897), 26–29.

18. *Thirteenth Annual Report of the Board of Park Commissioners of the City of Minneapolis* (Minneapolis: Harrison & Smith, Printers, 1895), 24.

19. For more on the growth of commercial amusements in this period that competed with what social reformers thought were more wholesome pursuits, such as spending time in parks, see: Lewis A. Erenberg, *Steppin' Out: New York Nightlife and the Transformation of American Culture* (Chicago: University of Chicago Press, 1984); Joanne Meyerowitz, *Women Adrift: Independent Wage Earners in Chicago, 1880–1930* (Chicago: University of Chicago Press, 1987); Kathy Peiss, *Cheap Amusements: Working Women and Leisure in Turn-of-the-Century New York* (Philadelphia: Temple University Press, 1986); Laurence Levine, *Highbrow Lowbrow* (Cambridge, MA: Harvard University Press, 1988); David Nasaw, *Going Out: The Rise and Fall of Public Amusements* (New York: Basic Books, 1993).

20. From 1892–1907 the park board operated the zoo. After then the zoo and nearly all of the animals moved outside of the park to a private zoo. Daniel Joseph Nadenicek, "Commemoration in the Landscape of Minnehaha: 'A Halo of Poetic Association,'" in *Places of Commemoration: Search for Identity and Landscape Design*, ed. Joachim Wolschke-Bulmahn (Washington, DC: Dumbarton Oaks Research Library and Collection, 2001), 72, 74.

21. Smith, *City of Parks*, 64.

22. *Sixteenth Annual Report of the Board of Park Commissioners of the City of Minneapolis* (Minneapolis: Harrison & Smith, Printers, 1898), 44.

23. *Sixteenth Annual Report of the Board of Park Commissioners of the City of Minneapolis* (Minneapolis: Harrison & Smith, Printers, 1898), 44. Smith, *City of Parks*, 99. St. Paul's Como Park, designed by Cleveland, developed a zoo in a similar manner to Minnehaha Park. Beginning with a few donations of animals, the zoo became a major attraction to the recreation park and pleasure ground. Unlike Minneapolis, St. Paul decided to keep the animals and during the 1930s, built large facilities to keep them and offered it as a free attraction for visitors. The Como Zoo continues to operate today; see Schmidt, "Pleasure and Recreation," 50.

24. Charles Loring, "With Apologies to Longfellow," *Minneapolis Journal*, May 17, 1904.

25. Nadenicek, "Landscape of Minnehaha," 74.

26. *Twelfth Annual Report of the Board of Park Commissioners of the City of Minneapolis* (Minneapolis: Johnson, Smith & Harrison, 1893), 3. For Loring the combination of beauty and practicality made Minnehaha an especially successful park.

27. *Ninth Annual Report of the Board of Park Commissioners of the City of Minneapolis* (Minneapolis: Johnson, Smith & Harrison, 1893), 4.

28. *Fifteenth Annual Report of the Board of Park Commissioners of the City of Minneapolis* (Minneapolis: Johnson, Smith & Harrison, 1897), 25. Cycling had emerged both as a sport and as a leisure activity in the 1870s, but by the 1890s cycling had become a favorite activity of middle-class women. Although there was debate over the appropriateness of women engaging in cycling, the activity became entwined with the all-American ideal Gibson Girl, "who participated in coed cycling, golf, tennis, and horseback riding." Steven A. Riess, *Sport in Industrial America, 1850–1920*, 2nd ed. (London: John Wiley & Sons), 42, 59.

29. *Sixteenth Annual Report of the Board of Park Commissioners of the City of Minneapolis* (Minneapolis: Johnson, Smith & Harrison, 1898), 44.

30. *Seventeenth Annual Report of the Board of Park Commissioners of the City of Minneapolis* (Minneapolis: Johnson, Smith & Harrison, 1899), 45–47.

31. Minneapolis Civic and Commercial Association, "Minneapolis, Where You are Always Welcome," 5.; Minneapolis Civic and Commerce Association, "Minneapolis," 1. Minnesota Historical Society Archives F613.M15 M514 1915, cover image. Nadenicek also discussed

Minnehaha as a "pilgrimage destination" for literary travelers in the late nineteenth century. He noted that this tourism waned into the early twentieth century, which coincided with the park board making increased interventions into Minnehaha's form; see Nadenicek, "Landscape of Minnehaha," 72.

32. Paula Lupkin, *Manhood Factories: YMCA Architecture and the Making of Modern Urban Culture* (Minneapolis: University of Minnesota Press, 2010), xx, xvi, 62.

33. Spain, *Women Saved the City*, 24.

34. Steven A. Riess, *Sports in North America: A Documentary History*. Vol. 6, *Sports in the Progressive Era, 1900–1920* (Gulf Breeze, FL: Academic International Press, 1998), xvi.

35. "Idea is Popular: Public Playground Movement Has a Good Start," unknown newspaper. Loring Scrapbook Collection, Box 1 Volume 1, 1871–1922, 61. Likely 1898. Folwell was a fervent believer in the importance of parks as public spaces. He co-wrote a treatise explaining the importance of parks in 1900, suggesting that the state should preserve parklands just as the city of Minneapolis had; see also: William Watts Folwell and Christopher W. Hall, "Minnesota Parks for Minnesota People," *Minneapolis Journal*, March 10, 1900. Minnesota Historical Society Archives SB482.M6 F54 1900.

36. "Idea is Popular: Public Playground Movement Has a Good Start," Loring Scrapbook Collection, Box 1 Volume 1, 1871–1922, 61.

37. "Dear Friend," mailer, July 13, 1899, Minnesota Historical Society Archives Loring Scrapbook Collection, Box 1 Volume 1, 1871–1922, 67.

38. "Dear Friend," Loring Scrapbook Collection, Box 1 Volume 1, 1871–1922, 67.

39. "Idea is Popular: Public Playground Movement Has a Good Start," Loring Scrapbook Collection, Box 1 Volume 1, 1871–1922, 61.

40. Robert E. Grese, *The Native Landscape Reader* (Amherst and Boston: University of Massachusetts Press in association with the Library of American Landscape History, 2011), 24; and see Richard E. Foglesong, *Planning the Capitalist City: The Colonial Era to the 1920s* (Princeton, NJ: Princeton University Press, 1968), 115.

41. David Dierdauer, "The Legacy of Theodore Wirth and How He Shaped the Minneapolis Park System," 2, 3, 8, Hennepin County Public Library. SB 482.M62 M647 2000 SCMC. 2, 3.

42. *Twenty-Fourth Annual Report of the Board of Park Commissioners of the City of Minneapolis* (Minneapolis: Harrison & Smith, Printers, 1906), 26.

43. *Twenty-Fifth Annual Report of the Board of Park Commissioners of the City of Minneapolis* (Minneapolis: Harrison & Smith, Printers, 1907), 37.

44. Cranz, *Politics of Park Design*, 63.

45. Burt Berlowe, et al., *Reflections in Loring Pond: A Minneapolis Neighborhood Examines its First Century* (Minneapolis: Citizens for a Loring Park Community), Hennepin County Central Library, 22. There were female recreation supervisors as well, but no description was found pertaining to their proper attire and appearance.

46. *Twenty-Seventh Annual Report of the Board of Park Commissioners of the City of Minneapolis* (Minneapolis: Harrison & Smith, Printers, 1909), 64.

47. Henrietta Jewett Keith, *Pipes O' Pan in a City Park: By a Daughter of Pan* (Minneapolis: Colwell Press, 1922), 57.

48. Smith, *City of Parks*, 128–35.

49. "Summary of Central District Report, 1919," Box 10, Folder 2. Minneapolis YWCA Collection, Social Welfare History Archives.

50. Minneapolis Civic and Commercial Association, "Minneapolis, Where You are Always Welcome," 21.

51. *First Annual Report of the Board of Park Commissioners of the City of Minneapolis* (Minneapolis: Harrison & Smith, Printers, 1884), 6.

52. David C. Smith, "Parks, Lakes, Trails and So Much More: An Overview of the Histories of MPRB Properties," (Minneapolis: Minneapolis Park and Recreation Board, 2008): 124–25.

53. Booth's call for gender-separated recreation facilities reflected national trends in recreation and reform theory at the time. *Twenty-Sixth Annual Report of the Board of Park Commissioners of the City of Minneapolis* (Minneapolis: Harrison & Smith, Printers, 1908), n.p. Special insert.

54. Smith, *City of Parks*, 127.

55. Smith, 127.

56. *Twenty-Sixth Annual Report of the Board of Park Commissioners of the City of Minneapolis* (Minneapolis: Harrison & Smith, Printers, 1908), 51. The playgrounds explicitly listed in that year's annual report were: Farview, Logan, Powderhorn Lake, North Commons, Jackson Square, Riverside, Minnehaha, Van Cleve, Elliot, Loring, Murphy Square, Stephens Square, and the Parade.

57. "Annual Report of Minneapolis Board of Park Commissioners 1908," 71, Hennepin County Public Library; Smith, "Parks, Lakes, Trails," 193–94.

58. "Annual Report of Minneapolis Board of Park Commissioners 1908," 71.

59. Cavallo, *Muscles and Morals*, 103.

60. Claude S. Fischer, "Changes in Leisure Activities, 1890–1940," *Journal of Social History* 27, no. 3 (Spring 1994): 453. See also: Carole O'Reilly, "'We Have Gone Recreation Mad': The Consumption of Leisure and Popular Entertainment in Municipal Public Parks in Early Twentieth Century Britain," *International Journal of Regional and Local History* 8, no. 2 (November 2013): 112–28.

61. Cavallo, *Muscles and Morals*, 102–4.

62. The Minneapolis Millers made their American Association baseball league debut in 1902. Games were especially popular entertainment as they could be attended by men, women, and children without social scorn, unlike theaters and dance halls; Rex Hamann, *The American Association Almanac: A Baseball History Journal: 1902–1952* (vol. 3, no. 1 September/October 2003), 9. On the professionalization of baseball and its relationship to social reform and urbanization, see Steven Riess, *City Games: The Evolution of American Urban Society and the Rise of Sports* (Champaign: University of Illinois Press, 1989). Kitten ball was the precursor to softball that was invented by Lewis Rober, a firefighter in Minneapolis, and debuted in 1895. It was a popular sport for men and women and was the only iteration of softball in Minneapolis until the 1930s. See also Smith, *City of Parks*, 133.

63. *The Success of Well Doing* (Minneapolis: Munsingwear Corporation, 1921), 39. Hennepin County History Museum Archives.

64. *The Success of Well Doing*, 39. Hennepin County History Museum Archives.

65. "Summary of Central District Report, 1919," Box 10, Folder 2, page 32. Minneapolis YWCA Collection, Social Welfare History Archives.

## Chapter 2

1. Sports journalists, ex-professional golfers, and devoted fans of the game all have tried their hand at being historians, but compared to other American sports, golf has drawn very little attention from the academic ranks. Books and articles fall into familiar categories: biography, origins of the game, legendary courses, and "great moments" of golf tournaments. For

the historian's survey and analysis, see George B. Kirsch, *The Rise of Golf in America* (Urbana: University of Illinois Press, 2013); Richard J. Moss, *The Kingdom of Golf in America* (Lincoln: University of Nebraska Press, 2009); and William W. Bremer's interpretive article, "Into the Grain: Golf's Ascent in American Culture," *Journal of American Culture* 4, no. 3 (1981): 120–32. Lane Demas, *Game of Privilege: An African American History of Golf* (Chapel Hill: University of North Carolina Press, 2017) is a recent, wide-ranging survey of race and golf.

2. Kirsch, *Rise of Golf*; and Moss, *Kingdom of Golf*.

3. Bremer, "Into the Grain," 121. Some readers may balk at extending the reasons why golf held such appeal and how it earned a place in the hearts and minds of Americans into this domain of historical perspective. However, sports historians have made such connections with good evidence and explication. For an example, consult Bremer's article. The concept of an American cultural imagination owes to University of Minnesota intellectual historian Professor David W. Noble.

4. Bremer, 121–22, 126.

5. Moss, *Kingdom of Golf*, xi.

6. For the founding and history of the Town & Country Club see Rick Shefchik, *From Fields to Fairways: Classic Golf Clubs of Minnesota* (Minneapolis: University of Minnesota Press, 2012); John A. Pfaender, *The First Hundred Years at the Town & Country Club* (St. Paul: Town & Country, 1988); Joel A. Rippel, *75 Memorable Moments in Minnesota Sports* (St. Paul: Minnesota Historical Society Press, 2003), 11; and Virginia L. Rahm, "The Nushka Club," *MHS Collections* 4 (Winter 1973): 303.

7. "The Town and Country Club of St. Paul," *Golf* 4, no. 1 (1899).

8. Kirsch, *Rise of Golf*, 13–17.

9. Joe Bissen, *Fore! Gone, Minnesota's Lost Golf Courses* (Boston, MA: Five Star Publishing, 2014), 90.

10. Shefchik, *From Fields to Fairways*; Rick Shefchik, "C.T. Jaffray: The Godfather of Minnesota Golf," *Minnesota Golfer* (Fall 2012): 26; David Smith, "The Mother of All Minneapolis Golf Courses: Bryn Mawr I, II," *Minneapolis Park History*, October 25, 2010, http://minneapolisparkhistory.com ; see Mary Lethert Wingerd, *Claiming the City: Politics, Faith, and the Power of Place In St. Paul* (Ithaca: Cornell University Press, 2001) for the possible motives other than convenience leading Minneapolis members to turn away from the Town and Country Club.

11. For a history of the Minikahda Club, see Shefchik's chapter in *From Fields to Fairways*, 23–50. Shefchik's book is a well-researched, interesting background on golf throughout the state. Bissen's, *Fore! Gone* is a worthwhile companion to Shefchik's work. Among the key Minikahda Club founders were Martin Koon, William C. Edgar, Walter Tiffany, and Harry Thayer.

12. William C. Edgar and Loring B. Staples, *The Minneapolis Club* (Minneapolis: Minneapolis Club, 1974), 5.

13. William Millikan, *A Union Against Unions: The Minneapolis Citizens Alliance and Its Fight Against Organized Labor, 1903–1947* (St. Paul: Minnesota Historical Society, 2001), 77.

14. David C. Smith, *City of Parks: The Story of Minneapolis Parks* (Minneapolis: The Foundation for Minneapolis Parks, 2008).

15. Businessman and country club member George A. Rhame as quoted in Shefchik, *From Fields to Fairways*, 213. Although never built, as early as 1903, plans for what would become Parade Park in Minneapolis included a public golf course.

16. Lincoln C. Cummings, "The Movement for Public Golf Links," *The American Golfer* 9 (1913): 488.

17. Andrew J. Schmidt, "Planning St. Paul's Como Park: Pleasure and Recreation for the People," *Minnesota History* 58, no. 1 (Spring 2002): 40–58.

18. Smith, *City of Parks*, 134–36. A quick look at matching names on the Minikahda Club membership lists and park board leadership reveals much about the background, rationales, and impetus for the municipal golf movement in Minneapolis. For municipal golf on the national level see George B. Kirsch, "Municipal Golf Courses in the United States: 1895–1930," *Journal of Sport History*, 32, no. 1 (Spring 2005): 23–44; and "Municipal Golf and Civil Rights in the United States, 1910–1965," *The Journal of African American History*, 92, no. 3 (2007): 371–92.

19. As quoted in Shefchik, *From Fields to Fairways*, 211.

20. Shefchik, *From Fields to Fairways*, 211.

21. "How to Build Your Municipal Golf Course," *American Golfer* 28 (April 4, 1925): 42, as cited in George B. Kirsch, "Municipal Golf Courses in the United States," 23–44.

22. Caspar W. Whitney, "Evolution of the Country Club," *Harper's New Monthly Magazine* 90 (December 1894): 16–33, in Steven Riess, ed., *Major Problems in American Sport History* (Stamford, CT: Cengage Learning, 2015), 178.

23. Norman Newhall, *The Minikahda Club, 1898–1998* (Minneapolis: The Club, 1998), 34–35.

24. Steven A. Reiss, "From Pitch to Putt: Sport and Class in Anglo-American Sport," *Journal of Sport History* 21, no. 2 (Summer 1994): 147–48; and Cindy L. Hines, "The Female Athlete in American Society, 1860–1940 (PhD diss., University of Pennsylvania, 1984), chapter 1.

25. Anne O'Hagan, "The Athletic Girl," *Munsey's Magazine* 25 (August 1901), 729–38.

26. As quoted in David L. Hudson, *Women in Golf: The Players, the History, and the Future of the Sport* (Westport, CT: Praeger, 2008), 120.

27. Anne O'Hagan, "Athletic Girl," 730.

28. Young-Quinlin apparently knew their customers had a wide-ranging vocabulary. *Minneapolis Morning Tribune*, June 6, 1916.

29. Kirsch, *Golf in America*, 17.

30. *Minneapolis Morning Tribune*, March 3, 1916.

31. *Minneapolis Morning Tribune*, March 3, 1913.

32. James E. Kelley, *Minnesota Golf: Ninety Years of Tournament History* (Edina, MN.: Minnesota Golf Association, 1991), 183.

33. "Colored People Talk of Organizing a Golf Club," *Minneapolis Tribune*, June 4, 1901, as discussed in David C. Smith, "First African-American Golfers in Minneapolis," *Minneapolis Park History*, October 29, 2010, http://minneapolisparkhistory.com.

34. Some physicians would turn away African-American patients, fearing the label of "black doctors." See Nancy J. Weiss, *Whitney Young, Jr. and the Struggle for Civil Rights* (Princeton, NJ: Princeton University Press, 1989), 38–47; Thomas E. Reinhart, *The Minneapolis Black Community, 1863–1926* (Collegeville, MN: St. John's University, 1970); David Vassar Taylor, *African Americans in Minnesota* (St. Paul: Minnesota Historical Society, 2002); Joseph B. Rosh, *Black Empowerment in 1960s Minneapolis: Promise, Politics, and the Impact of the National Urban Narrative* (master's thesis, St. Cloud State University, 2013); and Kirsten Delegard et al., *Research Guide To Minneapolis History: The Historyapolis Project* (Minneapolis: Augsburg College, 2014). This is an extensive, useful bibliography of sources, including a section on African Americans.

35. The TCGA, a group of African American golfers formed in the 1930s, requested "sanction and recognition" as an "official golf club" in August, 1951. Among several interesting aspects revealed by the hearing on the request was the TCGA's claim that "the whole problem is related to the ruling of the PGA barring Negro golfers from participating in PGA sanction tournaments."

36. *Minneapolis Star*, September 9, 1935.

37. *Afro-American News*, June 22, 1940.

38. This restriction would not be rescinded until 1961. For more background on the PGA's "Caucasion Only" clause and African American golfers in the Twin Cities, see Thomas B. Jones, "Caucasions Only: Solomon Hughes, the PGA, and the 1948 St. Paul Open Golf Tournament," *Minnesota History* 58 (Winter 2003–2004), 383–93; see also, Shefchik, *From Fields to Fairways*, 225–28.

39. Ball had moved to Chicago at age sixteen from Atlanta, where he had caddied for Bobby Jones as a youth. He won titles competing against white golfers in Chicago and Midwest tournaments and was a four-time winner of the United Golf Association's national championships of 1927, 1929, 1934, 1941. Among other accomplishments Ball became the first African American golf pro at Chicago's Palos Park public course. *The Chicago Defender*, May 13, 1939.

40. Pete McDaniel, *Uneven Lies: The Heroic Story of African-Americans in Golf* (Greenwich, CT: American Golfer, 2000), 51.

41. Joe Logan, "A Curious Episode Steers a Reputation Off Course at Cobbs Creek 80 Years Ago," http://articles.philly.com/2008-03-31/sports/25260300_1_black-golfers-usga-publinks. Ball was also a founding member of the United Golf Association (UGA). Perhaps as a result of his earlier protest, the United States Golf Association told Ball he was not invited to play in a 1933 Open tournament because of "his conduct" in the 1928 event. As a matter of ancestry, for those who follow such things, the USGA letter came from the organization's president, Prescott S. Bush. See Jimmie Williams, "U. S. Golf Body Bars Robert Ball: His Victory in Courts in 1928 Believed Cause," *Chicago Defender*, May 20, 1933.

42. "Smith Shoots 68 to Lead in St. Paul Open" *Chicago Daily Tribune*, July 14, 1934; and "Three Golfers Tie for St. Paul Title," *The New York Times*, July 16, 1934. For Horton Smith's resistance as PGA President see "On This Day in 1961: PGA Lifts Ban on Non-White Players," *Eurosport*, November 9, 2013, https://uk.sports.yahoo.com/blogs/bunker-mentality/day-1961-pga-lifts-ban-non-white-players-074304010.html.

43. Leo Bohannon, "In the Sport Light," *Minneapolis Spokesman*, August 17, 1934; and Jimmie Lee, "Golf Divots," May 15, 1936 and *Minneapolis Spokesman*, July 10, 1936.

44. Charles Hallman interview of Shirley Hughes in "Hastings tournament named for pioneering Black golfer," June 25, 2015, http://spokesman-recorder.com/2015/06/25/hastings-tournament-named-pioneering-black-golfer/.

45. Joyce A. Hughes, "Solomon Hughes, Sr." (unpublished manuscript, sent to author August 12, 2001). Jones, "Caucasians Only," 385.

46. Jones, 385–86; see also John H. Kennedy's account of the episode and legal issue in *A Course of Their Own: A History of African American Golfers* (Kansas City: Andrews McNeel, 2000).

47. Bessie Hughes, interview with author, August 2000.

48. *Minneapolis Spokesman*, August 13, 1948.

49. See issues of the *Minneapolis Spokesman*, August 13–14; Jones' "Caucasians Only," offers a more in-depth accounting of this aspect of the 1948 St. Paul Open.

50. Tom Crane to Ken C. Webb, reprinted in the *St. Paul Recorder*, July 27, 1951.

51. Calvin H. Sinette, *Forbidden Fairways: African Americans and the Game of Golf* (Chelsea, MI: Sleeping Bear press, 1998), 127.

52. This story of the San Diego Open is well told in a number of sources. For example, see Marvin P. Dawkins and Graham Kinloch, *African American Golfers During the Jim Crow Era* (Westport, CN: Praeger, 2000), Sinnette, *Forbidden Fairways*, John H. Kennedy, *A Course of Their Own: A History of African American Golfers* (Kansas City, MO: Andrews McNeel, 2000),

Al Barkow, *Golf's Golden Grind: The History of the Tour* (NY: Harcourt Brace Jovanovich, 1974); and Al Barkow, *Getting to the Dance Floor: An Oral History of American Golf* (NY: Atheneum, 1986).

53. *Minneapolis Spokesman*, July 4, 1952; *St. Paul Pioneer Press*, July 4–10, 1952; James Griffin, "Looking Back," *Insight News* (St. Paul), March 7–13, 1994; and Hallman, "Hastings Tournament," 3.

54. See Jason Gonzalez and Mike Kaszuba, "Golf in Minnesota hits tough times for players, courses," and "Shift in Course," *StarTribune.com*, August 18, 2014, http://www.startribune.com; Curtis Gilbert, "Skeptics greet St. Paul's effort to turn golf courses over to private management," *MPR News*, January 16, 2014, http://mprnews.org.

55. Bob Shaw, "The Brutal Metro Area Golf Market," *Twin Cities Pioneer Press*, March 29, 2016, http://www.twincities.com/2016/03/29/money-losing-metro-golf-courses-tee-up-a-tough-season/.

## Chapter 3

1. *Minneapolis Tribune*, April 28, 1959.
2. Carlton C. Qualey and Jon A. Gjerde, "The Norwegians," in *They Chose Minnesota: A Survey of the State's Ethnic Groups*, ed. June Drenning Holmquist (St. Paul: Minnesota Historical Society Press, 1981), 233.
3. Steven A. Reiss, *City Games: The Evolution of American Urban Society and the Rise of Sports* (Urbana: University of Illinois Press, 1989), 46; and Editorial Notes–Comments on Current Matters, *Putnam's Monthly* 9, no. 50 (February 1857), 112.
4. *Minneapolis Tribune*, December 16, 1868; *Minneapolis Daily Tribune*, November 7, 1873.
5. 1884 Minneapolis Board of Park Commissioners (BPC) Annual Report (Second Annual).
6. BPC Proceedings, December 5, 1885.
7. *Minneapolis Tribune*, February 3, 13, 15, 1884.
8. 1887 BPC Annual Report.
9. *Minneapolis Tribune*, Feb. 2, 13, 19, 1887.
10. *Minneapolis Tribune*, April 9, 1888.
11. *Minneapolis Tribune*, December 26, 1889.
12. *Minneapolis Tribune*, March 6 and 9, 1890.
13. *Minneapolis Tribune*, December 3, 1890, March 4, April 8 and May 3, 1891.
14. 1890 and 1891 BPC Annual Report.
15. *Minneapolis Tribune*, January 3, 1892.
16. *Minneapolis Tribune*, December 9, 1892.
17. *New York Times*, January 23, 1893.
18. *New York Times*, February 17, 1893.
19. *Minneapolis Tribune*, February 27, 1922.
20. R. Tait McKenzie, "The Anatomy of Speed Skating," *Appleton's Popular Science Monthly* 48 (December 1895): 188.
21. *Minneapolis Tribune*, January 10, 1896.
22. *New York Times*, February 12, 1923.
23. *St. Paul Daily Globe*, February 5, 1900.
24. 1902 BPC Proceedings, October 6, 1902; Dec. 7, 1903; February 6, 1905.
25. 1906 BPC Annual Report, Superintendent's Report.

26. Superintendent's Winter Recreation Report, Minneapolis Board of Park Commissioners, November 16, 1915.

27. *Minneapolis Tribune*, December 16, 24, 17, 1908; *Billboard*, December 26, 1908.

28. *New York Times*, January 10–11, 1937.

29. *Boston Daily Globe*, January 30, 1920.

30. *Minneapolis Morning Tribune*, February 21, 1920.

31. *Minneapolis Morning Tribune*, March 1, 1920.

32. *Minneapolis Morning Tribune*, March 2, 1920.

33. *Minneapolis Morning Tribune*, January 29, 1922; *Chicago Tribune*, February 17, 1922.

34. The Internet Hockey Database, accessed May 1, 2018, www.hockeydb.com.

35. *Minneapolis Tribune*, December 30, 1934.

36. *Preston Hollow Advocate*, January 1, 2007.

37. *Minneapolis Tribune*, February 28, 1929; Don Johnson, interview with author, September 4, 2014, notes in possession of author.

38. *New York Times*, January 25, 1932.

39. *Minneapolis Tribune*, January 20, 1936.

40. Records of Minneapolis Park and Recreation Board; Petitions and Communications Box 1, Folder 1931, Special Collections, Hennepin County Library.

41. Records of Minneapolis Park and Recreation Board; Playgrounds, Privileges and Entertainments Committee Box 3, Folder 1928, Special Collections, Hennepin County Library.

42. *New York Times*, October 14, 1935.

43. 1933 BPC Annual Report.

44. Records of Minneapolis Park and Recreation Board; Petitions and Communications Box 1, Folder 1933, Special Collections, Hennepin County Library.

45. 1934 BPC Annual Report.

46. *Minneapolis Tribune*, January 22, 1934.

47. *New York Times*, January 22, 1934; Louise Herou Scrapbook, Special Collections, Central Branch, Hennepin County Library.

48. *Minneapolis Star*, January 19, 1934.

49. *Minneapolis Star*, January 16, 1936.

50. *New York Times*, January 26, 1939; *Minneapolis Tribune*, January 16, 1947.

51. 1940 BPC Annual Report, Minneapolis Board of Park Commissioners.

52. Ann Kenne, "Tales from the Archives–Speed Skating at St. Thomas," University of St. Thomas Libraries Blog, https://blogs.stthomas.edu/libraries/2018/02/23/speed-skating-at-st-thomas; *Minneapolis Daily Times*, February 18, 1946.

53. 1948 BPC Annual Report.

54. *The American Legion Magazine*, September 1948.

55. *Minneapolis Star*, March 13, 1948.

56. *Minneapolis Star*, February 7, 1948.

57. *Minneapolis Tribune*, February 6, 1952.

## Chapter 4

1. John D. McCallum, *Big Ten Football Since 1895* (Radnor, PA: Chilton Book Co., 1976), 125.

2. Mike Wilkenson, *The Autumn Warrior: Murray Warmath's 65 Years in American Football* (Edina, MN: Burgess International Group, 1992), 160. The Rose Bowl's contract with the Big Ten and the Pacific Coast Conference had lapsed.

3. In the 1960s the Big Ten consisted of Minnesota, Wisconsin, Iowa, Michigan, Michigan State, Illinois, Northwestern, Purdue, Indiana, and Ohio State. More recent conference members are Penn State, Rutgers, Nebraska, and Maryland.

4. The University of Minnesota sits in the shadow of downtown Minneapolis. The Twin City area has a population of three million. Ohio State is in Columbus (metro area population 2.1 million), but unlike Minneapolis, the city has not had any of the major professional teams until recently (the NHL's Columbus Blue Jackets). And in Ohio, football is king. Northwestern University is in suburban Evanston—fifteen miles north of the Chicago loop. Northwestern is also the only private university in the Big Ten.

5. Steve Hunegs, "Ruminations on Gopher Football, Racism, WWII and Sandy Stephens from a Long-Suffering Fan," MINNPOST, November 23, 2011, accessed on May 30, 2019, https://www.minnpost.com/community-voices/2011/11/ruminations-gopher-football-racism-wwii-and-sandy-stephens-long-suffering-f/. There were other instances of teams holding out their black players. For example, two years later, Syracuse acceded to Maryland's demands not to field an African American player.

6. McCallum, *Big Ten Football*, 56.

7. "1934 National Champions," accessed on May 30, 2019, https://gophersports.com/sports/2018/5/21/sports-m-footbl-spec-rel-1934-champions-html.asp.

8. Stephen H. Norwood, "George Allen, Richard Nixon, and the Washington Redskins: The Drive to Win in an Era of Stalemate," in *DC Sports: The Nation's Capital at Play*, ed. Chris Elzey and Dave Wiggins (Fayetteville: University of Arkansas Press, 2015), 201.

9. *New York Times*, October 27, 2000.

10. Wilkenson, *Autumn Warrior*, 7

11. Wilkenson, 19.

12. S. Kaazim Naqvi, "O-H-I-O! Black Students, Black Athletes, and Ohio State Football, 1968–1976," *Journal of Sport History* 40, no.1 (Spring 2013): 115.

13. Ann M. Pflaum, interview with Sandy Stephens, May 3, 1999, University of Minnesota Library; and Fayette County Sports Hall of Fame, accessed April 24, 2017, http://www.fayettecountysportshalloffame.com/stephens.html.

14. Wilkenson, *Autumn Warrior*, 111.

15. Ann M. Pflaum, interview with Sandy Stephens.

16. Pflaum, interview with Sandy Stephens.

17. Fayette County Sports Hall of Fame, accessed April 24, 2017, www.fayettecountysportshalloffame.com/stephens.html.

18. Pflaum, interview with Sandy Stephens.

19. *Minneapolis Star Tribune*, May 14, 2015.

20. Wilkenson, *Autumn Warrior*, 22.

21. *Twin City Pioneer Press*, November 25, 2014.

22. *Twin City Pioneer Press*, November 25, 2014.

23. Wilkenson, *Autumn Warrior*, 341.

24. Charles H. Martin, *Benching Jim Crow: The Rise and Fall of the Color Line in Southern College Sports, 1890–1980* (Urbana: University of Illinois Press, 2010), 81.

25. John Sayle Watterson, *College Football History, Spectacle, Controversy* (Baltimore: John Hopkins University Press, 2000), 316–17; and Martin, *Benching Jim Crow*, 57.

26. Martin, *Benching Jim Crow*, 78.

27. Martin, 276, 278.

28. Kurt Edward Kemper, *College Football and American Culture in the Cold War Era* (Champaign: University of Illinois Press, 2009), 120.

29. McCallum, *Big Ten Football*, 87.

30. Wikenson, *Autumn Warrior*, 113.

31. *Minneapolis Star Tribune*, May 15, 2015.

32. Pflaum, interview with Sandy Stephens.

# Chapter 5

1. Jim Peltz, "Name that team: How major pro sports franchises came by their names," *Los Angeles Times*, December 14, 2013, http://articles.latimes.com/2013/dec/14/sports/la-sp-sports-nicknames-history-20131215/3.

2. David M. Krueger, *Myths of the Rune Stone: Viking Martyrs and the Birthplace of America* (Minneapolis, University of Minnesota Press, 2015), 5.

3. "Census-Bred Bitterness: St. Paul and Minneapolis have Locked Horns," *New York Times*, June 20, 1890.

4. Mary Wingerd, *Claiming the City: Politics, Faith, and the Power of Place in St. Paul.* (Ithaca, NY: Cornell University Press, 2001).

5. Jim Quirk, 'The Minneapolis Marines: Minnesota's Forgotten NFL Team," *The Coffin Corner* [Professional Football Researchers Association] 20, no. 1 (1998).

6. J. Thomas Jable, "The Birth of Professional Football: Pittsburgh Athletic Clubs Ring in Professionals in 1892," *Western Pennsylvania Historical Magazine* 62 (April 1979) 136–47.

7. "The Grim Reaper Smiles on the Goal Posts," *Cincinnati Commercial Tribune*. Dec. 3, 1905.

8. Steven R. Hoffbeck, "Bobby Marshall: Pioneering African American Athlete," *Minnesota History* (Winter 2004–05), 167.

9. Hoffbeck, 167.

10. Quirk, "Minneapolis Marines."

11. Quirk.

12. Hoffbeck, "Bobby Marshall," 167.

13. Chuck Frederick, *Leatherheads of the North* (Duluth, MN: Zenith City Press, 2007), 128.

14. Frederick, 36.

15. Frederick, 126.

16. Sid Hartman, *Sid Hartman's Great Minnesota Sports Moments* (St. Paul: MBI Publishing, 2006), 117.

17. Jim Bruton, *A Tradition of Purple: An Inside Look at the Minnesota Vikings* (New York: Skyhorse, 2011), 2.

18. Jeffrey T. Manuel and Andrew Urban, "'You Can't Legislate the Heart': Minneapolis Mayor Charles Stenvig and the Politics of Law and Order," *American Studies* (Fall/Winter 2008): 209.

19. Alan H. Levy, *Tackling Jim Crow: Racial Segregation in Professional Football* (Jefferson, NC: McFarland, 2003), 149.

20. Page Education Foundation, https://www.page-ed.org/.

21. Charles T. Clotfelter and Thomas Ehrlich, *Philanthropy and the Nonprofit Center* (Bloomington, IN: Indiana University Press, 1999), 294.

22. Amy Klobuchar, *Uncovering the Dome* (Long Grove, IL: Waveland Press, 1986), 25.

23. Brian Murphy, "Vikings: How Ex-GM Mike Lynn Made the Metrodome His Sugar Daddy," *St. Paul Pioneer Press*, June 22, 2012, http://www.twincities.com/2012/06/22/vikings -how-ex-gm-mike-lynn-made-the-metrodome-his-sugar-daddy/.

24. Brian Murphy, "Vikings lead the NFL—in Trouble," *St. Paul Pioneer Press*, July 13, 2012, http://www.twincities.com/2012/07/13/vikings-lead-the-nfl-in-trouble/.

25. Michael Silver, "Adrift on Lake Woebegone [sic]," *Sports Illustrated*, Oct. 24, 2005, https://www.si.com/vault/2005/10/24/8359371/adrift-on-lake-woebegone.

## Chapter 6

1. Jon Marthaler, "Soccer Insider: United FC to Salute Alan Willey, the 'Artful Dodger'" *Star Tribune* June 13, 2015, accessed July 10, 2016, http://www.startribune.com/united-fc-to -salute-alan-willey-the-artful-dodger/307236811/.

2. Cited in William P. Brenigan, *Early Minnesota Soccer History*, accessed July 29, 2016, http://homepages.sover.net/~spectrum/minnesota.html.

3. "Thistles. Vikings. Kicks. Kix: A Brief History of Soccer in Minnesota," *Special Collections: Hennepin County Library*, accessed July 11, 2016, http://hclib.tumblr.com/post/91071692065 /thistles-vikings-kicks-kix-a-brief-history-of.

4. "Retrospect: Celebrating the First Student from China," College of Science and Engineering: University of Minnesota, accessed August 3, 2016, https://cse.umn.edu/news -feature/retrospect-celebrating-the-first-students-from-china/.

5. Brian Quarstad, "Minnesota: A Rich Soccer History," *Fifty-Five-One: Voices from Soccer's North*, April 16, 2015, http://fiftyfive.one/2015/04/minnesota-rich-soccer-history/.

6. Patrick Reusse, "Reusse: Fans sure got their Kicks on the old Met's asphalt," *Star Tribune*, May 9, 2016, accessed July 10, 2016, http://www.startribune.com/fans-sure-got-their-kicks-on -the-met-s-asphalt/378595956/.

7. Ian Plenderleith, "NASL Soccer- The Rock 'N' Roll Years of the Minnesota Kicks," *St. Martin's Press: History Blog*, September 3, 2015, accessed July 12, 2016, http://www.thehistory reader.com/sports-history/nasl-soccer-the-rock-n-roll-years-of-the-minnesota-kicks/. The league folded in 1984 and a new version, the second-tier league in the United States, was reestablished in 2009.

8. Reusse, "Reusse."

9. Reusse.

10. Julian Shae, "The Best Player you Never Saw," BBC Sports, June 6, 2010, accessed July 14, 2016, http://news.bbc.co.uk/sport2/hi/football/world_cup_2010/8697346.stm.

11. Matthew Lane, "Throwback Thursday: Minnesota Kick's Alan Willey Scores Fives Goals Against Cosmos in Playoff Match," *NASL: It's Our Game*, June 30, 2015, accessed July 11, 2016, http://www.nasl.com/news/2015/07/30/throwback-thursday--minnesota-kicks-alan-willey -scores-five-goals-against-cosmos-in-playoff-match.

12. "Kicks Stun Cosmos," *Chicago Tribune*, August 15, 1978, accessed July 12, 2016, http:// archives.chicagotribune.com/1978/08/15/page/50/article/kicks-stun-cosmos-9–2.

13. Cited in "Briana Scurry: Against the Odds," *Famous Sports Stars*, accessed July 25, 2016, http://sports.jrank.org/pages/4329/Scurry-Briana-Against-Odds.html.

14. Caitlin Dewey, "Her Biggest Save," *The Washington Post*, November 2, 2013, accessed August 3, 2016, http://www.washingtonpost.com/sf/national/2013/11/02/her-biggest-save/.

15. Dewey, "Her Biggest Save."

16. Bill Dwyre, "Crossing the Line, *Los Angeles Times*, July 15, 1999, http://articles.latimes.com/1999/jul/15/sports/sp-56287.

17. For information on the Sons of Norway, its history and mission, see https://www.sofn.com/about_us/history/.

18. For more information on the Schwan's USA Cup see http://www.usacup.org/.

19. Interestingly, Buzz Lagos's assistant coach for the Blackhawks was Christian Akale, a graduate school friend of mine who established an intramural team for the History Department at the University of Minnesota. That got me playing the beautiful game. Soccer in the Twin Cities was an intimate community back then.

20. Karen Schneider, "Top Stars Coming out of Minnesota," *Minnesota Monthly*, May 2015, accessed July 12, 2016, http://www.minnesotamonthly.com/Lifestyle/People-Profiles/Kick-Start-Minnesota-Soccer-Stars-on-the-Cusp-of-Greatness/.

21. "Mukwalle Akale named in 21-roster for summer tournament with US U-20s," *SB Nation: Villareal*, accessed July 15, 2016, http://www.villarrealusa.com/2016/6/24/12027158/mukwelle-akale-named-in-21-player-roster-for-summer-tournament-with.

22. Schneider, "Top Stars." According to Schneider, "70,000 kids, state-wide signed up to play soccer in 2015; adult and youth hockey leagues had about 55,000 participants."

23. Frederick Melo, "Immigrant Populations Add to the Enthusiasm for St. Paul Soccer Stadium," *Twin Cities Pioneer Press*, August 3, 2015, accessed August 3, 2016, http://www.twincities.com/2015/08/03/immigrant-populations-add-to-enthusiasm-for-st-paul-soccer-stadium/.

24. Steve Brandt, "Less Baseball, More Field Sports for Minneapolis Neighborhood parks?" *Star Tribune* July 13, 2016, accessed July 16, 2016, http://www.startribune.com/less-baseball-more-field-sports-for-minneapolis-neighborhood-parks/386377461/.

## Chapter 7

1. Dan Truebenbach, "Edgerton: The Little Town that Could," City of Edgerton (website), accessed May 20, 2019, http://edgertonmn.com/events/basketball_legend.php.

2. Mark Steil, "Edgerton Remembers its Improbable 1960 Basketball Title," *Minneapolis Public Radio News*, March 26, 2010, https://www.mprnews.org/story/2010/03/26/edgerton-basketball-championship-50th.

3. Janice A. Beran, "Max J. Exner: Naismith's Roommate—Later Coach, Teacher and Public Health Physician," LA84 Olympic Foundation (website), accessed May 30, 2019, https://digital.la84.org/digital/collection/p17103coll10/id/11807/rec/19.

4. MSHSL 1968 High School Basketball Tournament Program.

5. "Williams Arena," University of Minnesota Golden Gophers (website), accessed May 30, 2019, http://www.gophersports.com/facilities/williams-arena.html.

6. Jim Byrne, "State Cage Tourney Ticket Demand Tops Supply by 10%," *Minneapolis Star*, February 2, 1956.

7. Jennifer Delton, "Labor, Politics, and African American Identity in Minneapolis, 1930–1950, *Minnesota History* (Winter 2001–2002), 420, accessed May 30, 2019, http://collections.mnhs.org/MNHistoryMagazine/articles/57/v57i08p418–434.pdf.

8. Marc Hugunin, "The Evolution of a Century of High School Basketball," Minnesota State High School League website, accessed May 30, 2019, https://www.mshsl.org/mshsl/Century_of_BoysBasketball.pdf.

9. *Minneapolis Star Tribune*, March 18, 1943.

10. See Randy Roberts, *'But They Can't Beat Us': Oscar Robertson and the Crispus Attucks Tigers* (Champaign, IL: Sports Publishing, 1999).

11. Kate Raddatz, "Minnesota Was the Birth Place of Intercollegiate Basketball," *CBS Minnesota*, March 16, 2017, accessed May 30, 2019, http://minnesota.cbslocal.com/2017/03/16/college-basketball-hamline.

12. Hugunin, "High School Basketball."

13. MSHSL 1971 High School Basketball Tournament Program.

14. Marc Huginin and Stew Thornley, *Minnesota Hoops: Basketball in the North Star State* (St. Paul: Minnesota Historical Society Press, 2006), 39, 41.

15. Hugunin, "High School Basketball;" and Huginin and Thornley, *Minnesota Hoops*, 43.

16. *Star Tribune*, March 4, 2014.

17. "Events and Discoveries," *Sports Illustrated*, February 22, 1960, accessed May 30, 2019, https://www.si.com/vault/1960/02/22/583743/events--discoveries.

18. Dan Truebenbach, "Little Town that Could."

19. Truebenbach.

20. Truebenbach.

21. Stiel, "Edgerton Remembers."

22. Truebenbach, "Little Town that Could."

23. Truebenbach.

24. Stiel, "Edgerton Remembers."

25. Truebenbach, "Little Town that Could."

26. Truebenbach.

27. Huginin and Thornley, *Minnesota Hoops*, 79.

28. Ross Bernstein, *Sixty Years and Sixty Heroes* (New Brighton, MN: Bernstein Books, 2008), 20.

29. MSHSL 1971 High School Basketball Tournament Program.

30. Sid Hartman, with Patrick Reusse, *Sid! The Sports Legends, the Inside Scoops, and the Close Personal Friends* (Stillwater, MN: Voyageur Press, 1997), 275.

31. Marc Hugunin, "Girls Making Up for Lost Time," Minnesota State High School League website, accessed May 30, 2019, https://www.mshsl.org/mshsl/GirlsBasketball_History.pdf.

32. Ellen Gerber, "The Controlled Development of Collegiate Sport for Women, 1923–1936," LA84 Olympic Foundation website, accessed May 20, 2019, http://library.la84.org/Sports Library/JSH/JSH1975/JSH0201/jsh0201b.

33. Huginin and Thornley, *Minnesota Hoops*, 39.

34. MSHSL 1967 High School Basketball Tournament Program.

35. Marian Benus Johnson and Dorothy E. McIntyre, *The First Era of Minnesota High School Basketball, 1891–1942* (Edina, MN: McJohn Publishing, 2005), xv.

36. Hugunin, "Lost Time."

37. *Austin Daily Herald*, April 3, 2018.

38. *Austin Daily Herald*, April 3, 2018.

39. Johnson and McIntyre, *Minnesota High School Basketball*, xv, xviii–xix.

40. Bernstein, *Sixty Years*, 72.

41. Hugunin, "Lost Time."

42. Hugunin.

43. *Star Tribune*, October 14, 2015.

44. *Star Tribune*, October 14, 2015.

45. Huginin and Thornley, *Minnesota Hoops*, 126.

46. Alan Schwarz, "Greatest College World Series Moments," *ESPN*, June 11, 2002, accessed May 30, 2019, http://a.espncdn.com/mlb/columns/schwarz_alan/1393596.html.

47. *Star Tribune*, March 3, 2016.

48. Jayne Solinger, "UConn Too Much for Gopher Women," April 5, 2004, *Minnesota Public Radio*, accessed May 30, 2019, http://news.minnesota.publicradio.org/features/2004/04/05_solingerj_gopherslose/.

49. *Star Tribune*, April 5, 2014.

50. *Star Tribune*, April 5, 2014.

51. Bernstein, *Sixty Years*, 9.

52. *Star Tribune*, October 5, 2017.

53. *Star Tribune*, October 5, 2017.

54. *Star Tribune*, May 8, 2018.

55. *Star Tribune*, April 14, 2018.

## Chapter 8

1. Carl Brookins, letter to the editor, *Star Tribune* (Minneapolis), Wednesday, November 11, 2015.

2. "Anti-Semitism in Minneapolis History," *Minnesota Public Radio*, October 18, 2017, https://www.mprnews.org/story/2017/10/18/anti_semitism_mpls_history.

3. Born in Ostrowiec, Poland, in 1897, Berger came to America at the age of sixteen. His parents and sisters stayed behind and eventually perished in Treblinka during the Holocaust. Berger built a theater empire and at one time owned as many as nineteen movie houses in Minnesota and neighboring states. He also operated Schiek's Cafe in downtown Minneapolis. After selling the Lakers, Berger became owner of the Minneapolis Millers of the International Hockey League, was a commissioner on the Minneapolis Park Board, and a founder and first president of Amicus, an organization that works with prisoners and helps ex-convicts to adjust to life outside of prison. Berger stayed active in civic affairs and philanthropic endeavors until his death at the age of ninety in 1988.

4. The author conducted the following interviews: Don "Swede" Carlson, August 21, 1988; Harold Gifford, October 26, 1988; Bud Grant, March 8, 1989; Sid Hartman, May 4, 1989; Tony Jaros, October 20, 1988; John Kundla, June 10, 1988; Bob "Slick" Leonard, January 8, 2010; George Mikan, June 7, 1988 and February 2, 1989; Vern Mikkelsen, May 10, 1988; Eva Olofson (widow of Vern Ullman), October 16, 1988; Jim Pollard, June 15, 1988; Dick Schnittker, March 3, 1989; and Don Smith (by correspondence), October 20, 1989.

5. The author consulted the following sources for this chapter: *Minneapolis Star*; *Minneapolis Tribune*; *New York Times*; *St. Paul Dispatch*; and *St. Paul Pioneer Press*; Stan W. Carlson, *The Minneapolis Lakers: World Champions of Professional Basketball* (Minneapolis: Olympic Press, 1950); Zander Hollander, ed., *The Modern Encyclopedia of Basketball* (Garden City, NY: Dolphin Books, 1979); Zander Hollander, ed., *The Pro Basketball Encyclopedia* (Los Angeles: Corwin Books, 1977); Leonard Koppett, *Championship NBA* (New York: Dial Press, 1970); Leonard Koppett, *24 Seconds to Shoot: An Informal History of the National Basketball Association* (New York: Macmillan, 1968); Robert K. Krishef, *Thank You, America: The Biography of Benjamin N. Berger* (Minneapolis: Dillon Press, 1982); and Carey McWilliams, "Minneapolis: The Curious Twin." *Common Ground* (Autumn 1946): 61–65.

6. Interview with Sid Hartman.

7. Sid Hartman with Patrick Reusse, *Sid: The Sports Legends, the Inside Scoops, and the Close Personal Friends* (Stillwater, MN: Voyageur Press, 1997), 69.

8. Bill McGrane, *Bud: The Other Side of the Glacier* (New York: Harper & Row, 1986).

9. Marc Huginin and Stew Thornley, *Minnesota Hoops: Basketball in the North Star State* (St. Paul: Minnesota Historical Society Press, 2006), 91.

10. Jim Pollard, interview with author, June 15, 1989.

11. Bud Grant, interview with the author, March 8, 1989.

12. Sid Hartman, "Lakers' Success Had Its Start Right Here," *Startribune*, December 10, 2015.

13. Sid Hartman, interview with the author, May 4, 1989.

14. John Kundla, interview with the author, June 10, 1988.

15. Vern Mikkelsen, interview with the author, May 10, 1988.

16. *Los Angeles Times*, 1971, cited in http://projects.latimes.com/lakers/player/elgin-baylor.

17. Huginin and Thornley, *Minnesota Hoops*, 101.

18. Vern Mikkelsen, interview with the author, May 10, 1988.

19. John Kundla, interview with the author, June 10, 1988.

20. Harold Gifford, interview with the author, October 26, 1988.

21. Stew Thornley, *Basketball's Original Dynasty: The History of the Lakers* (Minneapolis: Nodin Press, 1989).

22. Jim Pollard, interview with the author, June 15, 1989.

23. Eva Olofson, interview with the author, October 16, 1988.

24. *Minneapolis Star*, April 28, 1960.

## Chapter 9

1. E. M. Swift, "The Thrill of a Lifetime," *Sports Illustrated*, March 7, 1983, accessed May 31, 2019, https://www.si.com/vault/1983/03/07/628663/the-thrill-of-a-lifetime.

2. Swift.

3. *Star Tribune* (Minneapolis), February 6, 2004.

4. Ross Bernstein, *Frozen Memories: Celebrating a Century of Minnesota Hockey* (Minneapolis: Nodin Press, 1999), 134.

5. Gary L. Phillips, *Skate for Goal! Highlights from Minnesota's State Hockey Tournament* (Afton, MN: Afton Press, 1982), 4; *Star Tribune*, March 1, 1954.

6. Bernstein, *Frozen Memories*, 135; *Minneapolis Tribune*, March 1, 1954; and *Minneapolis Tribune*, February 28, 1960.

7. *New York Times*, March 9, 2014

8. *Minneapolis Tribune*, February 26, 1952.

9. *Minneapolis Tribune*, February 26, 1952; and *Minneapolis Tribune*, March 1, 1954.

10. British Columbia has a stick three feet longer, but it is bolted to the side of a building.

11. Ching Johnson and 1924 Olympian Taffy Abel became an imposing defensive presence for the Minneapolis Millers and subsequently the New York Rangers, when that team was formed in 1926.

12. *Star Tribune*, February 6, 2004.

13. Ross Bernstein, *More . . . Frozen Memories: Celebrating a Century of Minnesota Hockey* (Minneapolis: Nodin Press, 2007), 32.

14. *Minneapolis Tribune*, December 28, 1920.

15. *Minneapolis Tribune*, December 24, 1913, 11; and Bernstein, *Frozen Memories*, 29.

16. *Star Tribune*, February 4, 2004.

17. Swift, "Thrill of a Lifetime."

18. *Star Tribune*, February 4, 2004.

19. George Rekela, *A History of Professional Hockey in Minnesota: From the North Starts to the Wild* (Charleston, SC: History Press, 2014), 96.

20. Swift, "Thrill of a Lifetime."

21. Phillips, *Skate for Goal!*, 4. Ironically the first artificial ice rink in Minnesota was built in Eveleth, where kids already had a long winter of natural ice.

22. Swift, "Thrill of a Lifetime."

23. Swift.

24. Swift.

25. Swift.

26. US Census Bureau, Quick Facts, Edina, Minnesota, 2016, May 31, 2019, accesssd June 10, 2018, https://www.census.gov/quickfacts/fact/table/edinacityminnesota/PST045216.

27. Swift, "Thrill of a Lifetime."

28. *Brainerd Dispatch*, March 8, 2015.

29. Elizabeth Baier, "From Olympic to Amateur Rinks, Shattuck-St. Mary's Means Hockey," Minnesota Public Radio News, March 19, 2010, accessed June 15, 2018, https://www.mprnews.org/story/2010/03/18/shattuck-st-mary-hockey.

30. *Star Tribune*, February 20, 2014.

31. Bernstein, *Frozen Memories*, 17.

32. *Minneapolis Tribune*, January 8, 1924.

33. *Minneapolis Tribune*, January 24, 1924.

34. *Minneapolis Tribune*, January 26–February 4, 1924.

35. Bernstein, *Frozen Memories*, 158–59. Augsburg was an MIAC hockey power in the 1970s when Minneapolis South High graduate Ed Saugestad coached the team to a third-place finish in the 1971 NAIA championship. Augsburg won the MIAC title six years in a row from 1977 to 1982 and NAIA championships in 1978 and 1981. The Auggies run was aided by the building of an ice arena on campus in 1974. Some faculty were critical of President Oscar Anderson for this decision, but the arena, with two sheets of ice, became a money-maker for the college and increased its visibility in the Twin Cities. Indoor ice time was precious, and the arena was booked around the clock.

36. Nancy Dowd, the author of the novel on which the movie is based, was the sister of a minor-league hockey player who played on the Johnstown Jets with the three Carlson brothers, Iron Rangers from Virginia. Further confusing the story, however, is the fact that all three of the Carlsons—Jack, Steve, and Jeff—were to appear in the movie, but Jack was offered a contract with the Edmonton Oilers right before shooting began. Dave Hanson, a minor league journeyman, replaced Jack in the movie. Jack Carlson's pro career was short-lived, begging the question of how much in royalties he forewent from the movie, which has achieved cult status among cinephiles.

37. *New York Times*, January 15, 1928; and *Minneapolis Tribune*, February 14, 1928. Newspapers often mistakenly called the brothers the Hansons.

38. *New York Times*, January 15, 1928.

39. *Minneapolis Tribune*, January 20, 1928.

40. Bernstein, *Frozen Memories*, 37; and Seamus O'Coughlin, *Squaw Valley Gold: American Hockey's Olympic Odyssey* (Lincoln, NE: iUniverse, 2001), 67.

41. O'Coughlin, *Squaw Valley Gold*, 67.

42. *Minneapolis Tribune*, January 20, 1928.

43. *The Augsburgian* 1928, 89, cited in Phil Adamo, "The Hanson Brothers," unpublished paper, undated.

44. *Minneapolis Star*, December 11, 1931.

45. *Minneapolis Tribune*, December 20, 1931; and Minneapolis Tribune, December 30, 1931.

46. *Minneapolis Tribune*, January 5–15, 1932.

47. O'Coughlin, *Squaw Valley Gold*, 68.

48. Bernstein, *Frozen Memories*, 41.

49. *Minneapolis Tribune*, January 16, 1909.

50. *New York Times*, February 23, 2018.

51. Bernstein, *Frozen Memories*, 40.

52. Ross Bernstein, *Sixty Years and Sixty Heroes* (New Brighton, MN: Bernstein Books, 2008), 15, 26; and *Star Tribune*, February 6, 2004.

53. *Star Tribune*, February 6, 2004.

54. Bernstein, *Sixty Years*, 15.

55. Bernstein, 25.

56. Bernstein, 26.

# Chapter 10

1. The author conducted a series of interviews in 1987 to 1990 with Calvin Griffith, Griffith family members, and other Twins' employees. The author has also drawn on the *Washington Post*, the *Minneapolis Tribune*, and other newspapers and publications from the 1950s to 1980s.

2. The fictional Washington Senators' hero in the 1950s Broadway musical "Damn Yankees."

3. Calvin Griffith, interview with the author.

4. Griffith, interview.

5. Shirley Povich, interview with the author.

6. Griffith, interview. In 1987–88 the White Sox threatened to move if the city did not build a stadium to replace Comiskey Park, the oldest in the league.

7. Griffith, interview.

8. Griffith.

9. Griffith; for a discussion of baseball's expansion westward, see Benjamin G. Rader, *American Sports: From the Age of Folk Games to the Age of Televised Sports* (Upper Saddle River, NJ: Pearson, 2009), 231–33.

10. Griffith, interview.

11. Los Angeles Mayor Norris Poulson was instrumental in luring the Dodgers to California. See "Norris Poulson Reveals How Los Angeles Got the Brooklyn Dodgers in 1958," in *Major Problems in American Sports History*, ed. Steven A. Riess (Boston: Houghton Mifflin, 1997), 408–11.

12. Calvin Griffith, "Griffith Not Happy with Armory Stadium Site," *Washington Post*, January 17, 1958.

13. Griffith, interview.

14. Griffith.

15. Griffith.

16. Thelma Haynes, interview with the author. Griffith Stadium was about a mile and a half north of the National Mall near Howard University, a historically black college.

17. Griffith, interview.

18. Griffith.

19. Griffith.

20. Griffith.

21. Griffith.

22. Griffith.

23. Gerald Moore, interview with the author.

24. Griffith, interview.

25. Shirley Povich, interview with author.

26. Metropolitan Stadium was home to the Twins, the Minnesota Vikings, and the Minnesota Kicks. The Minnesota North Stars played in the adjacent Met Center.

27. Griffith, interview.

28. Griffith.

29. Jerold J. Duquette, *Regulating the National Pastime: Baseball and Antitrust* (Westport, CT: Greenwood Publishing, 1999), 51.

30. Griffith, interview.

31. Richard O. Davies, *Sports in American Life: A History* (Chicester, West Sussex: Wiley-Blackwell, 2012), 234.

32. Griffith, interview.

33. Wheelock Whitney, interview with the author.

34. Whitney.

35. Griffith, interview.

36. Griffith.

37. Griffith.

38. Jimmy Robertson, interview with the author.

39. Haynes, interview.

40. Whitney, interview.

41. Griffith, interview.

42. Povich, interview.

43. Griffith, interview.

44. Griffith.

45. Griffith.

46. Billy Robertson, interview with the author.

47. Haynes, interview.

48. Griffith, interview.

49. Griffith.

50. Griffith.

51. Griffith.

52. Griffith.

53. Billy Robertson, interview.

54. Tom Mee, interview with the author.

55. Natalie Griffith, interview with the author.

56. Calvin Griffith, interview.

57. Waseca is a town of about 9,500 people seventy miles south of Minneapolis.

58. Griffith, interview.

59. Ken Lenz, interview with the author.

60. Nick Coleman, interview with the author.

61. *Minneapolis Tribune,* September 29, 1978.
62. A reference to Alex Haley's main character in his 1976 novel *Roots.*
63. Griffith, interview.
64. Griffith.
65. Griffith.
66. Mee, interview.
67. Mee.
68. Griffith, interview.
69. Tony Oliva, interview with the author.
70. Charlie Daniels, interview with the author.
71. Haynes, interview.
72. Calvin Griffith, interview.
73. Griffith, interview.
74. Griffith.
75. Griffith.
76. Griffith.
77. Jimmy Robertson, interview.
78. Griffith, interview.
79. Griffith.
80. Povich, interview with the author.
81. Griffith, interview.

# Chapter 11

1. In this paper, the term *Organized Baseball* to refers to the entirety of major league baseball, which is the largest and longest-running professional baseball association in the United States. Whereas *major league baseball* refers specifically to the highest level of this baseball organization, *Organized Baseball* also includes affiliated minor leagues and developmental leagues within America and Cuba. *Organized Baseball* does not include collegiate leagues, independent leagues or, more pertinent to this paper, the Negro leagues and professional Cuban leagues. Historically, many writers refer to *Organized Baseball* in the shorthand as OB.

2. The 1960s Twins teams rostered about 25 percent of all Cuban talent in major league baseball. Statistics derived from Minnesota Twins rosters and place-of-birth searches on www.baseballreference.com. This search is only valid for Cuban players on the Minnesota Twins' major league roster, and the Minnesota Twins had many more Cubans in their minor league system who never made the major league roster. The largest producer of major league baseball players was, and continues to be, the United States.

3. Although there is variance in the date of Guilló's return to Havana, his journals clearly indicate that he was the first person to successfully disseminate baseball throughout Cuba. For more information, see Milton H. Jamail, *Full Count: Inside Cuban Baseball,* (Carbondale, IL: Southern Illinois University Press, 2000), 16–17, and Thomas F. Carter, *The Quality of Home Runs: The Passion, Politics, and Language of Cuban Baseball,* (Durham, NC: Duke University Press, 2008), 43.

4. Carter, *Quality of Homeruns,* 49.
5. Carter, 51.

6. Robert Elias, *The Empire Strikes Out: How Baseball Sold U.S. Foreign Policy and Promoted the American Way Abroad* (New York: New Press, 2010), 38–39.

7. Carter, *Quality of Homeruns*, 49–50.

8. Roberto González Echevarría, *The Pride of Havana: A History of Cuban Baseball* (New York: Oxford University Press, 1999), 180–82.

9. Jon Kerr, *Calvin: Baseball's Last Dinosaur, an Authorized Biography* (Dubuque, IA: William C. Brown, 1990), 15.

10. Brian McKenna, "Joe Cambria," Society for American Baseball Research (website), March 10, 2016, http://sabr.org/bioproj/person/4e7d25a0.

11. "Obituary: Joseph Carl Cambria," *Sporting News*, October 6, 1962, 50.

12. "Obituary".

13. Elias, *Empire Strikes Out*, chapter 3. The appearance of light-skinned Latinos on MLB teams was especially prominent when the United States was involved in World War I and World War II. See also Jeffrey Powers-Beck, "'Chief': The American Indian Integration of Baseball, 1897–1945," *American Indian Quarterly* 25, no. 4 (Autumn 2001): 508–38; and Bill Staples Jr., *Kenichi Zenimura: Japanese American Baseball Pioneer* (Jefferson, NC: McFarland, 2011).

14. Peter Bjarkman, *Baseball with a Latin Beat* (Jefferson, NC: McFarland, 1994), 200–205.

15. MLB's distinction between dark-skinned Latinos and black Americans resonates with Enlightenment-era racial "science." In 1775 Immanuel Kant wrote "On the Different Races of Man" and placed African blacks and aboriginal peoples (including Native Americans) at the "bottom" of the racial hierarchy in respect to civilization. Kant's system became the backbone of Georg Wilhelm Hegel's *Philosophy of History*, published in 1837, which was one of the dominant texts in justifying European colonialism in the name of spreading civilization. Although people like Charles Darwin, Thomas Huxley, and Franz Boas made convincing arguments throughout the next one hundred years to abandon such racial hierarchies, the example of MLB reveals that Kant's hierarchies remained in the twentieth century. In regard to race, MLB in the early twentieth century reveals that dark-skinned Latinos—being genetically descended from Africa but spatially affiliated with European colonialism—were somewhat "boosted" compared to black Americans. See Immanuel Kant, "On the Different Races of Man," *Race and Enlightenment: A Reader*, ed. Emmanuel Chukwudi Eze (London: Blackwell, 1997), 41–42.

16. Bjarkman, *Latin Beat*, 168–69.

17. Average Salaries in Major League Baseball, 1967–2009, Major League Baseball Player's Association, 2010, xiii, accessed May 31, 2019, https://www3.nd.edu/~lawlib/baseball_salary_arbitration/minavgsalaries/Minimum-AverageSalaries.pdf.

18. Although outside of the scope of this chapter, it is important to note that during this era baseball commissioner Ford Frick also attempted to make formal connections with the newly formed Nippon Professional Baseball League in Japan. American players were welcomed on Japanese teams beginning in 1952, and Japanese teams increasingly spent time in America during spring training. Essentially, Organized Baseball's attempt to control the pathways by which men could become baseball players extended not only to the Caribbean but also to Japan.

19. Japheth Knopp, "Negro League Baseball, Black Community, and the Socio-Economic Impact of Integration," *Baseball Research Journal* (Spring 2016), 73.

20. Bjarkman, *Latin Beat*, 204–5.

21. Echevarría, *Pride of Havana*, 336–37.

22. Echevarría, 48.

23. Echevarría.

24. *Damn Yankees* puts a baseball spin on the Faustian bargain, in which a Senators' fan makes a deal with the devil to turn the franchise into a winner. Five years after the first run of *Damn Yankees*, the Senators moved to Minnesota, and although likely without supernatural intervention, in 1965 the revamped Twins' team appeared in the World Series.

25. Echevarría, *Pride of Havana*, 303–4.

26. Organized Baseball players listed in Matt Kelly, "Winters in Cuba," National Baseball Hall of Fame (website), accessed March 11, 2016, http://baseballhall.org/discover/hall-of -famers-played-in-cuban-winter-league.

27. Echevarría, *Pride of Havana*, 333–34.

28. Stew Thornley, "Minneapolis Millers: 1959 Junior World Series vs. Havana," Stew Thornley (website), accessed March 11, 2016, http://stewthornley.net/millers_havana.html, 1994. Although they played in Minnesota, the Minneapolis Millers were a minor league affiliate of the Boston Red Sox.

29. Thornley.

30. Carter, *Quality of Homeruns*, 79.

31. Echevarría, *Pride of Havana*, 346–50.

32. Griffith's decision to move the Senators from Washington, DC, was based in part on his personal beliefs about blacks as a sporting audience (see page 20–21 of this chapter) as well as a long-standing dispute Griffith had with city officials over the occupancy and profit potential of Washington Stadium. See Jon Kerr, *Calvin*, 50–51.

33. Rosters are available at "1961 Minnesota Twins Statistics," Baseball Reference (website), accessed March 15, 2016, http://www.baseball-reference.com/teams/MIN/1961.shtml.

34. "Place of Birth Report," Baseball Reference (website), accessed March 15, 2016, http:// www.baseball-reference.com/friv/placeofbirth.cgi?TYPE=active&from=1961&to=0&DIV =countries&submit=Run+Query.

35. Retired player numbers are available from the Minnesota Twins website: "Twins Retired Numbers," Minnesota Twins, accessed March 16, 2016, http://minnesota.twins.mlb.com/min /history/retired_numbers.jsp. Despite his notable career achievements, Tony Oliva was never voted by journalists into the American Baseball Hall of Fame. From the 1980s until now, many fans and journalists debate his exclusion.

36. This familiar narrative is the subject of most of Oliva's monograph-length autobiographies, most recently encapsulated in Thom Henninger's ambitious biography, *Tony Oliva: The Life and Times of a Minnesota Twins Legend* (Minneapolis: University of Minnesota Press, 2015).

37. Henninger, *Tony Oliva*, 1. Pedro Oliva's birthdate has historically been in question because his original identifying documents were those of his younger brother Antonio. In older biographies it was common to report that Oliva was born in 1940. However, it is now agreed that Pedro Oliva was born in 1938.

38. Henninger, 4.

39. Henninger, 5.

40. Henninger, 10.

41. Henninger, 168–69. Hindered by international politics, Oliva was prohibited from seeing his birth family until a brief period in Mexico in the 1970s. Ultimately, Oliva married an American woman and has lived in America for the majority of his adult life.

42. Kevin J. A. Thomas, *A Demographic Profile of Black Caribbean Immigrants in the United States* (Washington, DC: Migration Policy Institute, 2012), 1–2.

43. See the entire *Flood v. Kuhn* case at "Flood v. Kuhn, 407 U.S. 258 (1971)," Justia (website), accessed March 20, 2016, https://supreme.justia.com/cases/federal/us/407/258/case.html.

44. Oscar Kahan, "Silver Bat for Cinderella Kid as Champion Hitter in Minors," *Sporting News*, January 24, 1962, 23.

45. Henninger, *Tony Oliva*, 11, 33.

46. Bob Addie, "Rollicking Ramos No Joke to Swatters," *Sporting News*, May 3, 1961, 5. If Ramos's 1961 regular season innings are included in the total, he threw 755 innings in an eighteen-month span. As a comparison, the highest innings pitched single-season total in the entire 1960s was Denny McLain in 1968 with 336, and McLain never played in the Cuban leagues. Like many Cubans, Ramos was recruited by Joe Cambria and signed his original Twins contract for $225 a month, a decision which necessitated his playing in Cuba in order to make more money. In the long run, the wear on Ramos's arm shortened his career; his last meaningful year was 1964 at the age of twenty-nine, and he was out of baseball entirely by age thirty-four. His MLB baseball statistics can be found at "Pedro Ramos," Baseball Reference, accessed March 18, 2016, http://www.baseball-reference.com/players/r/ramospe01.shtml.

47. Tom Briere, "Zoilo Stakes Quick Claim to Twin Post," *Sporting News*, November 29, 1961, 39.

48. Clifford Kachline, "Cuban Standouts Shun Own Land, Play Elsewhere," *Sporting News*, November 29, 1961, 46. Orestes "Minnie" Miñoso, perhaps the most well-known Cuban player in America, also decided to remain in America.

49. "Pedro, Alias Tony, Fouls Up Records, Wears Out Hurlers," *Sporting News*, October 20, 1962, 16.

50. "Pedro, Alias Tony."

51. Henninger, *Tony Oliva*, 41.

52. For information on Oliva's surgeries, see Henninger, *Tony Oliva*, 187. Henninger reports that Oliva generally remained affable during public appearances and has always been willing to sign autographs. Nonetheless, he also reports that Oliva regularly appeared at offseason conventions doing a shtick with fellow player Frank Quilici where Oliva's poor English was put on display for the audience's amusement. See Henninger, 106.

53. Henninger, *Tony Oliva*, 171. Numbers from "Tony Oliva," Baseball Reference (website), March 18, 2016, http://www.baseball-reference.com/players/o/olivato01.shtml.

54. Nick Coleman, "Griffith Spares Few Targets in Waseca Remarks," *Minneapolis Tribune*, October 1, 1978.

55. Coleman.

56. Howard Sinker, "Griffith: Talk Misunderstood," *Minneapolis Tribune*, October 1, 1978. Griffith's use of the word "colored" harks back to the Kantian distinction of races and civilizational hierarchy. Although Griffith may have felt that he was not racist, he put into practice the prevailing attitudes toward race in the United States in the early twentieth century.

57. Gary Libman, "Angry Carew Vows He Will Not Play for Griffith's Twins Again," *Minneapolis Tribune*, October 2, 1978.

58. Robert K. Fitts, *Remembering Japanese Baseball: An Oral History of the Game* (Carbondale, IL: Southern Illinois University Press, 2005), 152.

59. Fitts, 153. Wells reported that if he did not reach an agreement with the Hankyū Braves, then Griffith threatened to sell him to a team in South Korea. Politically speaking, South Korea was effectively a dictatorship until 1989.

60. Data aggregated from "Place of Birth Report," Baseball Reference (website), March 18, 2016, http://www.baseball-reference.com/friv/placeofbirth.shtml. As a comparison, the 1960s Twins regularly had more Cubans on their annual roster than they had any Latinos in the five-year period from 1979 to 1984.

61. "Place of Birth Report."

62. Dan Berry, "A Pitch is Framed by Diplomacy in Cuba," *New York Times*, November 29, 2015.

63. Statistics acquired from "MLB Team Payroll Tracker," Spotrac (website), September 15, 20018, http://www.spotrac.com/mlb/payroll/.

64. LaVelle E. Neal III, "Ex-Twins Star Oliva Misses Hall of Fame by One Vote," *Star Tribune*, December 9, 2014, http://www.startribune.com/oliva-misses-hall-of-fame-by-one-vote-on-disappointing-day/285115931/.


## Chapter 12

1. Sullivan fought in both St. Paul (1883) and Minneapolis (1887); Fitzsimmons fought in Minneapolis in 1891. Unless otherwise indicated, sources of information on fighters and their records throughout this chapter are from the Minnesota Boxing Hall of Fame's biographical sketches of honorees, Minnesota Hall of Fame (website), accessed March 15, 2017, http://www.mnbhof.org/Minnesota_Boxing_Hall_of_Fame/Welcome.html, and the boxing records website BoxRec, March 15, 2017, http://boxrec.com.

2. "The Maulers," *St. Paul Daily Globe*, November 27, 1883.

3. Needham also participated in a bout in Minneapolis in 1891 that lasted into the seventy-sixth round.

4. Many states at this time had rules prohibiting so-called "mixed race" bouts. Minnesota's rule to this effect remained on the books until 1923. Clay Moyle, *Billy Miske: The St. Paul Thunderbolt* (Iowa City, IA: Win By KO Publications, 2011), 176–77.

5. Martin was the first to claim the title, which remained in existence until 1926.

6. See Joel A. Ripple, *75 Memorable Moments in Minnesota Sports* (St. Paul, MN: Minnesota Historical Society Press, 2003), 7–10.

7. George A. Barton, *My Lifetime in Sports* (Minneapolis, MN: Olympic Press, 1957), 46–47.

86. Barton, *My Lifetime in Sports*, 47, 51.

9. See Eliott Gorn, *Bare-knuckle Prize Fighting in America* (Ithaca: Cornell University Press, 2010).

10. Minnesota Boxing Hall of Fame.

11. Attendance was 9559, with gate receipts of $41,864.

12. Gibbons and Grebs fought three times in extremely close fights, Gibbons winning by a newspaper decision in May of 1920 and losing in a similar manner in a rematch two months later. Grebs won the rubber match between the two in March of 1922 by a unanimous decision.

13. Barton, *My Lifetime in Sports*, 70, 72.

14. The county in which the City of St. Paul is located.

15. Minnesota Boxing Hall of Fame (website), March 15, 2017, http://www.mnbhof.org/Minnesota_Boxing_Hall_of_Fame/Welcome.html

16. The story of Miske's last fight is summarized from Moyle, *Billy Miske*, 73–76 and chapters 16 and 17.

17. See Moyle, *Billy Miske*, 176–79, for additional discussion of the racial issue, especially as it applied to the heavyweight division.

18. Louis avenged the loss to Schmeling two years later, on June 22, 1938, via a first-round knockout.

19. *St. Paul Pioneer Press*, January 16, 1936.

20. *St. Paul Pioneer Press*, January 18, 1936.

21. Savold lost by a twelve-round decision to Conn in 1942 and to Louis and Marciano (both by sixth-round knockouts) in 1951 and1952, respectively, when Savold was in the twilight of his career.

22. Armstrong appeared in bouts in 1938 and 1939, Robinson in 1942.

23. *Minneapolis Star Tribune*, April 13, 2018.

24. Yanez, whose boxing career consisted of a total of four fights, went on to become an iconic figure on the local boxing scene. He operated the White Bear Boxing Club (later known as the Mexican-American Boxing Club) for decades and helped establish a small but persistent Latino presence in Minnesota boxing.

25. *Minneapolis Tribune*, October 19, 1946; *St. Paul Pioneer Press*, October 19, 1946; and Scott Wright, "The Fighting Flanagan's: Boxing in Minnesota in the Postwar Era," *Ramsey County History*, 22, no. 2 (Winter 1987): 16–22.

26. Carol Thompson was murdered in her home in St. Paul on March 6, 1963. In what was to become one of the city's most sensational murder cases, her husband, T. Eugene Thompson, a prominent St. Paul attorney, was charged with hiring the killer with former boxer Norman Mastrian serving as the middleman. All three were tried and convicted and sentenced to lengthy jail terms for their roles in the crime.

27. Minnesota Boxing Hall of Fame. Most of Glen's fights before turning pro were fought in the navy where he was said to have run up a string of forty-four consecutive victories, but the competition would not have been as skilled as that faced by his brother.

28. *St. Paul Pioneer Press*, March 18, 1948.

29. Viscusi had proven to be too involved with promoting the careers of other fighters in his stable—such as featherweight great Willie Pep—and was not, in Del's mind, getting him the fights he needed.

30. *St. Paul Pioneer Press*, March 12, 1957.

31. The fight surpassed the previous record set in 1919 by the Gibbons-O'Dowd fight.

32. Akins won the title three months before the Flanagan fight but then lost it three months after the fight, in December 1958.

33. A copy of the news release and ad for the TV show was provided by Denny Nelson. Nelson, himself a former boxer, went on to become a world-class referee and judge of championship fights around the globe and in that capacity, was inducted into the Minnesota Boxing Hall of Fame in 2012. His son, Mark, who has followed in his father's footsteps, recently returned from Japan where he refereed his eightieth world title bout.

34. The Twins and the Vikings came to the city in 1961, and the North Stars came in 1967.

35. By 1977 boxing had entered the era of multiple champions in the same weight class, each recognized by a different sanctioning body—for example, the World Boxing Association (WBA), the International Boxing Federation (IBF), the World Boxing Council (WBC), the World Boxing Organization (WBO), and others.

36. The fights with LeDoux took place on April 22, 1976, and July 28, 1977.

37. He managed to gain draws against Spinks and Norton.

38. The fight took place in Annapolis, Maryland, in February, 1977.

39. LeDoux's career is well documented in Paul Levy, *The Fighting Frenchman: Minnesota's Boxing Legend* (Minneapolis: University of Minnesota Press, 2016).

40. See June Drenning Holmquist, ed., *They Chose Minnesota: A Survey of The State's Ethnic Groups* (St. Paul: Minnesota Historical Society Press, 1981), 73–91, 92–107.

## Chapter 13

1. Elliot Gorn, "Gouge and Bite, Pull Hair and Scratch": The Social Significance of Fighting in the Southern Backcountry," *American Historical Review* 90 no. 1 (1985): 20.

2. Scott M. Beekman, *Ringside: A History of Professional Wrestling in America* (Westport, CT: Praeger, 2006), 35–36.

3. Tourists to Humboldt can visit Frank Gotch State Park.

4. John Capouya, *Gorgeous George: The Outrageous Bad-Boy Wrestler Who Created American Pop Culture* (New York: Harper Collins, 2008), 8.

5. The origins of the word are unclear.

6. "Award-Winning Sports Writer Frank Deford Dies at 78," US *News and World Report*, May 29, 2017, www.usnews.com/news/sports.

7. Mechelle Voepel, "Iowa Remains Heartbeat of Wrestling," *ESPN Sports* March 2, 2011, accessed May 31, 2019, http://www.espn.com/college-sports/columns/story?columnist =voepel_mechelle&id=6163208.

8. Tim Hornbaker. "National Wrestling Alliance History," Legacy of Wrestling (website), May 3, 2011, accessed on May 31, 2019, http://www.legacyofwrestling.com/NWA_History.html.

9. Capouya, *Gorgeous George*, 121.

10. Interview with Northeast Minneapolis native Rich Renikoff, January 17, 2017.

11. Steven A. Reiss, "Tough Jews: The Jewish American Boxing Experience, 1890–1950," in *Sports and the American Jew*, ed. Steven A. Riess (Syracuse: Syracuse University Press, 1998), 73.

12. Hornbaker, "Wrestling Alliance History."

13. *Los Angeles Times*, June 4, 1990; and Ted A. Kluck, *Headlocks and Dropkicks: A Butt-Kicking Ride through the World of Pro Wrestling* (Santa Barbara: Praeger, 2009), 77.

14. Kluck, *Headlocks and Dropkicks*, 49.

15. Lee Cataluna, "A Villain Fans Loved to Hate," *Honolulu Advertiser*, August 19, 2007.

16. Brendan Maguire and John F. Wozniak, "Racial and Ethnic Stereotypes in Professional Wrestling," *Social Science Journal* 24, no. 3 (1987): 264.

17. *New York Post*, August 24, 2008; and John Capouya, *Gorgeous George*, xi.

18. Capouya, *Gorgeous George*, 5, 246.

19. George Shire, *Minnesota's Golden Age of Wrestling from Vern Gagne to the Road Warriors* (St. Paul: Minnesota Historical Society Press, 2010), 97.

20. Beekman, *Ringside*, 65.

21. Schire, *Minnesota's Golden Age of Wrestling*, 117.

22. Henry Jenkins, "Afterward, Part I: Wrestling with Theory, Grappling with Politics," in *Steel Chair to the Head: The Pleasure and Pain of Pro Wrestling*, ed. Nicholas Sammond, (Durham: Duke University Press, 2005), 311.

23. Sarah Burnett, "Before Trump, There Was Jesse Ventura—and an Improbable Victory," *PBS Newshour*, March 1, 2016, www.pbs.org/newshour.

24. *Washington Post*, November 4, 1998.

25. Maguire and Wozniak, "Racial and Ethnic Stereotypes," 266.

26. Kluck, *Headlocks and Dropkicks*, 46–47.

27. Ted Rueter, "Pro Wrestling Contributions to Americans' Culture of Violence," in *Pro Wrestling*, ed. Louise I. Gerdes (San Diego: Greenhaven Press, 2002), 28.

28. Nicholas Sammond, "Squaring the Family Circle: WWF Smackdown Assaults the Social Body," in Sammond, *Steel Chair*, 135, 149.

29. Lynn Rosellini, "The Birth of Modern Pro Wrestling: An Overview," in Gerdes, *Pro Wrestling*, 11–12.

30. Sammond, "Squaring the Family Circle," 135, 149.

31. Associated Press, "Ex-pro Wrestler Accused in Nursing Home Death," March 6, 2009, www.nbcnews.com/id/29534398.

# Contributors

**Sheldon Anderson** graduated from Minneapolis South High School in 1969 and Augsburg College in 1973, and received his PhD from the University of Minnesota in 1989. He is a professor of history at Miami University (Ohio), specializing in the history of sports, the cold war, and European diplomacy. He has authored *The Forgotten Legacy of Stella Walsh: The Greatest Female Athlete of Her Time* (2017); *The Politics and Culture of Modern Sports* (2015); *Condemned to Repeat It: 'Lessons of History' and the Making of U.S. Cold War Containment Policy* (2008); *A Cold War in the Soviet Bloc: East German-Polish Relations, 1945–1962* (2000); and *A Dollar to Poland is a Dollar to Russia: U.S. Economic Policy Toward Poland, 1945–1952* (1993). He also coauthored *International Studies: An Interdisciplinary Approach to Global Issues* (Fourth Edition 2018).

**Dick Dahl** has worked as a writer and editor for more than forty years. A 1971 graduate of St. Cloud (MN) State University with a bachelor of arts in journalism, he worked on a variety of publications in Minnesota before moving to Boston in 1987. There he began to specialize in legal journalism—first as a staff writer for a legal newspaper and then as a freelancer. He has written extensively for Harvard Law School and since returning to Minnesota in 2016, has become a frequent contributor to University of Minnesota Law School publications.

**Thomas B. Jones** is a professor emeritus at Metropolitan State University (St. Paul-Minneapolis). He graduated from the University of Minnesota (1964) with a bachelor of arts in history and received a Woodrow Wilson Fellowship for graduate study at Cornell University (PhD in history, 1968). He has taught US history at both the graduate and undergraduate levels and served as an academic administrator, faculty development director, and educational consultant. His writing includes articles and books on US history, sports, college teaching, faculty development, and liberal education. His most recent book is a sports mystery novel, *Bad Lies*.

**Jon Kerr** is author of *Calvin: Baseball's Last Dinosaur* (W. C. Brown Publishing, 1991). He has a master of arts in American history from the University of Minnesota (1978) and has been a journalist, educator, and writer for over forty years for publications including United Press International, the Associated Press, the St. Paul Pioneer Press, City Pages, the Twin Cities Reader, the Minnesota Suburban Press, the Riverview Times, the Prescott Journal, and others. He is also the author of several historical fiction works including his latest, *Mark Twain and The River of Timeless Temptation* (Old Man River Press, 2017).

**Brad Lundell** is a nonprofit executive, government affairs consultant, and freelance writer who has lived in Minnesota his entire life. He received his bachelor of arts in communications from Augsburg College in 1975 and his master of arts in public policy from the University of Minnesota in 1987. He has contributed to a variety of public finance and education funding issues during his forty-two-year career in public service.

**Shannon Murray** originally hails from St. Paul, Minnesota. After completing a history bachelor of arts at the University of South Dakota, she did graduate studies at the University of Calgary. Her master's thesis was a labor history of a series of strikes in the Minneapolis flour mills that contributed to the breakdown of semiskilled unions in the early 1900s. Her PhD dissertation, "Making a Modern Metropolis: Boosterism, Reform, and Urban Design in Progressive-Era Minneapolis," examined the ways civic leaders and social reformers used urban planning in their efforts to promote and maintain an economically viable and socially healthy city. She is currently and assistant adjunct professor in history at the University of Calgary and works as the indigenous programming manager for the Calgary Stampede.

**David C. Smith** is the author of *City of Parks: The Story of Minneapolis Parks*, a history of the celebrated Minneapolis park system, published by the Minneapolis Parks Foundation and distributed by the University of Minnesota Press. He has also written histories of more than 180 individual parks for the Minneapolis Park and Recreation Board's website, minneapolisparks.org, as well as park-related entries for MNopedia, an online encyclopedia of Minnesota created by the Minnesota Historical Society. He also maintains a proprietary website on Minneapolis history at minneapolisparkhistory.com. Prior to writing about parks, Smith was a Minneapolis-based corporate communications consultant and writer, a foreign service officer, and a Peace Corps volunteer. He grew up and went to college in St. Paul but now lives in Minneapolis.

**Tom Taylor** received his PhD from the University of Minnesota where he focused his dissertation research on twentieth-century Germany. He has taught for thirty years at Seattle University where he has offered a wide range of courses on modern European world history and methodology and historiography. Currently he is completing a comprehensive world history text that uses travel narratives to explore the significant events that have shaped the human story, for Pearson Publishing. He started playing soccer while in graduate school and still plays weekly.

**Stew Thornley** is a Minnesota sports historian who has written *Basketball's Original Dynasty: The History of the Lakers*, *On to Nicollet: The Glory and Fame of the Minneapolis Millers*, and *Baseball in Minnesota: The Definitive History*. He is an official scorer for Major League Baseball and the National Basketball Association.

**Blair Williams** completed his PhD in history at the University of Minnesota in August 2018. His dissertation, "Making Japan's National Game: Baseball, *Bushidō*, and Discourses of National Identity, 1868–2008," examines how Japanese baseball communities created, challenged, and reinforced characteristics of Japanese identity throughout the twentieth century. His dissertation is the basis of a forthcoming book that will bring the academic study of baseball in Japan to a general audience. In addition to his research, he has taught undergraduate classes in history at the University of Wisconsin-Eau Claire and St. Olaf College. Blair loves spending time with his three kids and wife, learning about photography, and participating in the annual tradition of Minnesota Twins fans saying, "There's always next year."

**Scott Wright** is professor emeritus of history at the University of St. Thomas in St. Paul, Minnesota. He attended the University of Minnesota where he received a bachelor of arts (American Studies, 1963), master of arts (Library Science, 1968) and PhD (American Studies, 1973). He served as library director at the then-College of St. Thomas from 1974 to 1979, and then shifted to the History Department where he taught until his retirement in 2010. His research and teaching focused primarily on US History, with a special emphasis on American thought and culture. He also received a Fulbright lecturing grant to Japan in 1979. In retirement he has published two volumes of fictionalized memoir, *Of Snapping Turtles and Packing Plants* (2012) and *Carrying the Mummy* (2015).

# Index

National Collegiate Athletic Association
(NCAA), 156, 170; and baseball championship, 129; and basketball championship,
129–30, 138, 145; and eligibility rules 74,
80; and football injuries, 86; and national
football championship, 69–70, 74–76, 78,
150–51; and national hockey championship, 153, 157–58, 164, 169, 170–1; and
scandals, 128–29
National Football League (NFL), 4, 6, 71,
72, 74–75, 80, 83, 85–88, 90, 91–95, 98–99,
100, 231
National Guard Armory (Washington, DC),
176
National Highway (Cumberland Road), 73
National Hockey League (NHL), 5, 54, 80,
116, 150, 153, 156–59, 161, 164, 170
National Hockey League Hall of Fame,
170–71
National Intercollegiate Athletic Association,
86
national speed skating championship, 53,
55–59, 61–62
National Urban League, 40–41
National Wrestling Alliance (NWA), 231, 240
National Wrestling Association, 235
Needham, Danny, 212
Negro baseball leagues, 195–96, 197, 200
Nelson, Byron, 54
Nevers, Ernie, 89, 91
New England Revolution, 111
New Jersey Devils, 158
New Prague Seals, 86
New York Central Park, 19, 21
New York Cosmos, 103–6
New York Giants (baseball), 8, 194
New York Giants (football), 92–94
New York Jets, 94
New York Knicks, 137, 141–42, 144
New York Mets, 156
New York Mills (MN) High School, 125
New York Liberty, 126
New York Rens, 136–38
*New York Times*, 49, 169
New York Yankees, 164, 174, 186
Newell, Hal, 223
Newman, Cecil E., 40

Neyland, Bob, 71, 72
Nicollet, Joseph, 234
Nightingale, John, 63
Nilsson, John, 49–50, 52
Nitschke, Ray, 70
Nixon, Richard, 176, 184
Nomellini, Leo, 71
Normanna Club, 48
Normanna skating rink, 49
North American Boxing Federation, 226
North American Soccer League (NASL),
103–6
North American Speed Skating
Championship, 60
North Carolina A&T, 75
North Commons Skating Club, 58
North Dakota State University, 166
Northeast (Minneapolis), 7, 233–35, 239
Northland Golf Club, 36
Northwest Hockey League, 158
Northwest Indoor Speedskating
Championship, 53
Northwest Kickers, 102
Northrup, Jesse, 33
Northrup, King & Company, 33
Norton, Ken, 224–25
Nortwedt, Olaf, 51
Norwegian Cup, 109
Ntsoelengoe, Patrick "Ace," 104
Nushkas, 31
Nussbaumer, Frederick, 33
Nye's Polonaise Room, 239

Obama, Barack, 208
O'Connor, Pat (boxer), 225–26
O'Connor, Pat (wrestler), 231, 236
O'Dowd, Mike, 214, 217
O'Hagan, Anne, 35
Ohio State University, 233; football, 67, 70–73,
82; basketball, 126, 130
Oklahoma State University, 229
O'Malley, Walter, 181, 185
Olberding, Mark, 122
Oliva, Pedro. *See* Tony Oliva
Oliva, Tony, 7, 189, 193, 200–207, 209
Olmstead, Frederick Law, 16
Olofson, Eva, 148